Twentieth Century Architecture 9

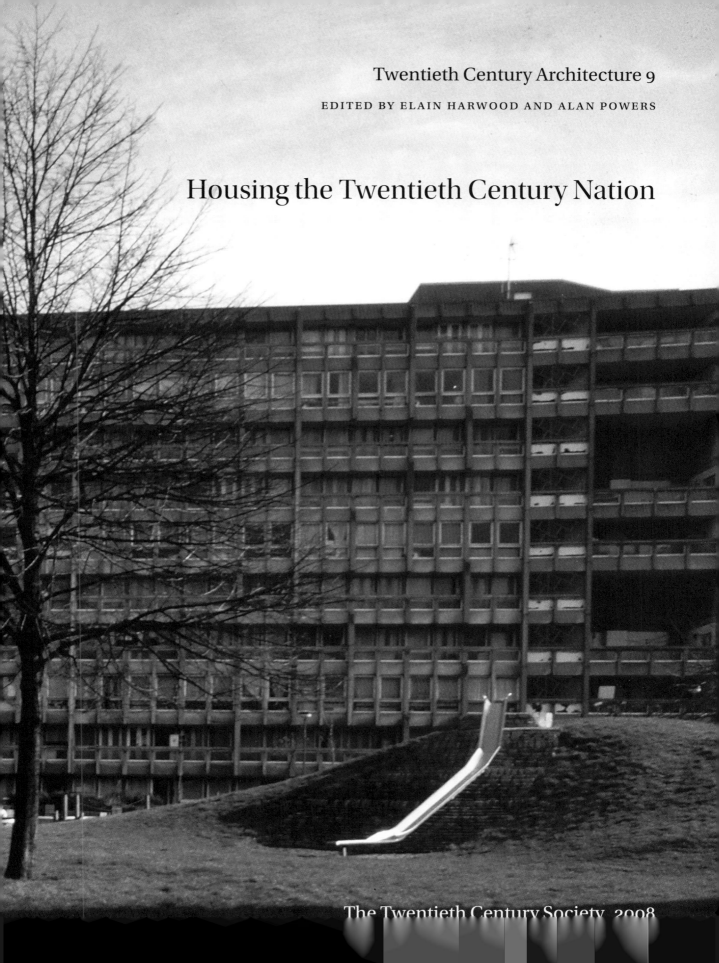

Twentieth Century Architecture 9

EDITED BY ELAIN HARWOOD AND ALAN POWERS

Housing the Twentieth Century Nation

The Twentieth Century Society 2008

TWENTIETH CENTURY ARCHITECTURE is published by the
Twentieth Century Society, 70 Cowcross Street, London EC1M 6EJ
© The authors 2008. The views expressed in *Housing the Twentieth
Century Nation* are those of the authors, and not necessarily those
of the Twentieth Century Society.

NUMBER 9 | 2008 | ISBN 978-0-9556687-0-8

Twentieth Century Architecture Editorial Committee:
Susannah Charlton, Elain Harwood, Alan Powers, Gavin Stamp
and Simon Wartnaby. Text Editor: Alison Boyd. We would also
like to thank Margaret Doyle, Liverpool Record Office, Liverpool
University Archives, Susanna Powers and June Warrington.

Designed and typeset in Utopia by Nye Hughes, Dalrymple
Printed in the United Kingdom by Henry Ling Limited, at the
Dorset Press, Dorchester, DT1 1HD

Every effort has been made to contact copyright holders, and the
editors would be glad to hear from those we failed to reach.

ENGLISH HERITAGE

The Twentieth Century Society was founded in 1979 to promote
and preserve architecture and design from 1914 onwards. For
information and membership details call +44 (0)20 7250 3857 or
contact www.c20society.org.uk.

Frontispiece: Robin Hood Gardens, by Alison and Peter Smithson
(1968–72), under threat in 2008. (Elain Harwood)

Contents

Contributors

JUDITH ALFREY is an Inspector of Historic Buildings with Cadw.

PETER CAROLIN was a partner in Colin St John Wilson & Partners (The British Library and other buildings), Editor of *The Architects' Journal* and Professor of Architecture at Cambridge. He has a particular interest in the work of Gunnar Asplund.

MICHAEL DRAGE worked in Byker from 1973 to 1984. Since then his practice has worked mainly on community and arts projects, notably the Live Theatre in Newcastle and urban design/heritage projects with the Civic Trust. He was a long-time member of the RIBA Community Architecture Group and of Newcastle Architecture Workshop.

MILES GLENDINNING is Director of the Scottish Centre for Conservation Studies, a research and postgraduate teaching unit within the School of Architecture at Edinburgh College of Art.

ELAIN HARWOOD is a historian with English Heritage. She is writing the Pevsner City Guide to Nottingham, and a major book on English post-war architecture.

ROLAND JEFFERY held director posts in housing associations before moving into the heritage sector. He has led the restoration of several historic buildings, the best known being Hawksmoor's Christ Church, Spitalfields and Shoreditch Town Hall. He currently works for The Princes Regeneration Trust, advising on heritage projects across the country.

BARBARA LINSLEY is Archivist for the Raveningham Estate in South Norfolk; advocate of affordable housing and vice-chair of one of the few parish councils in Norfolk to have achieved new housing in the village for rent to local people.

JONAH LOWENFELD is a writer living in Los Angeles. He has a M.Sc. from the Bartlett in Architectural History & Theory. This article was adapted from research conducted while living in London as a Fulbright Fellow.

JOHN PARTRIDGE CBE RA was a founder partner of Howell, Killick, Partridge and Amis (HKPA). The partners met at the LCC in the 1950s as the design team for Alton West Housing, Roehampton. The practice, which gained over 30 design awards, continued until he retired in 1995 and became a consultant.

JOANNA SMITH is a historian with English Heritage. She wrote *Behind the Veneer: the South Shoreditch Furniture Trade and its Buildings*, published in 2006.

MATTHEW WHITFIELD is completing a PhD on Liverpool's inter-war municipal flats, based in the Manchester Centre for Regional History at Manchester Metropolitan University.

CHRIS WHITTAKER studied at the AA School 1943-4 and 1947-51, then turned to planning, at Basildon and the LCC's Brandon Estate until 1960. He was an Associate with Trehearne & Norman, Preston & Ptnrs, 1960-65; for the MHLG/DOE 1966-72, he worked on the Barnsbury Environmental Study; and as a partner with Stephen George & Ptnrs, 1972-80, he had many Tenants' and Residents' Association clients.

Mass Housing as the Essential Twentieth-Century Building Type

ELAIN HARWOOD

Figure 1. The Lawn, Harlow, by Frederick Gibberd. Opening in May 1951, it was Britain's first 'point' block, marking a radical change in housing styles (author).

Most of us live in a twentieth-century dwelling. Not in a modernist icon, but in a house or flat designed with hundreds like it to fulfil modern expectations of comfort and sanitation. These, not the handful of cinemas, air terminals and lidos, will be the greatest abiding legacy of twentieth-century architecture, just as they prompted the greatest debates for their designers. This journal tells that tale, looking at private as well as public housing.

A century ago mass housing created by agencies other than private builders and developers was in its infancy. Liverpool Corporation had provided model dwellings as early as 1869 and Nottingham followed in 1877, but only London saw development on a large scale, with both luxury mansion blocks and working-class tenements. By 1908, the London County Council had turned from its celebrated flatted estates in Shoreditch and on Millbank, towards the building of cottages on the edge of the city. It was these, developed in short rows behind privet hedges on increasingly picturesque layouts inspired by Raymond Unwin's tract, *Cottage Plans and Commonsense*, which were to prove most influential.[1] Estates similarly inspired by Unwin and Barry Parker's suburban housing can be found across Britain, encouraged by Unwin's work after 1914 for the Local Government Board and its successors.

The Boer War had revealed the poor state of the nation's health, a situation little improved by 1914. In the aftermath of the Great War government and middle-class reformers began to provide the self-contained, dry and sanitary dwellings we now take for granted. Barbara Linsley shows how the garden suburb was reduced in the most rural locations to a single line of houses but nevertheless with the hedges and styling found in towns. The Bata estate at East Tilbury demonstrates the influence of garden suburbs as evolved in Czechoslovakia and brought home again. Threats to suburbia across southern England have prompted a campaign by English Heritage, which has included Jo Smith's research on Bata. This journal is the Twentieth Century Society's contribution. The building of flats was much rarer after 1920, save in London and Liverpool. Roland Jeffery looks at the dense rebuildings championed by the St Pancras Housing Association, while Matthew Whitfield shows that Liverpool City Council had a lively flat-building programme. Theirs was a battle for amenity and cost-effectiveness, in which issues of style were secondary; the most innovatively built flats have been the most difficult to maintain. Yet all too often windows have been replaced in London flats thoughtlessly and insensitively, while most of the Liverpool estates have gone completely.

Of greater concern to the Society, perhaps, is the loss and insensitive alteration of our post-war housing, amongst the most innovative in Europe in its architecture and planning. Peter Carolin and I hope to show that while European models provided an impetus, British sources also played an important role. Bilston, Dudley and Peterlee were unexpected locations for such idealism and, unappreciated, little survives there today. Cumbernauld has fared only a little better, though its townscape – and landscaping – can still be enjoyed.

Miles Glendinning highlights the perennial problem faced by housing –

1. Raymond Unwin, Cottage Plans and Commonsense, London, Fabian Society Tract no.109, 1902.

that while its significance, architecturally and socially, deserves the highest accolades, protective legislation is totally geared to the preservation of single one-off icons rather than wholesale areas. Conservation Areas largely lack the necessarily teeth, as local authorities are invariably owners and arbiters, and most will simply not designate social housing at all. A good example is Harlow, where – admirably - the first phases of the new town at Mark Hall are a Conservation Area, and their judicious mix of housing and landscape is beginning to be appreciated. Other parts of the town have fared less well. The Society has just learned of a threat to one of its most important developments, with demolition a possible option. When in 1960 Harlow was faced with the need to build at higher densities, the Development Corporation decided to hold a competition to encourage new design solutions. The young winner, out of some 60 entrants, was Michael Neylan with a scheme for Bishopsfield, built in 1963–6 and known locally as the Casbah. It comprises 239 units ranging in size from bedsits to five bedroomed houses. The flats are at the crown of the sloping site, built up over underground car parking to exaggerate the sense of a hill town, and the single-storey houses are strung out in pedestrian defiles below. The houses are partly open-plan with high, split-level living rooms, 'L'-shaped around rear patio gardens. Forty years on the units are still delightful places to live, and the close-knit plan has created a real community. A reconfiguration of the bedsit units at the top of the hill in 1993–5 by Florian Bagel seemed to revive the area, yet subsequent limited maintenance has prompted proposals for rebuilding as an 'economic' option. This limited focus, regardless of a building's worth or of green issues, are endemic in the housing industry.

This journal was prompted by research suggesting that there was almost no public housing in a fit state left to list – though Judith Alfrey may have a different experience in Wales. This has only served to increase the significance, therefore, of the few post-war housing estates that are listed, of which Roehampton (Alton) and Byker are perhaps the most interesting – and among the highly graded. Yet even here the question recently asked has been not 'should the windows be replaced', but 'how', the seven-year delay in listing Byker having allowed many alterations to be made, despite the local authority and conservation bodies working together towards a Conservation Plan in a manner to be commended. The articles by John Partridge and Mike Drage are uniquely first-hand accounts by those who were there. So, too, is Chris Whitaker's piece on a little-known estate for a very different market – which shows that problems faced by designers for the wealthy were similar to those serving modest means.

But what of the estates said to have 'failed'? What is failure – is it of the people, the idea, or both? Or are tenants the victims of changing fashion? Jonah Lowenfeld explores the 1980s' culture that attempted to redress an estate's problems from a totally negative mindset, and how it has taken another twenty years and an improved economy for change to be made.

The Smithsons wrote extensively about changing housing tastes in the 1970s.[2] They epitomise an era that attempted to determine how people lived their lives – not unkindly, but unrealistically. Peter Smithson said apologetically how he imagined council tenants to be people from similar backgrounds to his own – the optimistic, ambitious, skilled working class shorn in the 1970s and 1980s.[3] The demography of social housing has changed – as has that of the luxury market with an equally international flavour. A Bangladeshi community has grown up at Robin Hood Gardens which likes their building and uses it much as the Smithsons intended. In looking at housing, however, one is more aware than anywhere else of a lack of communication between housing and conservation lobbies, between dedicated residents groups and the wider public. Those 'ordinary' people who the Smithsons thought they were designing for still too often dismiss the value of modern housing. To all these groups, this journal is dedicated.

Figure 2. Bishopsfield, Harlow, by Neylan and Ungless, 1963–6, with sculpture, 'City', by Gerda Rubinstein, 1970 (part)

2. See, notably, Alison Smithson, 'The Violent Consumer, or Waiting for the Goodies', in *Architectural Design*, vol.44, May 1974, pp.274-8.

3. Although Peter Smithson's father was a travelling salesman.

1 Homes for Heroes: Local Authority Housing in Rural Norfolk, 1918–1923

BARBARA LINSLEY

Homes for Heroes: Local Authority Housing in Rural Norfolk, 1918–1923

BARBARA LINSLEY

ddison's 1919 Housing Act, fulfilling David Lloyd George's election prom-ise of 'homes for heroes' allowed the longstanding problems of insani-tary and overcrowded housing in rural areas, including Norfolk, to be addressed.[1] Speculative building for labourers had ceased to be economical after local by-laws and enforcement of the Public Health Acts after 1875 raised housing standards, while philanthropic building by landowners never regained momen-tum after the great agricultural depression of the same period.

In 1890, for the first time, all local authorities were empowered to build work-ing-class housing, but the unnecessarily complicated procedure and the higher cost of building in rural districts meant that almost no houses were erected there under the Act. A further Act of 1909 allowed local authorities to own the houses the houses they built or acquired for improvement, but by 1913 only 470 cottages had been built nationally under loans to local authorities, both rural and urban, only one tenth of the number demolished under closing orders. Norfolk, how-ever, had several enlightened councils. Erpingham Rural District Council (RDC) in the north, and Smallburgh and Blofield in the east, all built cottages using part III of the 1890 legislation after the amendments of 1909. The Sanitary Inspector for Smallburgh RDC had this to say about its twelve new cottages:

> They are soundly built at a minimum cost, £1,628 including land, [£135 13s
> 4d each] and though not beautiful from an artistic point of view, they should
> serve their purpose well. Each cottage has about twenty rod of garden and is
> let at or near £7 per annum. If only blocks like these could be erected in every
> village where wanted and let at £5 to £5 10s per annum, the labourer would
> have little cause for complaint as to his housing accommodation. But I fear
> this wish is utopian.[2]

Erpingham's cottage design was described by Depwade RDC in south Norfolk as 'that most generally considered suitable for rural districts. It has been adopted in several Districts and under favourable conditions appears to be practically self-supporting.'[3]

The small number of cottages built had little impact on the overall shortage but showed that some Norfolk councils were not reactionary laggards with regard to housing, as central government frequently portrayed RDCs. The dilemma of the rural districts was beginning to be generally recognised, that new housing would not be forthcoming in sufficient numbers unless the government provided financial support, whether for private enterprise or local authorities.

While some stockmen, the elite among farm workers, had their housing prov-ided with the job, at a nominal rent, their numbers were few. General labourers had to find their own accommodation in a nearby village or town at their own ex-pense, and then travel to work, so frequently the workers who received the lowest wages paid the highest rents. The tied cottage system, moreover, was seen as the principal device in maintaining a regime that condemned the agricultural worker to poverty and dependence. Where the employer was also the landlord, the twin threat of dismissal and eviction removed any vestige of independence from the low-paid farm worker.[4] This also seriously curtailed the freedom of his wife and

1. My PhD thesis examines the housing legislation of the inter-war period.

2. Norfolk Record Office (hereafter NRO), °7b, p.108.

3. NRO, DC/2/5/1, Depwade RDC Housing Committee Minutes, 1914.

4. Howard Newby, *The Deferential Worker*, London, Allen Lane, 1977, pp.182–3.

5. *Landworker*, October 1935, quoted in
W. H. Pedley, *Labour on the Land*, London,
P. S. King and Staples, 1942, p.74.

6. NRO, DC3/5/17, Great Witchingham,
Special Sanitary Committee, 1903.

7. Ian Cole and Robert Furbey, *The Eclipse
of Council Housing*, London, Routledge,
1994, p.50.

8. Public Record Office, part of the National
Archive (hereafter PRO), RECO 1/592,
Ministry of Reconstruction, memorandum
from Hayes Fisher on housing the working
classes.

children, who could also be formally tied to an estate even in the 1930s.[5]

Three bedrooms, the minimum required to separate boys and girls, were rare in country cottages.[6] Although the 1909 Housing and Town Planning Act simplified the procedure for dealing with unfit houses and encouraged councils to build, few local authorities were tempted. They were expected to charge an 'economic' rent for their properties which would cover the cost of the building and future maintenance. By 1913, however, the low wage issue was at the heart of discussions on rural regeneration, especially in Norfolk with one of the largest but lowest-paid agricultural workforces in the country.

By 1914, government was more willing to contemplate the direct involvement of the state and a major commitment to public expenditure as the only solution. In 1917, the conclusions of the Royal Commission on Housing the Industrial Population of Scotland, reporting after a five-year enquiry, showed that public and private sources of working-class housing had failed, and recommended that the state must accept direct responsibility. The report was controversial but sceptics in England became convinced.

When a Ministry of Reconstruction was established in 1915 to co-ordinate preparations for the restoration and improvement of normal industrial, trading and social conditions at the end of the war, housing was one of the first measures to be considered. The Treasury, however, was reluctant to commit itself to specific financial aid, without which local authorities would neither plan nor build. Lloyd George, wary of social unrest after the Armistice, pledged his Government to a wide-ranging programme of social reform, at the heart of which was a great housing campaign. For a government faced with massive unemployment as soldiers returned from the war, and with a genuine fear of revolution along Bolshevik lines, a dynamic house building campaign had appeal. By 1919 even Conservative members of the coalition government were backing a housing programme funded by the Exchequer that gave power of default over reluctant local authorities, breaking the stalemate found in counties like Norfolk and marking a permanent departure from previous housing policy.[7]

In 1918, local rural councillors, some of whom had houses of their own to let, remained unwilling to proceed with housing schemes. Moreover, it was often the councillors themselves, as farmers and landowners, who bore the brunt of increased rates. Faced with high prices for materials and increased rates of interest for loans, local authorities felt they were as unable as the speculative builders to erect working-class dwellings.

Christopher Addison, Minister of Reconstruction, was critical of the Local Government Board and Treasury's vague financial proposals to local authorities. He believed smaller authorities would not be able to raise the capital required or commit to programmes without Treasury support. The War Cabinet had already agreed in July 1917 that it would be necessary to 'substantially' aid authorities building 'housing for the working classes which is approved by the Local Government Board'.[8] Responses to the LGB's circular of 1918, which urged local authorities to submit building schemes, indicated that only 100,000 houses would be built nationwide – about a third of the minimum number thought to be required.

Addison took over at the LGB in January 1919, with the task of changing it into the Ministry of Health (MOH). He was wary of limiting the financial commitment of local authorities for their housing schemes, as he believed this would give them no incentive to economy. It was apparent, however, that otherwise local authorities would not build, and in February 1919 he acceded to their demands and limited their responsibility to an increase of one penny on their rates. A government subsidy would cover the difference between this and the actual cost of building, made law in July with the 1919 Housing and Town Planning Act, popularly known as Addison's Act.

The Act brought about two radical changes. An option to build became an obligation; local authorities were expected to provide for all working-class needs in their district, where they were not met by other means. Secondly, the principle of state subsidy for housing was enshrined in law. The sudden increase in the number and scale of housing schemes by local authorities proved that financial responsibility had been the stumbling block in the past.

In November 1918, Depwade RDC agreed to build 72 houses.[9] Although nowhere near the total needed, it was ambitious for a rural council without government funding and evidence of a change in policy at local level. But in February 1919 it resolved to build 300 houses, more than four times the number promised only three months previously and entirely due to the penny rate circular.[10] Few RDCs were either so enthusiastic or so prepared. Apart from a disinclination to trust the Government's penny rate pledge, some councillors made no distinction between local rates and government taxes – wherever the money came from the cost of providing the required houses would spell financial ruin both for the nation and for them.

Additional legislation was needed to make 'homes for heroes' a reality. The Acquisition of Land Act was passed in August 1919 to facilitate and cheapen compulsory land purchase for housing and the Housing (Additional Powers) Act in December 1919 offered grants to private builders prepared to erect houses of the same standard as those by local authorities. Councils such as Mitford and Launditch in central Norfolk, who did not wish to build themselves, welcomed this legislation, this authority being fortunate in containing part of the estates of Lord Leicester and Thomas Cook, both of whom built working-class housing. The council devolved their responsibilities on to the landowners and happily granted Lord Leicester £120 for a pair of cottages erected at Bintry. But this was exceptional, and other Norfolk RDCs were among the first to erect houses using Addison's Act.[11]

The Government's Manual on the Preparation of State-Aided Housing Schemes, published in 1919, stated that new public housing 'should mark an advance on the building and development which has ordinarily been regarded as sufficient in the past'.[12] The 500,000 houses it pledged to build were modelled on those of the Garden City Movement. The writings of Raymond Unwin, Barry Parker and Alexander Harvey emphasised simplicity and standardisation, and Unwin was an adviser on the 1919 legislation. In July 1917, Hayes (H.A.L.) Fisher, as President of the LGB, appointed a committee under the Liberal MP Sir John Tudor Walters to investigate the technical side of house building, including construction methods, economy and speed. The report of the Tudor Walters Committee in November 1918 was widely recognised as the first comprehensive treatise on the design of the small house, featuring many of Unwin's ideas such as the abolition of the parlour rather than reducing the size of the main living room, even if tenants desired one. The best economy would come not from following a single, standard plan, but from making the most of each site with regard to the position and aspect of the houses. To this end, the report recommended that each housing scheme employ an architect to design the layout and adapt type plans for the site. Norfolk RDCs followed this advice, but only because they did not have the specialist staff available in many urban authorities.[13]

By February 1920, Depwade had 98 houses under construction. In Norfolk, RDCs had a relatively simple procedure for choosing sites for their new houses. Parish councils would make recommendations which were followed up by an approach to the landowner. Some councils wrote to all the major landowners in the district asking if they would sell land for houses. If the landowner were amenable, either they or the council would suggest a price. Local authorities had compulsory purchase powers but most saw them as a last resort. By the end of 1919, Depwade had successfully agreed to purchase 41 sites, totalling 71.155 acres at £2670.10. They had failed to reach agreement on five sites and intended to make compulsory orders for them.[14] Landowners were aware of these powers

9. NRO, DC2/5/1, Depwade RDC Minutes, 11 November 1918.

10. NRO, DC2/5/1, Depwade RDC Minutes, 3 February 1919. By June 1919, the number had increased to 316 (Minutes, 2 June 1919).

11. NRO, DC7/1/34 Mitford and Launditch RDC Minutes, p.52 and 93.

12. Ministry of Health, Manual on the Preparation of State-Aided Housing Schemes, 1919, quoted in Brian Read, 'Homes for Heroes', Local History, no.85, May/June 2001, p.11.

13. The housing committee of Depwade RDC agreed to purchase twelve copies of the Tudor Walters Report in February 1919. NRO, DC2/5/1, Minutes, 3 February 1919.

14. NRO, DC2/5/1, Depwade Council Minutes, December 1919.

and rarely made a flat refusal. They could, and did, suggest other plots of land that might be more suitable, and some recommended a neighbour's land where they considered they had already done their duty. Small farmers often suggested the committee take land from larger farmers for building.[15] Where the development damaged crops the councils paid compensation.

In Norfolk's rural districts the sites were invariably agricultural. The new houses were grouped together where possible, most often in a straight line – against the advice of Unwin and the Tudor Walters report. If they could, they followed existing roads to minimise costs. Even though Norfolk RDCs were often building only a few houses in each parish, there seems to have been no attempt to insert these into spaces in existing house groups; rather the committees found it more convenient to buy one plot of land suitable for all the required houses.

Before large-scale mechanisation and transportation of building materials, cottages were built using local materials. These included flint from the fields and beaches, timber frame, clay lump, carstone and brick. Clunch and carstone were often used together as this how they occurred naturally. Flint was used in buildings all over Norfolk except in the far west. Clay lump is made of clay mixed with straw or horsehair and put into a wood mould, much like a large brick or breezeblock. It was used in the Breckland area from about 1800 to 1930. Brick, re-introduced to Norfolk in the fourteenth century, was the material of choice for the wealthy by the sixteenth century and by 1700 was used for most vernacular building.

Although Depwade RDC considered using clay lump in 1919, the National Housing and Town Planning Council argued against it, and the council dithered throughout the spring months, until it became too late to get the clay lump made in time and they abandoned the idea.[16]

The Ministry of Reconstruction had noted before the end of the war that any housing programme would have severe difficulties unless the Government took steps to control building supplies and labour. Most of the Ministry of Health's officials believed that it should be entrusted with the arrangements for materials. The Directorate of Building Materials Supply (DBMS) was set up to combat the predicted rise in prices for building materials once local authority housing schemes got underway, but was staffed by civil servants from the Ministry of Munitions and elsewhere, and as long as there were two departments the service proved an unsatisfactory and half-hearted attempt to control the price and supply of materials, effectively underwriting the big brick manufacturers who fixed the prices. Blofield and Flegg RDC spent a year trying to persuade the LGB and later the DBMS to allow them to purchase bricks locally. They had reached an agreement with a local brickyard but the DBMS insisted tenders to supply bricks for housing schemes should be sent through them.[17] This duplicated work and dragged out the proceedings. It was a sellers' market, and the building materials industry supplied those sectors offering the highest profits. The big building firms turned to industrial projects and the smaller ones to repair work. Local authority housing, which was not lucrative, was last in the queue for building supplies. By May 1920, the DBMS was suggesting local authorities should source their own building materials if they were able to do so locally, and on 1 July the DBMS was transferred to the MOH.[18]

When bricks were in especially short supply in 1920, the Government urged local authorities to consider 'special methods'. These were really just a substitute for building with bricks and were never popular with either builders or tenants. The advantages claimed for materials such as concrete blocks and pre-fabricated steel were speed, elimination of much skilled labour and equal durability to brick. Using ex-servicemen or the unemployed could overcome a shortage of skilled labour – but did not equate with speed. Large numbers of concrete houses needed to be built on each site to make them cost effective and they were not used in Norfolk's rural districts. A shortage of plasterers prompted the Govern-

15. NRO, DC22/2/45, Depwade Council Minutes, 1919-20 *passim*.

16. NRO, DC2/5/1, Depwade Council Minutes, 3 February, 10 April 1919.

17. NRO, DC15/1/13, Blofield and Flegg Council Minutes, 1919, *passim*.

18. PRO, HLG 49/4, Report of Committee, 12 May 1920.

ment to promote plasterboard, but again this was little used in Norfolk.

The new houses Depwade planned were to have a seventy-foot frontage where possible.[19] However, wrangling between the council and the Chief Housing Inspector over the inclusion of parlours took the best part of a year and delayed building. Some councils rejected non-parlour homes at first because they associated two-roomed cottages with older, inadequate housing. Generally speaking, older cottages had much better accommodation on the ground floor than upstairs. Those with a living room at the front and a scullery at the back compared favourably to new, non-parlour houses. The upper floor was the problem, as there were usually only two bedrooms in the attic space, opening one out of the other and with windows too small for either proper light or ventilation. The roof might not have a ceiling and if it were gabled, it was often impossible to stand upright except in the middle of the room. A desire not to duplicate these conditions may well have been behind a council's insistence on parlour houses, although many authorities showed it was possible to build a non-parlour house with three good bedrooms in the inter-war years.

19. NRO DC2/5/1, Depwade Council Minutes, 24 April 1919.

Another frequent disagreement between the Ministry, local authorities and tenants was over the external appearance of the new houses. The Tudor Walters Report had rejected any form of external ornamentation on economic and aesthetic grounds. Unwin believed that proportion and good arrangement would give an inherent attractiveness to new developments at little or no extra cost. He later criticised local authorities for not relating buildings to one another or to the site. For him, the overall effect of 'grouping' was more important than individual houses, and the effect he desired could not be achieved by using all semi-detached houses. As with many other aspects of the housing problem, the rural situation was not specifically considered – layout and grouping could not improve the appearance of very plain houses erected in single figures.

Following the Tudor Walters Report, the plans recommended to local authorities by the MOH retained only the general Georgian characteristics of neat, hipped roofs and symmetrical disposition of doors and windows. No wonder they were called 'boxes with lids'. The Ministry's architects, including Unwin, believed external features should derive from internal arrangements. Local authorities and their tenants preferred the gables and bay windows of speculative builders, so the rise in costs and a shortage of materials in 1920 actually led to a more varied style being acceptable to the Ministry.

Slate was the preferred roofing material, but where tiles were available locally, their use was encouraged. Tiles are more porous than slate and so have to be laid at a much steeper pitch, as with thatch, a traditional Norfolk material. If following a doctrine of simplification, with no broken rooflines, the roof when laid with tiles would have to be of a great height – wasting space and using more bricks in the higher gables. Therefore the MOH allowed the use of dormer windows, projecting wings, and an L shaped ground plan in parlour houses. Red pantiles were a popular Norfolk roofing material and were used across the county in the new houses. A few even had thatched roofs.

Smallburgh RDC purchased two sites in Hickling, paying £100 for two acres. The houses built on these two sites were based on their survey under the 1919 Act. The scheme was approved by the Housing commissioner and the ministry of Health, and adopted by the council on 25 November 1919. The same plans were used for both sites, with one block of four cottages, a central archway giving access to the back of the middle two. The architect, Edward Boardman, an Arts and Crafts architect based in Norwich noted for How Hill, a holiday house at Ludham, planned to use thatch for the roofs of the cottages at Mill Lane, Hickling, but changed this to tiles when he invited tenders in March 1920. The council accepted a tender of £3,280 build the four cottages in April 1920. However, due to the building materials shortage, the builder was unable to get pantiles for the roofing. Boardman managed to obtain a price for thatch that worked out at the

Figure 2. Cottages at Mill Lane, Hickling (the mill is in a field directly opposite). The thatch is in good order and, although plastic guttering has been added and the windows replaced, the original neo-Georgian style has been kept. Edward Boardman was the architect here and for several Norfolk RDCS (author).

Figure 3. Houses at North Burlingham, Blofield RD, by George Skipper (author).

20. Information and photograph by kind permission of Olive Harvey.

21. NRO, DC2/5/1, Depwade Council Minutes, November 1919.

same cost as tiles. The Housing Commissioner approved this in June 1920. The cottages were completed, with their thatched roofs, by March 1921.

For houses in North Burlingham, Blofield RD appointed as its architect George Skipper, a local rival of Boardman better known for his commercial work in Norwich before the war, including the Norwich Union building on Surrey Street and Jarrold's department store. It is likely that both architects adapted plans recommended by the MOH for working-class housing. Skipper's large, three bed-roomed, parlour houses illustrate the varied rooflines permitted by the MOH when the materials shortage was at its height. Loddon and Clavering RDC used a very similar design in their houses in Ditchingham. These were also semi-detached and have an extended roof down to single-storey height at the back of each property over the scullery. Unlike the Burlingham houses, those in Ditchingham have more typical orange-red Norfolk pantiled roofs. Loddon and Clavering were among the first councils to build using Addison's Act.

The same family has occupied No.35 Sun Road, Broome, since it was completed in 1921. Mr Harvey, the first tenant, was the carpenter employed by local builder Hood to fit the houses here and in Ditchingham, a couple of miles away. The family had been living with Mrs Harvey's mother and were glad to have their own home.[20]

Depwade RDC, following Ministry guidelines adapted for rural use, made provision for a bath, 'to be fixed later if required and as much storage space and cupboard room as possible.'[21] Water supplies were a perennial problem in Norfolk's rural districts where there was invariably no piped water supply. Much time was devoted to the provision of wells on the new sites; in some districts, surface wells were sufficient, in others, deeper bores had to be sanctioned and increased the cost of the scheme considerably. Sometimes, on larger sites, water was piped into the new houses; on others, it had to be drawn from a well and carried to the house. The provision of an upstairs bathroom, which became common in urban developments, was a non-starter in rural districts where the water for the bath had to been carried upstairs and down again afterwards. Baths were provided for use in the scullery. Fixed baths in bathrooms only became possible in local authority houses with the advent of water and sewerage systems, often only in the 1960s.

The Tudor Walters Report of 1918 recommended houses of a high standard. It argued that it would be uneconomical in the long run to add to the already large supply of houses that would soon be inadequate. The report proposed a minimum size of 855 square feet and an optimum of 1,055 square feet excluding stores. The 1919 *Housing Manual* produced by the MOH recommended even higher space standards; averaging 900 square feet for a three bed-roomed non-parlour house and 1,080 square feet for a parlour house. These standards were exceeded in the optimistic early post war years. Detractors often criticise the uniformity of council housing – but what needs to be highlighted is the high standard of amenity. Even without a fixed bath in a bathroom, the new council houses provided a level of comfort and convenience not previously experienced by the working classes of rural Norfolk.

At a recommended eight houses to the acre, the early houses built by Norfolk RDCs had an average garden size of 350 square yards – considered the optimum size for a man to cultivate profitably and easily by spade in his leisure time. Depwade RDC preferred fruit bushes rather than chestnut pailings to divide the plots. It supplied decent-sized sheds built of brick, and ditches with a live fence of whitethorn or myrobella at the boundaries.[22] As gardens were an important resource for the tenants, councils went to great lengths to ensure decent topsoil was left and even supplied rabbit proof fencing when tenants complained of predation. Poultry houses were sanctioned provided they were not close to the houses but where 'the poorer class of tenants' had erected 'unsightly' fowl houses close to the property, they were asked to remove them.[23] Occasionally even pigstyes were permitted provided they were at the end of the garden and none of the neighbours complained.

In the post-war boom of 1919, the Government was prepared to fund 'homes for heroes' at an average cost for a six-roomed house of £1,000 rather than risk revolution. The whole process of planning, building and managing the new houses was a novelty, and inevitably took time, and the building and materials industries could not meet the demands placed on them. The costs of building and the rents charged quickly became too high. The new houses were intended for the working classes, yet setting rents that Norfolk labourers could afford was highly problematic.

When it was apparent that not enough houses were going to be built by the end of the first year to fulfil Government claims, the MOH, in September 1919, tried to speed up the process, leading to increased prices and shortages of materials and labour. The building industry increased production but still could

22. NRO, DC2/5/1, Depwade Council Minutes, 8 September 1919.

23. NRO, DC2/5/1, Depwade Council Minutes, 13 June 1921.

Figure 4. No.35 Sun Road, Broome, a three bed-roomed parlour house, Loddon and Clavering RD (author).

Figure 5. Mrs Harvey and three of her daughters outside No.35 Sun Road, Broome, when it was completed. Her daughter Olive, not in the picture, took over the tenancy when she retired and returned home to nurse her mother. The houses had iron-framed windows that have since been replaced with double glazed uPVC windows. The earth closet was in a separate brick building to the side of the house that is now used for storage. The large scullery at the back of the house was converted to a separate kitchen and bathroom in the 1960s by the RDC (Olive Harvey).

not cope with a flood of local authority housing schemes. The slump of 1920–1 transformed the balance of political forces. The power of labour was undermined and an insurance against social unrest was no longer needed. A policy of reducing public expenditure in line with orthodox economic theory ended the 'homes fit for heroes' campaign, the Government declaring it could now not afford to provide five-roomed houses at an average cost of £320.[24] In July 1921, the Government decided to limit the subsidy to houses already with approved tenders; private enterprise also lost the grant on houses started after July 1921. This about-face left local authorities large and small struggling to meet their commitments.

The situation in Depwade RDC illustrates perfectly what happened across the country when the Government called a halt to further expenditure on housing. In March 1921, its housing committee resigned when the council refused to sanction the building of another sixteen houses to complete building on various sites. Those councillors who were against building on the grounds of cost now had the Government on their side. A new committee was formed and agreed not to build the houses, against the advice of the Clerk, who pointed out that sites where building had started could be completed and still claim the subsidy. This would cease in June 1922 and the council would be left with small pieces of land difficult to sell or let profitably. The rapid about-turn of council and Government had repercussions. The contractor put in a claim for breach of contract for £2,385, eventually settling for £250 after the Ministry intervened.

Captain Tighe, the Housing Inspector for Norfolk, stated in June 1921
That no further building in rural areas would be sanctioned, that no work is to be done in connection with the preparation of plans or obtaining tenders, that all sites should be let with a view to ultimate sale.[25]

Selling sites in 1922 that had been purchased in 1919 involved losses to all the councils, as potential buyers offered less than cost price, and there were conveyancing fees. Depwade RDC had 300 houses in their original housing scheme that had been sanctioned by the MOH. When building ceased they had completed 98.[26] In 1919, the Government had pledged to build 500,000 houses in three years. By March 1920, local authorities had built only 1,250 houses. By 1921, completions had risen to 25,000. The original target of 100,000 houses in the first year was not reached until March 1922. In England, Scotland and Wales fewer than 176,000 houses were built under the 1919 Act.[27] Depwade had managed to provide 32.7 per cent of their proposed total; nationally local authorities built 35.2 per cent, showing that small rural district councils were as capable of administering housing schemes as the large urban authorities.

While Addison's Housing Act of 1919 did not solve the housing problem in rural Norfolk, it was an admirable achievement. Without it the RDCs would not have built, as indeed most of them had not under previous Housing Acts. Extreme economic circumstances, some of which could not have been forecast or alleviated by control of the market, disadvantaged the housing programme. Changes in the balance of political power put an end to housing schemes that had barely started. Nonetheless, they had responded to the new demands placed upon them and rose to a challenge that many civil servants would have preferred to hand to County Councils. Housing committees across the county put in place the administrative procedures required to run the schemes effectively and efficiently in spite of being short staffed after the war. Many were disconcerted by the sudden termination of their building. Later, without the lengthy bureaucratic supervision of central government, local authorities were able to continue building, within new financial constraints imposed by successive Governments.

24. A. Sayle, *The Houses of the Workers*, London, Fisher Unwin, 1924, p.132.

25. NRO, DC2/5/2, Depwade Council Minutes, 1 July 1921.

26. *Eastern Daily Press*, no.15,450, 30 March 1921, p.7.

27. Mark Swenarton, *Homes Fit For Heroes, the Politics and Architecture of Early State Housing in Britain*, London, Heinemann Educational, 1981, p.122.

2 Housing Happenings in Somers Town

ROLAND JEFFERY

Housing Happenings in Somers Town

ROLAND JEFFERY

The St Pancras House Improvement Society was founded in 1924 by a group associated with the Magdalen College Mission in Somers Town, the area of London between Euston and St Pancras stations.[1] Developed on suburban brickfields and pastures from the 1790s, Somers Town mostly comprised four-storey terraced houses, with, at its centre, a formal polygon of semi-detached villas. The arrival of massive construction works for the London railway termini – Euston, Kings Cross and later St Pancras - damaged the area as properties were allowed to deteriorate from the 1840s and jerry-built infill on once spacious gardens pushed up the density. By the 1920s, when Somers Town formally celebrated its centenary, it was one of central London's most squalid slums.

Magdalen Mission, in common with other missions and settlements founded and funded by the Oxford and Cambridge colleges, combined social work with its Christian evangelism. It was staffed by clergy whose stipends were met by the college and by volunteer undergraduates who would spend their vacations, or a year following graduation, at the Mission. Many of the Oxbridge missions and settlements were effective at propounding the Christian Socialism of F. D. Maurice, combining reformist, even radical, political views with practical action and religious practice, usually of the High Church sort. This work was made possible by ancient college endowments and middle-class generosity. Among the strengths of the settlement model was that those volunteering lived on site amidst the slum conditions, which highlighted the need for practical action.

The Society's founder was Father Basil Jellicoe (1899–1935), a priest of mercurial charm, a charismatic preacher and cousin of Admiral Earl Jellicoe of Scapa. He suffered from a manic-depressive illness and met an early death, possibly at his own hand.[2] When active, however, he could summon prodigious reserves of energy and his 'piercing eyes and lively, mobile face' shines out of the many photographs taken during the period of his work with the Society.[3] In launching the St Pancras House Improvement Society he was implementing a dream of the previous Magdalen Missioner, the Reverend Ivo Hood, who in 1904 proposed setting up a 'four per cent philanthropy' dwellings company funded by Magdalen graduates to implement slum clearance. The First World War intervened and this scheme was stillborn.

The new Society's first response to the Somers Town slums was the purchase in 1925 of seven houses in Gee Street for £430 each. They did basic repairs and converted them into self-contained flats, offering marginally more privacy than the typical multi-roomed tenement. Irene Barclay, recruited in 1925 as the Society's Secretary and first housing manager, recalled that 'they were in a shocking state of dilapidation. Had they been in Knightsbridge they would probably have cost three times the price, been gutted and renovated and sold for £2,000 to £3,000 apiece.'[4] Fr Jellicoe had already raised the money for this purchase by touring the country in a little car, speaking at meetings organised by churches, West End hostesses, Rotarians, working men's clubs, schools and colleges. He quickly became famous and, as Barclay recalled, 'His meetings were highly dramatic. He would wait for perhaps a minute before starting to speak, then,

Figure 1. St Joseph's flats on opening. (All photographs from the St Pancras Housing Association Archive unless otherwise noted.)

1. The name changed to St Pancras Housing Society in 1944, St Pancras Housing Association in Camden in 1970, and to St Pancras Housing Association in 1989. Today it operates within the Origin Group as St Pancras Housing.

2. Kenneth Ingram, *Basil Jellicoe*, Canterbury, The Century Press, 1936.

3. Irene Barclay, *People Need Roots*, London, National Council of Social Service, 1976, p.20.

4. ibid., p.22.

Figure 2. Father Jellicoe in Clarendon Street (n.d.)

Figure 3. Gee Street housing, the Society's first project – reconditioning commencing.

Figure 4. Irene Barclay, n.d.

throwing off his cloak and advancing on his captive audience he would say "Now I am going to tell you about Somers Town", and tell them he did, to great effect, ending with: "Before I came here today you didn't know. Now you do there is no excuse for you. You must help." And help they did. Money came in at the rate of £1,000 a month.'

Irene Barclay (1894–1989) was the first woman in Britain to qualify as a chartered surveyor. In its infancy housing management was a female domain, its first professional body being the Society of Women House Property Managers, founded in 1913 by Octavia Hill and others. At St Pancras, housing managers were invariably female until the late 1960s, and were known by tenants as 'the landladies'. Surveying had, however, remained an exclusively male profession. Immediately after the Sex Disqualification Removal Act of 1919, Barclay was encouraged to train as a surveyor by her lady supervisor at the Crown Estates office in Regents Park, where she was manager of the Crown's run-down working-class housing just a few yards east of the grand Nash Terraces. After qualifying in 1922, she worked in the Welwyn Garden City office of Louis de Soissons but soon determined to use her professional skills for more urgent social purposes and started her own practice with another freshly qualified woman, Evelyn Perry. Barclay and Perry's pioneering housing surveys in slum areas of London, working house by house and visiting every room without invitation from the slumlords or prior announcement to the tenants ('I think they were ready to admit us because they realised we were on their side') broke new ground.[5] Their surveys were far more thorough than those undertaken by the London County Council, which declared 'clearance areas' for wholesale demolition on the basis of largely external physical surveys, a practice it continued until the 1960s.

Apart from their thoroughness, Barclay and Perry's work had huge value as propaganda, for they documented the level of overcrowding and financial circumstances of many occupants alongside the chronic disrepair and lack of amenities of the built fabric. As Barclay wrote later,

> I learnt to know intimately the typical terraced house, built in the early nineteenth century for single family occupation, once charming, with dainty iron balconies, some with little gardens. When I knew the inside of the houses they had three, four or five families in the eight rooms, two of which were in the basement, dark, damp with rotten floors, overrun with rats and black beetles. … There was a back yard WC and a wash-house with a coal-fired copper. The family on the top floor had the great advantage of some privacy – there was room for a gas cooker on the landing, and no needed to pass

5. ibid., p.15.

26

*through a person's domain to reach his own, so there was no sound of tramp-
ing feet overhead. On the other hand, if the roof leaked, and it often did, there
was little chance of avoiding the rain. … And on the top floor the chimney
was more likely to smoke.*[6]

The first Barclay and Perry survey was commissioned by a group of Chelsea resi-
dents shocked at the slums in their wealthy borough. They included the actor
Ernest Thesiger and James McDonnell QC, fresh from his celebrated defence of
Roger Casement and who spent much of his wealth, derived from estates around
Rye, on art – boasting that he owned more portraits than the National Portrait
Gallery. They were unlikely activists, but armed with Barclay and Perry's survey
they took out private prosecutions of local slum landlords (because the local
authority failed to use its statutory powers to do so), noisily publicising their
court victories and thereby galvanising the 'much offended' council into action.
They also published Barclay and Perry's reports to right-thinking individuals as
propaganda. Subsequent surveys by Barclay and Perry covered St Marylebone,
Shoreditch, Southwark, Victoria and Pimlico, Fulham, North Kensington and
Paddington; and outside the metropolis they looked at Birmingham, Manchester
and Edinburgh.[7] The foreword to the *Survey of Victoria and Pimlico* was aimed
at the residents of the wealthier parts of Westminster, many of whom occupied
prestigious enclaves just yards from the slums, and tackled the reluctance to use
rate income to subsidise housing schemes, declaring that:

> *the City of Westminster has exceptional rating resources compared with
> the rest of London and it may be regarded as the centre of Empire … . The
> Committee … will feel rewarded if this larger survey succeeds in enlightening
> public opinion, strengthening the hands of all engaged in similar work, and
> paving the way for remedial action, which is neither so difficult nor so costly
> as is commonly supposed.*[8]

These surveys prompted the founding of the St Pancras House Improvement
Society in 1924, one of many such. With Father Jellicoe as its first Chairman it was
rapidly propelled to national prominence, capitalising on middle-class concern
about inner-city housing conditions since the close of the First World War, when
the plight of returning troops had elevated housing conditions to a new prominence and the Liberal Party slogan of 'Homes Fit For Heroes' was born. The political response was a flurry of legislation enabling local authorities to act against
slumlords and to subsidise new housing developments by local authorities and
private companies, but none took off. Local authorities were given a responsibility under the 1919 Housing and Town Planning Act to meet the housing needs of
their areas, but had inadequate financial powers and there was strong ratepayer
pressure not to subsidise housing from the rates. Indeed, the reluctance of the
Conservative councillors at St Pancras Metropolitan Borough to act in Somers
Town was the main spur to the formation of the St Pancras Society with its practical, Fabian approach.[9] It was assisted by fundraising, based on Anglo-Catholic,
Free Church, Fabian and upper middle-class networks. Because it caught the
climate of concern the Society won widespread coverage in the national press,
at first out of all proportion to actual achievements.

Within months, the modest start made by upgrading existing slum properties was seen as inadequate, and the St Pancras Society started to raise funds
for larger clearance and new-build developments. Alongside the fundraising
for gifts, it began to sell non-convertible loan stock. This was an extension of
the 'five per cent philanthropy' that had flourished in the nineteenth century
(becoming four per cent philanthropy as yields fell). Model housing – mostly
tenements but occasionally cottage estates – was built in working-class areas and
investors received a 5% return on their loan stock. In London the East End Dwellings Company and Metropolitan Dwellings Company, joint stock companies
that sought to distribute profits, led the field. It was a form of ethical investment
that seldom performed as well as more speculative stock, but was secured on

6. ibid., p.14.

7. For example, the *Victoria Ward
Westminster Survey of Housing Conditions*,
Westminster Survey Group, April 1927;
*Survey of Housing in the Royal Borough of
Kensington*, Kensington Housing Asso-
ciation, February 1932; *Survey of Housing
Conditions in St Andrew's Ward, Edinburgh*,
Edinburgh Council of Social Service, 1931.

8. *Victoria Ward* survey, ibid.

9. Barclay, *op.cit.*, p 24. See also Irene
Barclay, *The St Pancras Housing Association
in Camden: What it is and Why: a History*,
London, St Pancras HA, 1972.

10. John N. Tarn, *Five Per Cent Philanthropy*, Cambridge University Press, 1973.

11. It became a registered charity only later.

12. Malcolm J. Holmes, *Housing Is Not Enough – The Story of St Pancras Housing Association*, London, St Pancras HA, 1999.

property assets.[10] The St Pancras House Improvement Society was incorporated under the Industrial and Provident Societies Acts as a public utility undertaking with a memorandum that dedicated it to social housing and to not distributing profits.[11] The loan stock was unsecured, so its purchase was an ethical rather than an investment decision.

Apart from the dwellings companies there were two other strands of social housing in London at that time: the great metropolitan trusts and the London County Council. The large charitable trusts of Peabody, Samuel Lewis and Guinness were endowed by their founders with fortunes enabling them to charge rents affordable to respectable working-class households with a regular income. However, after a period of rapid growth they struggled to expand in the 1920s as building costs had risen and their funds were extensively committed. Many of their tenement flats were sixty or more years old, and dated in their lack of sanitary provision and grim, cramped accommodation. The LCC's first initiatives in the 1890s were inherited from the Metropolitan Board of Works, whose primarily interest in roads and drainage infrastructure overflowed into housing when they acquired sites alongside road improvements. These early LCC estates seemed by the 1920s to be inadequate, and Irene Barclay was critical of the Boundary Estate in Shoreditch, and the Millbank Estate, Pimlico. While she admired their beguiling Arts and Crafts detailing, by Owen Fleming and his young team of mainly Architectural Association graduates, she argued that they failed the dwellers of the worst slums because only about eighty per cent of them were typically re-housed on the completed estates. The densities in the slums were so high that this was felt to be inevitable. Those fortunate enough to be re-housed were typically in employment with regular wages. 'The rest', Barclay noted, 'went where they could, to escalate slum conditions by overcrowding the neighbourhood'. The LCC's low-density cottage estates on London's periphery suited only those who could find skilled work in the new outlying industrial estates or who – even less likely – could afford commuter fares. So neither the LCC nor the housing trusts addressed all the issues of areas highlighted in the Barclay and Perry surveys, where casual labour, poverty wages and unemployment were endemic.

The twin concerns of producing housing at rents the poorest residents could afford, and of maintaining the entire existing communities intact by rebuilding on the same site, became hallmarks of Barclay's projects and of the work of St Pancras House Improvement Society. The third hallmark was the range of non-housing provision that soon followed, from loan clubs to put professional sharks out of business, social facilities for children, mothers and the elderly, a furniture scheme, holidays for tenants and their children, and welfare funds. The recipe was rapidly copied and Barclay and Jellicoe were soon involved in schemes across central London.[12]

The Society chose as its architect Ian Hamilton, nephew of General Sir Ian Hamilton, First World War hero of the Dardanelles and who first encountered the Society when an undergraduate at Magdalen College, Oxford. Sir Herbert Warren, the poet, educationalist and reforming President of Magdalen, recommended him to Jellicoe as one concerned with social housing and able to challenge the assumption in 1924 that the extent of disrepair in the slums and their low yields made the 'Housing Problem' insoluble. Not a few landlords, Barclay and Perry found, preferred their tenants not to pay rent as this relieved them of the obligation to repair. Even if the rents were paid, the sums the poor could afford gave a low return. Local authorities had powers under several statutes passed between the London Public Health Act of 1891 and the Housing, Town Planning Act in 1909 to compel landlords to keep their houses 'in all respects reasonably fit for human habitation and to recover costs for repairs from landlords who failed to observe their duties'. But most failed to use them, either from a political reluctance to challenge owner's property rights or because of the cumbersome and costly procedures necessary for even modest and temporary improvements.

They saw the lack of economic return on slum property as the principal obstacle. Ian Hamilton contributed to Jellicoe's pamphlet, *The Englishman's Home*, which ran to several editions and which challenged the complacency of this market view of the problem. Hamilton, Jellicoe said, carried out his work 'in the spirit of a sanctified lark'. He invariably wore an Eton wing collar and an immaculate suit, even when visiting the poorest tenements, but his patrician demeanor belied a profound commitment to improving the housing conditions of the poorest, which became his life's work.

Hamilton's architecture was always thoughtful, sometimes charming, with a careful choice of brick, skillful detailing with brick and, often, Roman tile on edge. But it is principally remarkable for a relentless cost-consciousness achieved without meanness. His architectural idiom was a practical version of a formula that became the almost unvarying uniform of London's inter-war social housing. It was composed of several elements. The outer, 'public', faces of the load-bearing brick blocks were neo-Georgian with subtly updated proportions to the façades and rhythm of white sash windows. The inner 'private' elevations boasted a more modern arrangement of long concrete access balconies cantilevered from the floor slabs, with brick parapets, concrete refuse chutes to communal waste chambers and stair towers. These Janus-faced blocks were normally four stories, with a fifth floor rising into a lofty, tiled mansard roof, and arranged in symmetrical Beaux-Arts layouts as far as the sites allowed. The inner courtyards had play areas and simple landscaping, while the Georgian outward face had more formal perimeter walls and gates that gave a corporate identity to the whole as an 'estate' development.

It is difficult to pinpoint the emergence of this form. It had few precedents before 1914, for the Peabody Estates built from the 1860s onwards adopted a functional style, while the dwellings companies used an eclectic classicism and the traditional staircase plan, made into an economic proposition by mean dimensions while given some distinction by cast-iron staircase balustrades. The LCC estates of the 1890s adopted Arts and Crafts styling but stuck to the staircase plan, often only serving two flats per floor, while for cottage estates its architects preferred a stripped-down vernacular. But by the 1920s the neo-Georgian model had arrived, reflecting a widespread shift in taste in domestic design, not only in England, after 1900. In 1921–2 the Guinness Trust completed their Kennington Park Road tenements with touches of neo-Georgian styling, designed by their favoured architects, Messrs Joseph. In 1924 Ian Hamilton designed the first flats for St Pancras, St Mary's, not built for another eighteen months but immediately exhibited as a cardboard model on a fundraising tour made by Jellicoe in his car. The LCC was building its first estate in the idiom at Tabard Gardens, Southwark (planned in 1915 but not realised before 1924), and the Collingwood Estate at Brady St, Whitechapel, and Whitmore Estate in Shoreditch immediately followed.[13]

Without exception, housing societies after St Pancras adopted this formula, as did the LCC under their long-serving Chief Architect, G. Topham Forrest. There were subtle differences in the colour of brick, and later in the 1930s a few balconies became more streamlined and details showed a knowledge of Willem Dudok and Art Deco. However the basic formula remained remarkably constant. Although the workmanship, especially of the brickwork, was exceptionally good, the designs were driven by cost. The open access balcony arrangement saved on expensive staircases. It enabled all flats to be dual-aspect, if well-lit only on one side, and the balconies were even suitable as closely supervised toddlers' play areas. The concrete floor slabs used the well-established technique of reinforcement with mild steel and gave superior sound insulation and fire resistance, while allowing the balconies to be cantilevered from them.

The St Pancras flats designed by Hamilton were among the best and most humane of the type. They never included the 'Simplified Type' built by the LCC as

13. A watercolour of 1924 by Cyril Fairey for the LCC Councillors shows an LCC estate, probably a prototype rather than one actually built. (see back cover)

Figure 5. Ceremonial burning of papier maché models of vermin. The fire is being lit by General Sir Ian Hamilton, uncle of the architect.

Figure 6. Bedding being fumigated.

late as 1926 with shared bathrooms on landings, an arrangement continued from the earliest LCC flats of the 1890s but deemed unacceptable by Barclay, who commented ironically: 'The London [County Council] blocks were too close together and the flats without baths – but in the early years of the century who would have thought of giving the people who did the dirtiest work bathrooms?'

Both housing societies and local authorities were to find that improving existing stock inevitably cut the number of households that could be accommodated, as more kitchens and bathrooms had to be provided. The move to wholesale rebuilding may have been driven, therefore, by the St Pancras Society's insistence on re-housing *all* the existing tenants on site. Two other factors ruled out refurbishment as a satisfactory strategy for St Pancras: bed bugs and dry rot. The common bed bug (*Cimex Lecularlis*) was endemic in the slums and no safe *in situ* chemical treatment was available. Barclay recalled that 'these insects ... feed on blood and attack the soft bodies of children unmercifully. They thrive on stuffy warmth and live in woodwork and plaster ... Directly these old buildings were touched clusters and bunches of these vile insects were uncovered. I remember seeing a cross taken down from a wall and its exact outline remained for a few seconds in living bugs.'[14] When tenants moved to their new flats all their furniture, bedding and clothing was sealed inside the St Pancras traveling 'bug van'-cum-removals vehicle, to be fumigated with fearful Zyclon B gas and then thoroughly aired for 24 hours. Only such drastic treatment prevented the bugs from moving with the tenants. The Society's own publicity and fundraising film, *The Terror that Walketh by Night*, dramatised infestation with Expressionist alarm.[15] Dry rot (*Merulius Lacrimans*) also thrived in the slums, encouraged by damp from disrepair and humidity from overcrowding. It was not until the late 1930s that a chemical treatment was developed, and it was made safely and commercially available only in the late 1940s. This ushered in the possibility of wholesale refurbishment of older houses as an urban renewal strategy; in the inter-war period it was not feasible.

The most ambitious buildings by the St Pancras Society were in Drummond Crescent, Euston. All means were used to assemble funds, from a month of prayer before the Blessed Sacrament at Pusey House, Oxford, endorsements from Neville Chamberlain, Minister of Health, to letters in *The Times*. John Galsworthy described an experience of a visit in *Swan Song* (the final part of the *Forsyte Saga*), and became an active fundraiser for the Society. The Prince of Wales became a shareholder, amidst appropriate publicity, and within nine months the purchase price was raised and 69 houses and some open land were bought

14. Barclay, *People Need Roots*, *op.cit.*, p 23.

15. 1935; current location unknown.

for £26,000. The fifth Annual General Meeting in 1929 saw the start made on St George's flats, the first development of what *Housing Happenings*, the Society's bulletin, dubbed a 'mini Garden City', designed by Ian Hamilton.[16] The Chairman of the LCC performed the rite of commencement of the scheme, which involved a dramatic demolition by explosives of some of the site's slums, probably the first use of such a stunt. The foundation stone was laid by Admiral Lord Jellicoe and was filmed for newsreel distribution by the Gaumont Film Company, the first of many uses of film to promote the St Pancras Society's work. Amenities included corner shops run by traders already on the site; a rooftop nursery school complete with playground, paddling pool and ornamental fountain; communal gardens, individual allotments, and clothes-drying areas. When completed in 1931 St Christopher's, across the north of the site, were the only low-cost flats in London totally equipped by electricity, with hot water and portable fires: the height of modernity at the time yet affordable to those on low incomes.

From the start Ian Hamilton's blocks featured ceramic reliefs in Doulton's polychrome stoneware designed by Gilbert Bayes (1872–1953), one of the material's most effective champions.[17] Jellicoe ensured the Society's first flats were named St Mary's, and bore a Bayes Virgin in the style of the Della Robbia workshop. The circles of clothes-drying lines in the courtyards each had Doultonware finials and the centre of the spokes had a more elaborate embellishment. Over the following decade more than 300 finials, lunettes, fountains and ornaments were commissioned for the Society. Many were based on the motifs or life stories of the saints after whom the blocks were named, so St Joseph's flats had a bag of carpenter's tools in the centre of the drying area. Others used illustrations from Hans Andersen or the Grimm Brothers – Sleeping Beauty, the Little Mermaid and the Goose Girl – or nursery rhymes, such as the 'Four and Twenty blackbirds' at St Christopher's. When the Society developed an estate in York Rise, Kentish

16. *Housing Happenings*, no.3, 1929.

17. Louise Irvine and Paul Atterbury, *Gilbert Bayes, Sculptor 1872–1953*, Shepton Beauchamp, Richard Dennis, 1998, pp.51–2.

Figure 7. A small child in a slum tenement, Little Drummond Street.

Town, designed by Hamilton on land granted by the London Midland and Scottish Railway to re-locate people displaced by the expansion of Euston Station on condition that some of their workers were housed there, Bayes adopted motifs from the insignia of the railway company as finials. It was an enlightened and successful series of commissions giving humanity and interest to the common areas of the estates, which were rarely generous in scale. Sadly, estate modernisation and theft has severely reduced the number of surviving examples, though a programme funded by the Heritage Lottery Fund has seen limited restoration and may encourage more.

Returning from a period of recuperation in 1927, Basil Jellicoe resigned as Missioner at Magdalen Mission to concentrate on his role as Chairman of the

Figure 8. Gilbert Bayes modelling a dragon.

Figure 9. Typical Gilbert Bayes washing posts.

House Improvement Society, and his widespread social activism and preaching. He was in great demand as an inspirational speaker and champion of the housing cause, and was the nationally known public face of the Society. He was, however, increasingly difficult to work with on account of his intensely personal approach (like most charismatic leaders he was no team player), and his unreliable health. He was regularly away for weeks at a time on speaking tours or on retreat at religious houses or rural vicarages during bouts of depression, so that the Society's Committee and the staff at Barclay and Perry began to develop ways of managing his absences. With worsening health from 1928, Jellicoe's breaks became more frequent and he was deeply hurt to discover that he was not indispensable. Eventually, after a year's absence on sick leave he agreed in 1934 to resign, broken and bitter, accepting a small pension from the Society for he had never held a clerical living. Even in his last year of life, during bouts of serious illness, he remained active, rolling out the St Pancras model of social housing, founding the St Richard's Housing Society in Sussex and becoming Chairman of the Isle of Dogs Housing Society in the London docks. Jellicoe died in 1935 after a protracted and especially severe depression. His memorial is an arch at the entrance to St Michael's Cottages in New Street, Penzance, an urban replacement for fishermen's slum cottages built by the St Michael's Housing Society, which he helped start in 1931. A memorial plaque on the site 'erected by his friends' pointedly makes no mention of his work in Somers Town or, indeed the capital city. It is dedicated in memory of 'the Pioneer of the better housing of God's children'.

In the metropolis, expansion of the Society's work was an objective from the start, achieved by encouraging other housing societies to replicate the model. Barclay and Perry took the lead, through their conditions surveys, with informal but enthusiastic support from the Society's Committee members. Fr Jellicoe's passionate oratory often launched things and supported fundraising, and there

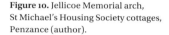

Figure 10. Jellicoe Memorial arch, St Michael's Housing Society cottages, Penzance (author).

was a free exchange of technical expertise. The St Marylebone Housing Society grew out of a Barclay and Perry survey in 1926, as did the Lambeth Housing Association and Southwark Housing Society, the Stepney Housing Trust and Bethnal Green Housing Society. The St George's Housing Society, in Shadwell and notable for the active leadership by the local Jewish community, and the Isle of Dogs Housing Society followed in 1930.[18] Barclay and Perry now had several junior staff and acted as contract housing managers for most of the new societies, a commercial arrangement but one carried out more in a spirit of selfless duty than for profit.

Many of the off-shoot societies adopted the same architectural idiom as St Pancras with four- or five-storey flats, and most used Ian Hamilton as their architect. Several also commissioned finials and decorations in Doultonware from Bayes, of which a few survive more or less intact today. Unfortunately, inappropriate window replacements and poor maintenance have compromised some of these attractive and hardwearing buildings, but the layout and some of Hamilton's recognisable character and detailing survives. Among the best are the

18. Stepney Housing Trust, Isle of Dogs HS and Bethnal Green HS are today merged into the East London Housing Association.

Janet Street Estate on the Isle of Dogs, and the Shipton Street Estate in Bethnal Green. The latter even included a public house – The Globe – with ambitions along the lines of Fr Jellicoe's own pub – The Anchor – in Somers Town. Jellicoe was dismayed equally by the abuse of alcohol and the narrow-mindedness of the teetotal Coffee House Movement, so decided to open a pub himself as a calculated counter-blast. It boasted elegant Hamilton facades and a well-fitted mahogany lounge, in stark contrast to the run-down drinking houses and bottle shops of the area. Jellicoe's embrace of a moderate enjoyment of drink, instead of encouraging teetotalism, was widely discussed and – though he soon ceded management to the Restaurant Public Houses Association – the publicity attracted, indeed courted, by the 'publican-priest' did much to promote the 'improved public house movement' and a more understanding attitude to the consumption of drink. The Anchor seems to have been Jellicoe's own project rather than a Housing Society initiative, though the Society's Committee often met in its upper room. Later sold to a brewery, it was clumsily converted to flats in the 1990s but still stands at the corner of Chalton and Aldenham Streets in Somers Town.

The Society expanded closer to home through the North St Pancras Group, formed to carry out work in Kentish Town. This operated almost as an autonomous entity, issuing its own loan stock and acquiring land in its own name. There were confused and difficult relationships with the parent body, which could not decide whether the Group should be integral to it or independent. Some members of the North Group were out of sympathy with the pronounced Anglo-Catholic atmosphere of the Society's publicity and fundraising. Their own fundraising did not lack flair, however. Leonard Day, their Vice Chairman and a keen amateur photographer, led the Society to use film as a propaganda medium. Using techniques of cross cutting, montage and dissolves, a number of short documentaries told the story of the Society's work. Large captions were intercut with hand-held footage of the slums and more composed shots of architectural models of the proposed replacements. Workmen were shown building the new flats, followed by newly-installed tenants delighted with their new homes. They are especially powerful when they juxtapose the affluence of much of London – swells arriving at Claridges and luxury flats for sale in the West End – with the poorest slums, as in *Paradox City*, directed by Leonard A. Day and Gerald E. Belmont in 1934. These films and their energetic use in fundraising events across the country were ground-breaking, and deserve to be better known, both for their contribution to the British documentary tradition and to charity fundraising techniques. As well as *Paradox City* there was *On Top of the World*, featuring the rooftop children's nurseries built on the top of Ian Hamilton's flats.[19]

The North Group commissioned a large neo-Georgian estate in Athlone Street, Kentish Town, completed in phases by 1938 to Hamilton's design and again boasting a rooftop nursery school, which remains in use. The Group harnessed the wealthy and well-connected residents of Hampstead and Highgate to the cause and boasted a letter head with no fewer than 43 august names, from the Archbishop of Canterbury as Patron, via Lady Stewart as Organising Secretary, Free Church ministers, Rotarians and the rabbi of the local synagogue, to avowed socialists such as J. B. Priestley.

The Society's most interesting architectural commission of the 1930s came from yet another off-shoot of the parent body. The South West Group was persuaded to remain an integral part of the Society, although sometimes acting as part of the North Group. Kent House in Ferdinand Street, Kentish Town, designed by Connell, Ward and Lucas and the Society's first venture into concrete architecture and modernism, was promoted jointly. Some North Group members clearly had an appetite for architectural experiment, for Kent House represented a very different architectural programme from Hamilton's work. The debates throughout the 1930s on how to renew the nation's aging housing stock and increase its supply (especially to support the massive immigration in the South East) were

19. Now at the National Film Archive. A television documentary *Somers Town* (dir. Richard Broad, 1984) also at the National Film Archive, includes clips from other St Pancras films apparently lost in recent years.

Figure 11. Kent House, Ferdinand Street, Kentish Town.

fought on technical as much as political grounds. The North Group at St Pancras followed these intently. *Housing Happenings* reported that

> the Committee of the North Group has given much thought to the question of reducing building costs without reducing quality ... and has decided to make an experiment of building a block of flats in reinforced concrete in Ferdinand Street ... We have accepted plans by Messrs Connell, Ward and Lucas, the well-known architects in reinforced concrete. The plans are attractive with provisional estimates showing a considerable saving as compared to brick.

The commission arose from identical concerns to those faced by the traditional buildings, of how to achieve decent family housing within rigorous cost constraints. Godfrey Samuel of Tecton also supplied an outline scheme, turned down by the Society because it felt he used the site less well.[20] The selected design filled the tiny site but had to be modified in the event to placate the LCC, the twenty flats being reduced to sixteen when the rear block was rotated ninety degrees on plan and entirely separated from the front block. As with all St Pancras commissions the occupiers of the slum houses at the front of the site were to be all decanted into the rear block before demolition began.[21] Other traditions survived in this forward-looking building. Models of bugs and bug-infested wood were ceremonially burnt on site as the existing slums came down, the ashes ceremonially mixed into the new concrete footings.

As well as strikingly clean modernist lines, the blocks were innovative in their details, with built-in flower troughs providing structural stiffening to the balcony fronts and private balconies which were said to be 'large enough for a baby to sleep on or even for meals or sitting out.'[22] The common access balconies to the rear doubled as clothes drying areas whilst more extensive airing was available on the communal flat roof. Back-to-back fireplaces meant that one fire heated both main rooms, plus the kitchen oven and hot water boiler, making the electric cooker superfluous in winter. Windows stretched the whole length of the flats on both elevations. This and the relative lack of structural beams and columns (what columns there were coincided with internal door frames to minimise their presence) internally created a pared-back, sleek effect very different from the Society's neo-Georgian flats. The cost of Kent House was budgeted at £400 per flat, a tough challenge for a small development on a constricted site, but came in below this. An existing fish and chip shop was replaced on the ground floor, which was otherwise cut away, the front block being raised on *pilotis*. *Paradox*

20. Letter from Lady Stuart to Godfrey Samuel of Tecton, March 1934, British Architectural Library SaG/1/2(ii); whereabouts of Tecton's drawings unknown.

21. *Architects Journal*, vol.79, 21 June 1934, p.885

22. *Housing Happenings*, No.17, 1934.

23. *Housing Happenings*, No.21, Summer 1936. Press coverage included *Architects Journal*, vol.82, 19 December 1935, pp.909–15; *Building*, vol.11, January 1936, p.21.

24. John Allan, *Lubetkin, Architecture and the Tradition of Progress*, London, RIBA Publications, 1992, pp.320ff.

25. Robert J. Esau, *Connell Ward & Lucas and Early Modern Low-income Housing*, RIBA Research Award Report, 1994, RIBA, London.

City included an on-screen appeal for the building whilst Leonard Day's *Castles in Chalk Farm* (1936) included footage of reinforced concrete being poured and captured the pioneering atmosphere.

Kent House originally boasted 'Tintocrete' self-coloured canary yellow concrete to the stairs, balconies and landings, red paint on the balcony ironmongery and turquoise paint on the steel window frames. *Housing Happenings* reported that, at the opening, speakers 'referred to the bright and cheerful colours, novelty and practical utilities of Kent House'.[23] For most of their life the blocks have been painted white, perhaps in line with the later idea that modernism of the heroic age is 'white architecture', but in recent years the original colours have been partially reinstated. The building has become easily the best known commission of the St Pancras Society and a symbol of an architectural style that might have developed rapidly in social housing if the Second World War had not intervened.

Unfortunately the lightweight monolithic structure of Kent House, 4½- inch thick in-situ concrete, which gave the building such striking lean and tidy lines, did not perform well thermally – especially in winter when the inner surfaces were prone to condensation. Amyas Connell was at the time involved with Berthold Lubetkin and others in a MARS Housing Research Group on insulation and some of Connell Ward and Lucas's private housing schemes of the 1930s used wood wool or double leaf cavity wall construction.[24] But – presumably because this was an experiment designed to demonstrate the low costs of the method used – the permanent cork shuttering pioneered by Lubetkin or fibre board used elsewhere was omitted, and Kent House relied on thermal plaster alone. This problem led to the blocks being refurbished by Jeffrey Fairweather Architects in 1980–2, when insulation was applied to the exterior (rather than inside, in order that tenants could remain in occupation) which almost tripled the thickness of the walls. This has seriously diminished the elegance of the windows, and the size and proportions of balconies, doors and other details, giving a rather bunker like aspect to what were originally light elevations. At the same time the access balconies and stairs, once elegantly spare in their detailing and open-sided, were glazed in around a new lift tower and the elegant *pilotis* compromised with cumbersome gates. Kent House has since been listed Grade II, so perhaps its original elegance and complete colour scheme may one day be restored.

Kent House was the only foray of Connell, Ward and Lucas into social housing, in spite of their concern to use new technology to reduce its cost. Other proposals, including an ambitious scheme for miners' housing in Wales were not realised.[25] It is interesting to compare the Society's most regular architect, Ian Hamilton, with Connell, Ward and Lucas. With his patrician background, dress and demeanor, Hamilton pursued a life-long commitment to decent, homely working class housing and its cost-effective construction within a traditional architectural language. Like many avant-garde architects of the 1930s the younger firm espoused left-of-centre politics and advocated a new architecture of social inclusion, but made its living designing houses for comfortably-off patrons. The Association immediately reverted to updated forms of Hamilton's 1920s' model, starting with their York Rise Estate in Kentish Town of 1938. These middle-of-the-road architectural preferences lasted well after the Second World War.

ACKNOWLEDGEMENTS

The author is grateful to Malcolm J. Holmes at Camden Local History Library, custodian of the SPHA archive; to June Warrington and Joanna Smith at English Heritage; Charles Hind at the British Architectural Library; and Sue Woods at the National Film Archive. Unless otherwise credited, photographs are used by kind permission of the Origin Group, within which St Pancras Housing today operates.

3 Lancelot Keay and Liverpool's Multi-Storey Housing of the 1930s

MATTHEW WHITFIELD

Lancelot Keay and Liverpool's Multi-Storey Housing of the 1930s

MATTHEW WHITFIELD

Before 1930, Liverpool stood virtually alone outside London as an authority willing to turn to flats as a solution to its housing problems. Government funding after 1930 and especially after 1933 made flats a more attractive proposition for most major British cities, especially those in the north of England with a legacy, like Liverpool's, of ageing nineteenth-century housing stock. Nevertheless, Liverpool's municipal flats demonstrated a distinctive policy compared with those elsewhere in the country. Whilst technologically unremarkable – built with concrete floors and load bearing brick walls, these buildings strove for a new way to house people and were, in their own way, defiantly modern.

Other cities followed the new trend for multi-storey re-housing, but were of varying scales and adopted different models. The Quarry Hill flats in Leeds, designed by R.A.H. Livett, quickly became the talismanic municipal housing project of the period, owing to their rationalist Mopin system of construction, sheer size and prominent position towering above the city centre.[1] But Liverpool constructed five times as many flats as Leeds in the period 1933–39, and achieved an innovative house style all its own.[2] The shifting form and stylistic appearance of Liverpool's multi-storey schemes through the 1930s show the evolution of architectural thought both in municipal housing and the British architectural scene as a whole. The construction of these buildings is a story of well-intentioned municipal energy harnessed for the purposes of a stylistically significant architecture. The architectural language utilised was sufficiently new and fashioned into suitably meaningful messages that their role in British modernism deserves reassessment.

The figure who oversaw this pioneering period in Liverpool's housing history was the Corporation's Director of Housing, Lancelot Herman Keay (1883–1974). An efficient public servant, Keay as an architect was committed to expanding the possibilities of public housing. Appointed in 1925 as an Architectural Assistant to Liverpool's dynamic City Engineer, John Brodie, he quickly assumed more authority within the housing operations of the Corporation and, by 1930, headed a separate department as Director of Housing.[3] Keay was appointed because he was a supporter of multi-storey housing and had a firm vision of how flats could demonstrate civic enterprise. He represented a fulcrum around which an existing enthusiasm for flats and a subsequent influx of architectural talent into the Housing Department were balanced. He was a conduit and an enabler, who could exploit the context in which he found himself to produce bold and innovative plans.

The first municipal housing in the United Kingdom was constructed in Liverpool, when in 1869 St Martin's Cottages were provided by the Corporation as 'model dwellings' along the lines of those previously built by philanthropic and corporate interests.[4] That these 'cottages' were multi-storey flats was no accident – high land values in the central area of the city coupled with the need to re-house as many people as possible in sanitary conditions made building upwards an economic and practical necessity. Iain C. Taylor argues that the Corporation was motivated principally by hard-headed business interests; when no private

Figure 1. St Andrew's Gardens, parabolic pedestrian archway (all illustrations courtesy of Liverpool Record Office, Liverpool Libraries (352/HOU) save where otherwise noted).

1. Anthony Bertram, *Design*, London, Penguin, 1938. A model of Quarry Hill is used as the front cover of this compendium of BBC Radio lectures from October 1937 on the subject of modern design and architecture.

2. Alison Ravetz, 'From Working Class Tenement to Modern Flat: local authorities and multi-storey housing between the wars' in Anthony Sutcliffe (ed), *Multi-Storey Living: The British Working Class Experience*, London, Croom Helm, 1974, p.123.

3. John Brodie (and his City Engineer's Department) acquired a reputation for competence and innovation, engineering a comprehensive road system to prepare the city for the motor age and deriving national fame for his invention of the football goal net.

4. City of Liverpool Housing Department, *Housing Progress 1864–1951*, Liverpool City Council, 1951.

5. Iain C. Taylor 'The Insanitary Housing Question and Tenement Dwellings in Nineteenth-century Liverpool' in Sutcliffe, *op.cit.*, esp. p.67.

6. Taylor (ibid) outlines figures which indicate that Liverpool had the highest population density in Britain by the late nineteenth century, pp.43-5.

7. *Liverpool Post and Mercury*, no.21125, 23 February 1923, p.5.

8. Liverpool City Council, Housing Committee Minutes, 16 October 1924.

9. Ravetz (*op.cit.*, pp.122-50) explores the rationale for multi-storey housing schemes in Britain as a whole during this period, including economic, social, ideological and architectural factors. Liverpool's peculiar circumstances (its unskilled, casual labour market, a long history of extreme overcrowding and existing experience with tenements) led to this potent political consensus.

enterprise came forward to develop the Corporation's site it was compelled to build itself so as not to lose money or face embarrassment.[5] Once this Rubicon of political philosophy had been crossed, Liverpool slowly developed an intermittent but identifiable pattern of municipal tenements, reaching a high in the years immediately before the First World War. As an alien form of housing to England (though not to Scotland), Liverpool's commitment to the flat was a remarkably forward-looking solution to exceptional conditions of dirt, disease and overcrowding compared with cities of similar size and circumstances.[6]

The political momentum in Liverpool Corporation following the First World War consolidated the choice of flats. It eagerly adopted the housing programme promoted by central government with the 1918 Tudor Walters Report, calling for 'Homes Fit for Heroes', and the 1919 Housing (Addison) Act. There was a general determination that something must be done about the city's still-crumbling housing stock. Initially caught up in the national emergency programme, by the mid–1920s the Liverpool Corporation was able to focus on its particular needs. After a financial scandal in the Housing Department in the early 1920s, John Brodie assumed all authority for housing within his City Engineer's Department. By 1925, pressure was growing from Liverpool's cultural elite for the Council to appoint a qualified architect to take charge of housing and champion design quality. The University of Liverpool's Vice-Chancellor, Dr Adami, supported by Professor Charles Reilly of the School of Architecture, attacked the Council's record on public building in 1923, claiming that the 'leave it to Brodie' attitude had reaped disappointing results.[7] Lancelot Keay had previously worked for the Birmingham Corporation, where there had been an antipathetic attitude towards flats; his sympathies with the aims of the councillors at Liverpool made him the ideal candidate for the post of Architectural Assistant to Brodie. Perhaps the most significant intellectual and policy shift came in 1924 when members of the Corporation's Housing Committee visited Amsterdam to explore the municipal construction of concrete cottages. However, what most impressed the deputation was the widespread and successful use of multi-storey tenements in the city's new public housing schemes. The Chairman of the Housing Committee, Thomas White, produced a glowing report and at the same meeting a resolution was passed to explore the possibility of building large-scale tenement blocks in Liverpool's central core.[8]

Following the Amsterdam trip, building flats became a policy initiative by the Council as a whole. Along with many in the Conservative group, White was a progressive who cared about the city's housing conditions. The momentum towards multi-storey housing was, however, part of a coalition of interests across the whole Council. Conservative councillors saw the economic interests of the city threatened if large numbers of working-class citizens were relocated exclusively to suburban cottage estates on the edge of the conurbation, away from the fiercely competitive casual labour market on the dockside, while Labour saw a threat to their electoral stability if large numbers of their traditional voters were decanted from central wards *en masse*. For the left wing of the Council there was the additional aesthetic and philosophical appeal of large, flatted housing schemes along the lines of those constructed by Socialist authorities in cities such as Vienna.[9]

Lancelot Keay's entry into this fecund political scene in 1925 was a catalyst for a process that was already gaining momentum. Brodie had drawn plans for two very large 'clearing house' schemes to the north and south of the city centre, and when these ten-storey blocks were refused subsidy by the Ministry of Health, Keay began work on designs for scaled-down five-storey developments for permanent occupation on the same sites. Many plans were produced for city centre flats, despite the difficulty of building them. Arthur Greenwood's Housing Act of 1930 was designed to make it easier to clear overcrowded slum housing. Subsidies were now given on a per-person basis rather than the 'per house' funding which had encouraged new housing on low-rise, low-density suburban estates. Moreover, the Act offered an extra 25 shillings for forty years per person re-housed in flats on sites with a value above £3,000 per acre.[10]

With the legislative framework in place for multi-storey housing, Keay focused on achieving the ambitious goals he had set himself and his department. The 1930 Act required local authorities to outline a five-year plan to clear and redevelop their slums. The Liverpool Corporation proposed a total of 5,000 dwellings per year up to 1936 with 3,000 of them produced from slum clearance and subsequent re-housing. The remaining 2,000 were to be new cottage developments subsidised by the 1924 (Wheatley) Housing Act, which remained in force until 1933.[11] Since his arrival in Liverpool, Keay had lobbied the Housing Committee for a larger staff for his department, appointed on a more permanent basis. After 1930 this became even more of a priority, and Keay was particularly keen to increase the number of architectural staff to assist with design work. There was a growing tradition in the Housing Department of appointing students from the Liverpool School of Architecture (which could be reckoned the most important in Britain between the wars) as interns during their summer vacations, especially after the Depression in the United States ruled out the office placements previously fostered by Reilly. Instead he began to encourage more of his students to pursue careers in public service. In Keay's office, much of the extra workload was taken up by these interns, who also proved to be a rich source of talented permanent staff.

REGENT ROAD

Two separate but interdependent factors conspired to ensure a decisive break with the design practice of the 1920s. Keay's artistic impulses had hitherto drawn him towards a neo-Georgian aesthetic, and the designs led by him before 1930 made heavy use of nostalgic domestic detailing such as oriel and bay windows, traditionally-paned windows and classical motifs such as urns. The first change of direction came with his visit to Berlin in July 1931 for the International Housing and Town Planning Congress, which exposed him to the avant-garde of communal flat schemes, by both municipal authorities and private industrialists for their workers. Their belief in tenement living as a positive virtue rather than a necessary evil, and encouragement of modern designs to reflect modern social

10. Marian Bowley, *Housing and the State, 1919–1944*, London, George Allen and Unwin 1945, p.136, footnote 2. She describes the housing legislation after 1930 as the 'Third Experiment' since the First World War aimed at improving Britain's housing. This is explored further in Francis Newbury, *Liverpool's Flats 1919–1939, Policy and Design of Central Area Redevelopment by the Liverpool Housing Department*, Liverpool School of Architecture, unpublished MA thesis, 1980.

11. Liverpool City Council, Housing Committee Minutes, 27 November 1930.

Figure 2. A Stadium for Liverpool, student diploma design by John Hughes, 1930.

Figure 3. Regent Road, perspective, 1931.

values, was an evident inspiration. Together with the Chairman of the Housing Committee, Hugo Rutherford, Keay presented a positive report of all they had seen in Germany, praising the 'ingenuity and ability displayed by the various architects'.[12] Keay's appointment of John Hughes from the Liverpool School of Architecture in August 1931 was the second factor in favour of a break with the practice of the 1920s and a decisive movement towards handling flats in a modern idiom.[13] Some of Hughes's student drawing work had already been published to some acclaim.[14] It is likely that Keay appointed him because these showed him handling modern design proficiently.

John Hughes produced designs for new housing at Regent Road in October 1931. This was his first work for the Liverpool Corporation, produced within two

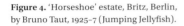

Figure 4. 'Horseshoe' estate, Britz, Berlin, by Bruno Taut, 1925–7 (Jumping Jellyfish).

months of his appointment that August. The drawings were never utilised, but indicate a new architectural direction for the Housing Department. Regent Road adjoined the docks and an associated industrial area. It was considered a suitable site for housing as part of a long-term master plan which envisaged the area immediately inland of the docks as a zone to be developed with high-storey tenement dwellings, with heavy industry relocated to spacious sites on the fringes of the conurbation. After Hughes had drawn up his scheme, there followed a long dispute between the City Council and the owners of the Regent Road site over cost; the scheme was abandoned as agreement could not be reached and the Ministry of Health would not sanction a loan to purchase the land.

The plan was for three residential blocks, six or seven storeys in height, the most distinctive element being a central semi-circular block. The layout was an 'open courtyard', albeit one partly enclosed by two protruding shop units along Regent Road; these elements were to be used frequently in built schemes such as Myrtle Gardens. The perspective drawing shares many similarities with that for the later St Andrew's Gardens, but with some important deviations. Most obviously, the design for Regent Road included one characteristic feature of

12. Liverpool City Council, Housing Committee Minutes, 23 July 1931.

13. Liverpool City Council, Housing Committee Minutes, 27 August 1931.

14. An exhibition of architectural students' work was held at the Walker Art Gallery in July 1930. A design for a stadium in reinforced concrete by John Hughes was reported widely in the architectural press, including *Architect and Building News*, vol.124, 11 July 1930, pp.53–4 ('we admit to being distinctly impressed with both Mr Hughes and his stadium') and a piece by Maxwell Fry, *Architects' Journal*, vol.72, 16 July 1930, pp.87–8.

International Style modernism, a white stucco finish, that linked it to the most progressive architecture of Germany and the Netherlands. However, the commitment to smooth, white painted surfaces appeared to die with the scheme, as St Andrew's Gardens and all subsequent multi-storey public housing in Liverpool up to 1939 turned to golden-brown bricks. The evidence of the plans for other projected schemes indicate that a white stucco was the intended and, indeed, preferred finish for the Corporation's modern flat developments, but that concerns about the maintenance of such surfaces in the highly polluted air of the city centre made brick a more realistically affordable option. The skilled plasterers essential for such large jobs also appeared to be in short supply in Liverpool during this period.[15] Despite such setbacks, Keay's personal preference for a white finish persisted, for in a 1935 lecture he criticised some flats he had seen in northern Germany, 'nearly all carried out in brickwork without a stucco face', as 'heavy and ponderous'.[16] Many of the schemes designed before 1939 showed a stuccoed effect in their perspective drawings but not in their final execution.

While the reality of building imposed restrictions, a design could aim at an undiluted modernism. Regent Road was designed with a 'low-pitched slate roof' but the perspective drawing indicates that this would have been disguised by a partially-open roof canopy providing sheltered access for residents to a space for drying or perhaps recreation.[17] To all intents and purposes this was to be a flat roof. In addition, while brick banding was used to create the impression of horizontal strips of windows at St Andrew's Gardens, the windows at Regent Road were shown grouped into an almost continuous strip.

John Hughes's early efforts set the standard for his later work. One of his inspirations was evidently the Hufeisensiedlung or 'Horseshoe' estate at Britz, a suburb of Berlin, almost certainly mediated through Lancelot's Keay's aesthetic conversion at the 1931 Berlin Housing Congress. Built to plans by Bruno Taut in phases between 1925 and the early 1930s, the estate was one of the earliest attempts to apply functionalist theory to public housing on a large scale, with a large horseshoe-shaped block at its heart that gave it its name. It sought to provide its residents with the clean air of the suburbs without sacrificing any of the community cohesion of old neighbourhoods. Keay's expressed his enthusiasm for the German schemes he had seen in an official report, in which he praised 'the breadth of vision exercised in the layout of the various estates'. He noted that 'practically every scheme is designed on modern lines' and cited Britz as an example of 'the skilfulness exhibited in the layout and the design of the buildings'.[18] Though applied by Hughes to a central urban site, the similarity of ideas between Taut's design and that for Regent Road (and later for St Andrew's Gardens) are unmistakable. The curve of the main block at Regent Road is shown with the same terminal arms housing shops, the central space has similar landscaping, and the architecture is drawn from the same intellectual tradition of the honest exposition of unornamented materials.

ST ANDREW'S GARDENS

The construction of St Andrew's Gardens was the single most significant staging post in the evolution of Liverpool's inter-war housing, providing much of the imagery and design that has come to symbolise the city's municipal housing of the 1930s. Alone amongst Liverpool's inter-war tenements a large portion survived unaltered to the end of the twentieth century to enjoy the statutory protection of listing. Today, a single block survives as student housing, the horseshoe-shaped Block 'D', and as a distillation of the design ethos of Liverpool's Housing Department through the 1930s. This was an ethos that was open to, and accepting of, change: in legislation and political atmosphere, in the architectural *Zeitgeist* across Europe, in personnel and in ideas within the department, which produced a new kind of housing for Liverpool.

Superficially, the planning and construction of St Andrew's Gardens followed

15. Liverpool City Council, Housing Committee Minutes, 27 August 1931.

16. L.H. Keay, 'Working Class Flats: a Solution to the problem of Re-housing', extracts in *Town and Country Planning*, vol.3, no.11, June 1935, pp.92–4.

17. Described by Lancelot Keay when reporting on Hughes's new design for Regent Road. Liverpool City Council, Housing Committee Minutes, 1 October 1931.

18. L.H. Keay and Hugo Rutherford, 'Report for the Housing Committee on the International Housing and Town Planning Congress, Berlin', presented in Liverpool City Council, Housing Committee Minutes, 23 June 1931.

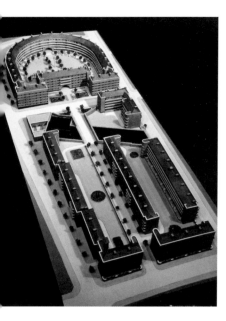

Figure 5. St Andrew's Gardens, model on display in June 1935.

a pattern established since the end of the First World War. A large site on and around Trowbridge Street occupied by an abattoir and hide market became available in the late 1920s, and the Council had to decide how to use it. It knew that flats were required to re-house those who would be displaced by Keay's ambitious plans for the newly designated Gerard Street 'Clearance Area' scheme under the 1930 Act. The Act targeted small parcels of land where sufficient of the property could be declared insanitary that the local authority gained the power of compulsory purchase to clear the site.[19] An alternative location for this decanting programme was that of the former workhouse, diagonally opposite Trowbridge Street at the top of Brownlow Hill, but after much deliberation by councillors, this prestigious site was sold to the Archdiocese of Liverpool for its Metropolitan Cathedral. The Trowbridge Street site was large enough for all the required dwellings, and had scope for expansion to the east and west as it was situated amongst more housing that could easily be designated as unfit by the Chief Medical Officer of Health.

The first perspective drawings to illustrate the St Andrew's Gardens scheme in 1932 bore John Hughes's signature, and presumably encapsulated his ideas on working-class housing. These were to be repeated in virtually all the Corporation's major tenement schemes for the remainder of the decade, and occupy a mid-point between Liverpool's tradition of municipal tenements before 1930 and the authentic modernism sweeping through the architecture of Europe. One of the most readily identifiable motifs is the horizontal treatment of the fenestration, including the banding of brickwork between windows to give the impression of a continuous line across each storey. Perhaps the most self-conscious reference in his work to European modernism of the period, these windows were frequently cited as a practical and healthy innovation in the tenement programme, giving lighter, more airy flats that would benefit residents. Keay had previously claimed at Regent Road that horizontal windows allowed 'a very much larger amount of window space per room', rather as Le Corbusier claimed in his 'five points' refined at Stuttgart's Weissenhofsideulung exhibition in 1927.[20] Hughes probably agreed that sash windows, such as those in Liverpool's Blackstock Street development of the 1920s, were unsuited to their task, both stylistically and practically. The argument that simply rotating a window from a portrait to a landscape position admits more light and air is unproven, but the application of such modernistic devices marked a genuine attempt to solve sanitary problems and was the most significant aspect of Hughes's work. A truly modern treatment would have used actual strip windows, larger and with more openings for more effective ventilation, but here was an indication that a building to meet present day needs was being designed with the truth of its purpose reflected in its finished form.

The structural honesty of St Andrew's Gardens was further expressed with the introduction, for the first time in English public housing, of what were described as 'sun balconies'. These were provided by cantilevering the building's concrete floor slab outwards by a few feet, with a brick balustrade to enclose the outdoor space that tenants could now enjoy. Although not every flat in the scheme enjoyed this privilege, the balconies were a first acknowledgment that a flat need not be the poor relation to a house, but that the form itself demanded particular design innovation if it was reach its full potential as a housing type.

The other striking aspect of Hughes's architecture was its strong geometry. At St Andrew's Gardens, the dominant motif was the semi-circle, which defined the plan of block 'D' and the archways that pierced the blocks through their axis along St Andrew's Street, the thoroughfare through the spine of the development. Narrower openings in the ground floor of the blocks, including those giving access to the stair towers, were fashioned into the shape of a parabolic arch, a distinctive form that complemented the organic shapes throughout the scheme. The stair towers themselves were made distinct from the main housing blocks by their elevation as 'bull-nosed' turrets, echoing the shape of block 'D'. This block

19. Bowley, *op.cit.*, pp.138–40.

20. Liverpool City Council, Housing Committee Minutes, 1 October 1931.

was known locally as the 'bullring' due to its distinctive shape, in addition to the site having previously been an abattoir.

Aside from these curvaceous accents throughout the development, other features were loyal to the modernist doctrine of the straight line, used coolly and without fanfare or embellishment. Despite the apparent dichotomy between the organic and strictly manufactured elements of the scheme, both strands of thought were executed with impeccable simplicity. The absence of any traditional forms of applied decoration united the varied building lines, plans and elevations into a harmonious and recognisably modernistic whole. The fenestration was the clearest evidence of this design philosophy, with the banded windows wrapping around corners and the parallel glazing bars continuing unbroken and unabashed by the apparent obstacle of the building's edge. Another attempt at modernist linear authority can be observed in the brave, if clumsy, attempt to simulate the appearance of a flat roof, with the top storey stretched upwards as a parapet to disguise the traditional pitched roof behind. In the urban terraces of Georgian Britain such a device was the habitual method of achieving a civilised, uniform building line, but in the 1930s, when flat roofs were being used freely in the most innovative modern buildings of Europe, the pretence of flatness was second best. Nevertheless, the overall effect, at least from the surrounding streets, added to the impression of planar simplicity and disciplined rectangularity.

St Andrew's Gardens has often been compared to the major public housing projects built in Socialist-controlled Vienna during the 1920s.[21] The monumental nature of developments like Karl Marx Hof was echoed in the expansive scale of schemes such as St Andrew's and, appeared to inspire such striking design motifs as the semi-circular archways and grouped balconies. However, Keay had led a delegation of housing officials to inspect Vienna's housing achievements as early as 1926 and been somewhat unimpressed.[22] No formal report was offered to the Council on the trip, and he was dismissive of the Viennese tenements because the back-to-back flats he had seen there were too small and had insufficient ventilation and amenities for the British council tenant.[23] Other English authorities were more directly inspired by the example of Vienna, Leeds in particular, but any similarity with Liverpool's housing seems to have been incidental. It is possible that John Hughes wished to replicate something of the monumental flair of those photogenic blocks, but there was no policy that officially recognised the example Vienna had set.

Figure 6. Karl Marx Hof, Vienna, by Karl Ehn, 1926 (Stephen Kauffman).

Figure 7. Gerard Gardens, main entrance, 1936.

21. Ravetz, *op.cit.* p.134 explores how English local authorities seemed most impressed by the possibilities suggested by communal houses in Vienna, despite the intrinsically more interesting housing being developed in Germany and elsewhere; Eve Blau, *The Architecture of Red Vienna*, Cambridge, MIT, 1999.

22. *Liverpool Echo*, no.14586, 27 September 1926, p.10; no.15688, 13 April 1930, p.14.

23. ibid, no.15688, 15 April 1930, p.14.

24. Alan Powers, 'Liverpool and Architectural Education in the Early Twentieth Century', in Joseph Sharples, ed., *Charles Reilly and the Liverpool School of Architecture, 1904–1933*, Liverpool University Press, 1996.

25. L. H. Keay, 'The Redevelopment of Central Areas', in *RIBA Journal*, Third Series, vol.43, 23 November 1935, p.63; *Liverpool Daily Post*, no.25078, 20 November 1935, p.6; City of Liverpool, *Housing 1937*, Liverpool Housing Department, 1937, p.41.

The Gerard Street developments were the only realisation of an ambitious plan to comprehensively redevelop an entire district of Liverpool's central core, immediately north of the city's cultural heart of William Brown Street and St George's Hall. It demonstrated the continuing influence of John Hughes on the design culture of the Housing Department, although an additional signature amongst the drawings suggests that Leon Berger, a new Architectural Assistant recently graduated from the University of Liverpool, collaborated on the design or at least the perspectives. The completed building at Gerard Gardens broadly repeated the modernistic form established by Hughes at St Andrew's Gardens. The only discernible difference appears to be a loosening of the linear theme in favour of a more rounded aesthetic across the whole building. Wings were 'bull-nosed' into the main block rather than each constituent part being set alone in a rectangular uniformity. In addition to these more curvaceous lines, a new decorative method emphasised the horizontal banding of the windows, with a deeper tone of brick used to unify the window line rather than the bands set in relief at St Andrew's Gardens.

A further significant influence on Hughes's architecture is revealed by the Gerard Street scheme. The influence of Bruno Taut appears to give way here to a more expressionist tendency derived from Erich Mendelsohn, who lectured in Liverpool in 1933.[24] Hughes's final year stadium design was clearly in thrall to Mendelsohn's mastery of emotive curvature laid on top of a disciplined and functional canvas. Hughes's distinctive bull-nosed turrets made their first appearance at Gerard Gardens, as did the banded windows and the illusion of a flat roof. Mendelsohn's 1926 department store design for Schocken in Stuttgart was a model for these sweeping, expressive motifs, whilst Hughes was evidently impressed by his Berlin Metal Workers Union Building with its creative method of handling a corner site. Gerard Gardens displays the same arrangement of three interlocking blocks turning around an important corner to produce a civically-minded scheme with the understated flourish of modern lines. Liverpool's multi-storey flats of the 1930s did not belong to any particular architectural school, nor, in their pleasing inconsistencies, did they constitute a school of their own. Mendelsohn himself represented an inventive confusion about the nature of modern design; inserting heretical curves where the ascetic functionalist would have balked, and delighting at times in axial symmetry where theoretical modernism demanded an asymmetry related to purpose. Whilst difficult to classify easily as fully modernist, schemes such as Gerard Gardens were receptive to this worldwide architectural conversation on modern building.

The strict axial symmetry of Gerard Gardens could be explained by its forming part of a larger master plan. Well before the introduction of the 1935 Housing Act, Keay anticipated the setting up of 'Redevelopment Areas' in districts of slum housing. As a result, Liverpool was the first local authority in Britain to apply for the new powers of clearance and re-housing under the new rules.[25] 'Redevelopment Areas' replaced the cumbersome 'Clearance Areas' of the 1930 Act by granting local authorities more comprehensive powers of compulsory purchase based on the occurrence of overcrowding rather than insanitary property. Keay had sat on a committee at the Ministry of Health, convened to consult experts on how the new legislation should be drafted, hence his advance knowledge. Gerard Gardens was the vanguard of a larger development, an individual scheme funded under the 1930 Act but also forming a cornerstone of what was planned to become the Central Redevelopment Area (CRA).

The earliest design for the area, dated September 1934, shows an aerial view of the scheme with the spine of the development, a new 120-foot wide road, slicing diagonally through the planned new housing and connecting the East Lancashire Road in the north with the soon-to-be-opened Mersey Tunnel in the south. Gerard Gardens and Gerard Crescent are depicted in the southeast corner, whilst the rest of the development area is laid out in a series of large courtyard-style

blocks. A later plan, dated March 1936, shows a shift away from the enclosed curvature of the first scheme towards a series of regimented, parallel blocks with open ground on all sides. What unified both schemes was an evident desire to see more high-storey dwelling blocks than had been attempted before, releasing land on the ground for public gardens. Developing tenement blocks in such central areas had always suffered from the twin problems of the low availability and high cost of land; Redevelopment Areas embodied Keay's argument that true efficiency in re-housing could only be achieved with economies of scale. If an entire district could be purchased, cleared and rebuilt as one unit, without the myriad of individual legal issues that accompanied the smaller 'Clearance Areas' of the 1930 Act, then a plan could be devised which would see the most effective use made of precious land.

The surviving perspectives of the CRA demonstrate how holistic the scheme was intended to be. The image projected is a high-rise Utopia with elegantly pedestrian avenues intersecting with traffic routes, lush yet urbane planting to soften the angular solemnity of the residential blocks, and shop units designed with a cool glamour that could as easily house a fashion boutique as a greengrocer's. Leon Berger's 1936 drawing of a proposed recreation centre for the area encapsulates much of the expressionistic modernism implicit in all the designs. The architects were aware of the striking effect that rebuilding an entire district could have, and set their ambitions accordingly. The repetitive simplicity of the plans for a central pedestrian thoroughfare cutting through the heart of the largest blocks is an arresting sight on such a large scale.

Neither the CRA nor any of the Housing Department's other Redevelopment Areas were realised, because the 1935 Act failed to address the issue of business relocation. A series of appeals by businesses against compulsory purchase orders made the acquisition of sufficient land impossible. Nevertheless, the sheer scale of the Liverpool Corporation's ambitious schemes indicates Keay's comprehensive vision for the transformation of Liverpool's inner core. This scale

Figure 8. Gerard Gardens, design for a recreation centre by Leon Berger, 1936.

Figure 9. Myrtle Gardens, a view from a balcony towards the shops.

Figure 10. Caryl Gardens, the main entrance.

of conception was intrinsically linked with the nature of the proposed designs; where functionalism was appropriate in planning, it was appropriate in appearance. With a growing architectural staff channelling new ideas into the growing workload of the Housing Department, an identifiable design culture was established that, by the mid–1930s, had the confidence to plan for a comprehensively and rationally rebuilt city.

MYRTLE GARDENS

This scheme represented John Hughes's last significant work for the Housing Department before leaving Liverpool to become Deputy Director of Housing in Manchester. It was the apotheosis of his housing work, encapsulating the ideas implicit in the earlier schemes. The shops at the terminus of the blocks fronting Myrtle Street created a holistic modern community housing unit, providing residents with some of the shared facilities they could expect as part of their new multi-storey lifestyle. At the time of construction, these semi-circular shops along Myrtle Street must have been the most architecturally advanced in Liverpool, despite their status as basic community services.

Myrtle Gardens was also notable for having flat roofs, making real the architectural illusion attempted at St Andrew's and Gerard Gardens. Indeed, one of the initial perspectives depicts a floating canopy above the actual roof level of the Crown Street entrance, indicating the public use of the flat roof as a sheltered terrace, drying area or promenade. This canopy was not built, and there is no evidence that the flat roof was used by anybody other than maintenance staff. Nevertheless, the use of a fully modernist device on such a large scheme indicated a commitment to contemporary methods of construction and a desire to maintain the modern lines of the building as much as possible.

CARYL GARDENS

The targets for re-housing that the Housing Department set itself through the 1930s were onerous, especially for a relatively small staff. Despite the new members of staff acquired by Keay, and the regular procession of architectural students during summer vacations, the core of the housing staff remained as it had been during the 1920s, with old hands seeing out their municipal service. The copious design work was shared between the architectural staff, young and old, and as a result there was little consistency between one scheme and another. Caryl Gardens best represents this state of affairs. Wilfred Twiss was named as the principal Architectural Assistant on the project, a more mature architect who had not attended the Liverpool School and who evidently had a different design emphasis from that of his younger colleagues.[26]

The main entrance on Caryl Street was modern in style, albeit with some jazz-deco concrete dressings suggesting a more frivolous tone. Above the main entrance arch were the rectilinear sun balconies familiar in other large schemes of the 1930s, but elsewhere on the main elevations were elongated bay windows typical of the 'domestic' tenement blocks of the previous decade. The end portions of each wing were stuccoed and painted white, but had chalet-style shutters on either side of the windows, a detail typical of Caryl Gardens' distance from the modern idiom pursued elsewhere in the city. From the available drawings there is no conclusive evidence as to who was the designer, under Keay's leadership, but it is possible to see in Caryl Gardens the survival of an older tradition within the Housing Department which could not be brought into a fully successful synthesis with the new style.

Aside from the discordant aesthetic of Caryl Gardens, the scheme was significant for the comprehensive social facilities provided for the residents of its 312 flats. The recreational facilities were second to none. Large playgrounds were provided for children of all ages, with accommodation for a Boys' Club and a Girls' Club, which offered a formal programme of sporting and other recreational pastimes. These clubs were designed to be shared with the surrounding neighbourhood, including residents of the adjoining Warwick Gardens. Most

26. Twiss, a man in his 40s, was credited as the official assistant on Caryl Gardens in 'Redevelopment in Central Areas of Liverpool', *RIBA Journal*, Third Series, vol.46, 23 January 1939, pp.293–8. It is not known which other housing schemes he contributed to.

Figure 11. Corlett Street, perspective by Edgar Farrah, 1937.

CITY OF LIVERPOOL HOUSING · CORLETT STREET SCHEME · FALKNER STREET FRONTAGE

CITY OF LIVERPOOL HOUSING · CORLETT STREET SCHEME · SOUTH EAST ASPECT remarkably, Caryl Gardens included a Chapel of Rest for residents who passed away. The social mission of the Housing Department thus extended from the cradle to the grave.

CORLETT STREET

As one of the last tenement schemes completed in Liverpool before the outbreak of war ceased all production, Corlett Street suggested an entirely new direction for the Housing Department. The 138 flats on the site were constructed with two innovations that indicated a more serious-minded modernism within the architectural team. Firstly, Corlett Street was one of the first major multi-storey developments in the city to include internal staircase access to all flats, as opposed to the balcony access system employed on every previous tenement block since 1918. These internal staircases were grouped so that each landing gave access to just two flats, and only ten flats were served by the stairwell in total (eight if the ground floor flats were excluded). This move increased privacy and reduced inconvenience and noise for residents. Secondly, the flats were grouped into three parallel blocks to maximise sunlight and air, a method based on the *Zeilenbau* layouts from Germany.[27] Lancelot Keay had become a late convert to this theory of parallel spacing, initially preferring the courtyard block plan typical of traditional Dutch flats (hence the name 'Gardens' attached to the majority of Liverpool's flat schemes of the period). However, once he was convinced of the functional arguments of *Zeilenbau* planning, future schemes strove to meet this ideal wherever possible.[28]

The actual design of the blocks at Corlett Street was perhaps the closest that the Housing Department reached in the 1930s to achieving a purely modern design without any form of organic or expressionistic interpretation. The original perspectives of 1937 by Edgar Farrah, a young Architectural Assistant in the ascendancy after the departure of John Hughes, show a strictly cubic scheme with dual-aspect balconies and building lines completely free from any decorative embellishment. Additionally, a white stuccoed finish inspired by the best-regarded examples of European modernism was intended, and the scheme as planned would have constituted the most significant example of International Style modern architecture in Liverpool at the time. That the finished building did not have stuccoed walls but opted for the rustic brick that had become a near-inevitable feature of the Corporation's multi-storey housing of the period, detracts little from the overtly modernist spirit of the scheme.

CONCLUSION

Through these examples of Liverpool's housing practice, it is possible to identify a partial, yet striking, view of the aesthetic influences on the buildings that did so much to advance the city's reputation as a patron of municipal architecture. Though tenement flats were not a new building type in 1930, least of all in Liverpool, they attracted those who, as architects or councillors, wished to advance a particular philosophical cause. The most famous examples of public housing from Austria, Germany and the Netherlands were published widely in the architectural press, but it was personal visits, most particularly that made by Lancelot Keay and Hugo Rutherford to Berlin in 1931, which seemed to mark significant changes in policy. It is interesting to try to determine the precise nature and depth of these foreign influences and broader social trends with which they belonged. Above all, it was the academic transmission of modern architectural ideas though the Liverpool School of Architecture which was to provide an ideological underpinning for architects such as John Hughes, Leon Berger and Edgar Farrah. Technologically unadventurous, Liverpool's 1930s flats are only a footnote in the larger story of European modernism between the wars, but as an example of how innovative aesthetic and social ideas were transmitted into British architecture they are invaluable.

27. John R. Gold, *The Experience of Modernism: Modern Architects and the Future City 1928–1953*, London, E. and F.N. Spon, 1998, pp.51–2. The original idea was by Theodore Fischer who applied the system to a 'garden city' style development in Munich in 1919. The most significant examples in the 1920s were by Ernst May, Frankfurt City Architect. Walter Gropius disseminated the idea to modernists through the Bauhaus.

28. Lancelot Keay, addressing the RIBA on 'Housing and the Redevelopment of Central Areas' on 18 November 1935, announced that 'the best result is admittedly obtained by planning blocks in parallel running north and south' (*RIBA Journal*, vol.43, 23 November 1935, p.61).

4 'Work Collectively and Live Individually': The Bata Housing Estate at East Tilbury

JOANNA SMITH

Bata

SHOE...ER...O THE WORLD

'Work Collectively and Live Individually': The Bata Housing Estate at East Tilbury

JOANNA SMITH

'At its outskirts the rough country road turns into a concrete highway, over which one rolls into a lively twentieth century industrial city. Here is electric power, here are assembly lines turning out cheap shoes, here are prefabricated houses and multi-story [sic] buildings raised by efficient, standarized construction methods. Most exciting of all, here is modern graciousness and decency. Here is order. ... Here is the achievement of advanced methods of planning and construction applied to industrial plant and housing alike.'[1]

This paean to the city of Zlín, now near the eastern border of the Czech Republic, celebrates the achievements of a single business, the Bata Shoe Company. From modest origins, the firm grew in the inter-war years of the twentieth century to become one of the world's largest shoe manufacturers and retailers. An outcome of this prodigious growth was the recreation of Zlín as, in effect, a company town provided with modern factories, housing and community facilities. Bata was also an international organisation, with overseas companies and manufacturing sites across the globe. These company satellites were conceived and built as 'mini-Zlíns', planned, like the company headquarters, on Garden City tenets and designed in a thoroughly modern idiom reflecting concerns for simplicity, spaciousness and economy. One of the key maxims of the company's founder, Thomas Bata, was to 'work collectively and live individually.'[2] This was given architectural expression through a differing approach to industrial and communal buildings and family housing. While concrete or steel framing and modular planning predominated for the manufacturing and public buildings, the characteristic residential unit was the brick-built semi-detached family house. Between 1930 and 1941 this model was replicated over a dozen times on several continents. In 1933 it was used to create an industrial settlement at East Tilbury in Essex, near the north bank of the River Thames. This was conceived on a grand scale, with forty factories and thousands of houses proposed, although only a fraction of this was realised. But much of what was built still remains, an unexpected modernist village in the relative isolation of the estuarine marshes.

'SHOEMAKERS TO THE WORLD': THE BATA ORGANISATION

The ancestors of Thomas Bata (in Czech Tomáš Bat'a), 1876–1932, had been cobblers in the Moravian town of Zlín from the seventeenth century. In 1894 Thomas set up in the shoe making business with his brother Antonin, and by 1918 was running the largest shoemaking concern in Czechoslovakia, including a first shop. During the difficult post-war years the business focussed on expanding its retail outlets and penetrating foreign markets. In the early 1920s companies were established to sell Bata shoes in Holland, Denmark, Yugoslavia, Poland and England. Economic difficulties at the Zlín plant peaked in 1922, after which the firm began an extraordinary expansion, extending its sales to Asia, particularly India. The redevelopment of Zlín then began in earnest, facilitated by Bata's political control of the municipality following his election as mayor in 1923.

The Bata Company was now a worldwide shoe empire, all co-ordinated from

Figure 1. Advert depicting the Bata shop at No.72 High Street, Grays, Essex, published in the *Bata Record*, 25 April 1958 (Bata Limited)

1. Jan Pokorny and Elizabeth Hird, 'They Planned it that Way', *Architectural Record*, vol.102, no.8, August 1947, p.68.

2. Eric J. Jenkins, 'Utopia, Inc., Czech Culture and Bata Show Company Architecture and Garden Cities', *Thresholds*, no.18, 1999, pp.60–3; Henrieta Moravciková, 'Social and Architectural Phenomenon, the Batism in Slovakia', *Slovak Sociological Review*, vol.36, no.6, Autumn 2004, pp.519–43.

Figure 2. Statue of Thomas Bata by Joseph Hermon Cawthra, erected in 1955 outside the factory at East Tilbury. (English Heritage).

3. Anthony Cekota, *Entrepreneur Extraordinary, The Biography of Thomas Bata*, Rome, International University of Social Studies, 1968, p.347; Jean-Louis Cohen, 'Zlín. An Industrial Republic', *Rassegna*, no.70, 1997, pp.42–5.

4. National Archives, BT 271/51 Report by the Trading with the Enemy Department, Board of Trade, February 1945.

5. Jan Bata had originally gone to a new Bata settlement in the USA, at Belcamp, but had to leave following blacklisting by Britain and America because he maintained contact with the companies under Nazi control. National Archives, CO 852/478/12.

Zlín. It controlled the entire process of shoe making, from the production of raw materials through to the marketing and sale of the finished goods. But even in the late 1920s Bata's approach of a 'one-world economy' was challenged by the growth of national protectionist policies, as the industrialised countries raised customs barriers and restricted imports in response to the global economic crisis. To circumvent these restrictions Bata founded 22 (of an eventual total of 29) overseas companies between 1929 and 1932.[3] Manufacturing sites were established in Germany, Switzerland, France, Croatia, Poland, England, the Netherlands and in India between 1931 and 1936.

This prodigious growth was maintained despite the untimely death of Thomas Bata in a plane crash in July 1932. Control of the company then passed to his stepbrother, Jan Bata, while his seventeen-year old son, also Thomas, learnt the business. Jan continued his brother's approach, developing a global organisation run by a complex and opaque 'mass of interlocking holding and operating companies', with ultimate control largely residing with a trust in Switzerland.[4] But during the Second World War the organisation fractured, with some factories under German control and others, such as East Tilbury, supplying the Allies. In 1940 Thomas Bata Jnr established a new settlement at Batawa, Canada, and a new company to oversee the wider organisation while Jan Bata established a new settlement in neutral Brazil in 1941.[5] In 1945 the factories in Eastern Europe were nationalised and a legal battle ensued over ownership of the remaining businesses between Jan and Thomas. From this conflict emerged the Bata Shoe Company, led by Thomas Bata Jnr, with its headquarters in Toronto, Canada. The company continues today, a family owned business headed by Thomas G. Bata, the grandson of the founder, now based in Lausanne, Switzerland.

The British operation began in 1924 with the foundation of the Bata Shoe and Leather Company Ltd in London, principally concerned with selling imported products.[6] Following the decision to expand into manufacturing the British Bata Shoe Company Ltd (hereafter British Bata) was established in 1933.[7] Closely modelled on the mother company, British Bata acted as both producer and distributor, controlling every aspect of shoe manufacture. The principal site was at East Tilbury, which focussed primarily on the manufacture of rubber and leather footwear, but after 1940 other facilities were acquired. These included factories at Maryport (Cumbria), Dudley and Cumnock in Scotland. Company-owned plantations in Nigeria supplied the rubber, a tannery in Leicester produced the leather and a mill in Chorley, Lancashire, manufactured the textiles. By the 1950s British Bata employed around 5,000 people, over 3,000 of which worked at East Tilbury. By 1964 the company owned 300 retail shops and was Britain's largest exporter of footwear.[8] But by this date manufacturing was already beginning to shift overseas. From 1970 British Bata began to contract, first selling off its subsidiary works in the UK, then its retail shops and the company housing at East Tilbury. By the end of the twentieth century its workforce had dwindled to 150.[9] British Bata disposed of the main factory in 1997 and went out of business in 2006.

Although technically separate, British Bata had essentially always been an offshoot of the main corporation, its management having a distinctively Czechoslovakian slant.[10] In 1935 Thomas Bata Jnr worked at East Tilbury as assistant general manager and, after the Second World War, made regular visits and often attended the opening of new buildings. Being part of a global organisation also brought benefits for the workforce, including opportunities for overseas travel, and the community at East Tilbury enjoyed an international character that few Essex villages could match.

6. Jane Pavitt, 'The Bata Project: a Social and Industrial Experiment', *Twentieth Century Architecture*, no.1, *Industrial Architecture*, 1994, p.34. Cekota, *op.cit.*, p.382.

7. Pavitt, *op.cit.*, p.34.

8. British Bata Shoe Company Limited, *British Bata*; East Tilbury, 1964.

9. Patrick Wright, *The River: The Thames in Our Time*, London, BBC Worldwide, 1990, p.59.

10. In 1940 58% of British Bata shares were owned by the Swiss Trust and Westhold Inc., the holding companies set up by Thomas and Jan Bata. National Archives, BT 271/51.

Figure 3. The factory entrance at East Tilbury, published in 1964 in the company pamphlet *British Bata East Tilbury* (Bata Limited).

Figure 4. [opposite] The sports and recreation facilities at East Tilbury, published in the 1954 company pamphlet *Working with Bata* (Bata Limited).

Figure 5. The cultural centre erected as a memorial to Thomas Bata, 1933 (State Gallery Zlin).

BUSINESS PHILOSOPHY AND THE ROLE OF ARCHITECTURE AND PLANNING

Thomas Bata underpinned his business with a combination of modern production methods, notions of welfare capitalism and a competitive management system. Some of his ideas and methods were taken from American and European practice, filtered through a Czechoslovakian cultural tradition of 'practical idealism' that sought to incorporate 'oppositional concepts, such as communism and capitalism, modernity with tradition, and social programs with profiteering, while capitalising on the opportunities that arose from that combination'.[11] This philosophy continued to shape the organisation beyond Bata's death and the post-war realignment of the company.

To acquaint himself with the latest developments in manufacturing and business methods Thomas Bata visited the United States three times, in 1904, 1911 and 1919. On his last trip he toured the largest US shoe company, Endicott and Johnson at Binghampton, Johnson City, where the works were surrounded by workers' housing, schools, parks and sports fields. He also visited the Ford plant at River Rouge, Detroit, to observe mass-production techniques. Bata's response to Ford's methods was, reportedly, 'If an automobile can be made and sold like that, why not shoes?'[12] This kind of manufacturing relied heavily on mechanisation, rationalisation and standardisation of process, efficient factory design and the reduction of skilled labour. It went hand-in-hand with new approaches to organisation, exemplified by Frederick Taylor's 'Scientific Management' theory.

In 1924 Bata introduced a new management system, supposedly influenced by European models such as the Carl Zeiss factories in Germany.[13] This was based on departmental autonomy, with a financial interest in the quality and quantity of the output (and the sharing of profit, losses or wages) reaching down to workshop or production line level. Bata regarded this as 'a genuinely cooperative organisation, everyone working for himself and for all'.[14] The labour force, unskilled and semi-skilled, was recruited young, moulded to a company ethos and subjected to strict discipline. But this was ameliorated by modern working conditions, reasonable levels of pay and the provision of a wide range of facilities, including accommodation. From 1916 onwards the company began to construct residential districts in Zlín, as well as shops, cinemas, sports facilities, schools, medical facilities and churches.

By the mid–1920s architecture and planning had become central to evolving company identity. Their approach combined the precepts of the Garden City Movement – low-density housing, a heavily landscaped setting, the separation of manufacturing and residential areas, a civic core, and a street pattern that avoided monotony – with modernist design and industrialised construction. Bata's preference was for simplicity, spaciousness, straight lines and economy in

11. Jenkins, *op.cit.*, pp.60–3.

12. Cekota, *op.cit.*, pp.52–3, 74, 90.

13. Cohen, *op.cit.*, p.42.

14. Jenkins, *op.cit.*, p.63.

Figure 6. The administrative building, built in 1937-8 (State Gallery Zlin).

Figure 7. Zlin housing (Elain Harwood).

15. Kotera was probably exposed to the movement when he visited London in 1905. Jiri Musil, Vladimir Slapeta and Jaroslav Novak, 'Czech Mate for Letchworth', *Town and County Planning*, vol.53, no.11, November 1984, pp.314-15.

16. ibid, p.315.

17. Thomas Bata is said to have returned from his visit in 1919 with a plan of an American factory that was used as a model. Vladimír Šlapeta, *Bat'a: Arckitekture und Urbanism*, Zlín, Zlín State Gallery, 1991, p.108.

18. The motto was 'we have no right to make the customers pay one single cent more for shoes because of our buildings'. Bata is said to have devised a system of building with gangs of 18 men, working with standardised and interchangeable units, and an organised schedule of deliveries of materials, that enabled a standard factory of about 50,000 sq ft to be constructed in five weeks. Cekota, *op.cit.*, pp.223, 225.

19. Shannon Ricketts, 'Batawa, an Experiment in International Standardisation', *Society for the Study of Architecture in Canada Bulletin*, vol 18, no.2, September 1993, pp.80-87.

20. Šlapeta, *op.cit.*, p.106.

construction. These ideals were realised by a team of architects and engineers, and an in-house building department that drew upon home-grown talent as well as European and American experience.

Czechoslovakia's first garden suburb had been founded in Prague in 1912, and one of the leading proponents of the movement in the country was Jan Kotera (1871-1923).[15] Kotera was invited to design a family house for Bata in Zlín in 1911 and produced a scheme for the first company housing district in 1916. Although only a small part of this was completed, a similar approach was used by Kotera's pupil, Frantisek Lydie Gahura (1891-1958), when planning the rapid expansion of Zlín from the mid-1920s. Gahura, who was not employed directly by the company but by Thomas Bata, was later joined by another architect, Vladimir Karfik (1901-96), who acted as head of construction for the company from 1930 to 1946. Gahura and Karfik took elements of garden-city planning, such as a central axis that combined an open landscape with municipal and cultural buildings, but located the factory at the heart rather than the periphery of the town, reflecting the company's dominant role.[16]

American factory design was influential too.[17] In 1924 an in-house construction department was established with 'well-trained management, designers, administrators, blue-prints, patterns, a loss-calculating system, material specifications, machinery and work methods'.[18] This enabled the application of mass-production techniques for company building facilitated, in 1927, by the development of a construction system by Gahura and the engineer Arnost Sehdal for a reinforced-concrete frame. This modular system was used for a wide range of company buildings, including factories, public and social buildings, but was sufficiently flexible to allow for differentiation between them. The most notable examples of its use were Gahura's Bata Memorial (1933) and Karfik's seventeen-storey administration building (1937-8). By 1938 the construction department, headed by Karfik, had 38 members of staff.[19]

Czechoslovakia was receptive to avant-garde architecture in the 1920s and 1930s, particularly in Prague and Brno, which contained many modern buildings. The approach of the Bata company to its housing was to optimise space, sunlight and air, but its preference remained, until the 1940s, for individual residential units. Some blocks of flats, with no more than four flats per unit, were built in Zlín in 1928 but Bata rejected multi-storey or communal buildings because he believed that 'the man who has a flat in a building with a garden is more stable, and instead of following politics would rather potter about in the garden or sit out on the lawn, so he doesn't go to the pub or political meetings'.[20] Two types of

Figure 8. Aerial view of the Bata settlement with East Tilbury village and the river Thames beyond, taken in 2005 (English Heritage, NMR).

accommodation predominated, semi-detached two-storey family houses, and hostels or dormitories – which might be larger multi-storey buildings – for single workers. As with the design of factory and communal buildings, economy was an important consideration, resulting in standardised house plans and fittings. But Bata's motives in becoming a large-scale builder of housing have also been attributed to his 'irresistible need to influence all aspects of his life and those who worked for him'.[21]

Having developed the prototype of a rational industrial settlement, Bata then reproduced it in his satellites. These were conceived as complete communities, laid out to a common pattern. The company architects provided the general plans and designs for important buildings at each satellite and, in line with the collectivist notions of the day, seem to have worked collaboratively, amending or revising colleagues' plans or designing particular elements of different settlements as required.[22] The head organisation provided machinery, instructors to train the locally-recruited workforce, managers and a social model. In turn, the satellites established their own building departments to construct and, when necessary, adapt the company's designs.[23] After the war the organisation abandoned its uniform approach to building design but the same architects were used by both the parent and secondary companies. The British firms Katz and Vaughan, and Watkins Gray International, designed buildings in the 1950s and 1960s for various Bata companies.[24]

THE DEVELOPMENT OF EAST TILBURY

A historic settlement already existed at East Tilbury. This owed its existence in part to its strategic location, at the point where the River Thames significantly narrows from its wide estuary mouth for the first time, on a gravel terrace that rises slightly above the low estuarial marshland. Yet despite the opening of a branch line from the main London to Southend railway in the 1850s, and its relative proximity to the town of Tilbury, two miles away, East Tilbury remained a modest settlement.

In October 1931 the Bata Shoe Company advertised for a 600-acre site by the Thames. One of the respondents, William W. Wilson, was the owner of St Clere's Hall, situated just north of East Tilbury village. His estate, which ran from the railway line to the river, seems to have been chosen for a number of reasons. One was its geology: the gravel below the marsh facilitated construction as it precluded the need for piled foundations. Another reason was the high unemployment in Tilbury, a consequence of the contraction in shipping and dock

21. Cekota, *op.cit.*, pp.224–5.

22. There does not seem to have been a policy of allowing individual responsibility for whole satellites or colonies. See http://momoneco.kotka.fi (transcript of a lecture by Henrieta Moravciková, 'Batovany-Partizánske: An exemplary Slovak Industrial Town').

23. See the account of the construction office, Moravciková, ibid.

24. Bronek Katz was a Polish-born architect, recommended following his work at the Festival of Britain in 1951 (Pavitt, *op.cit.*, pp.43–4). Following a prototype Bata store in the early 1950s in Cyprus, the firm was made responsible for several new branches (including the refitting of the Oxford Street store in 1956) and a bachelor hostel and houses at Cité Bata, near Dakar. *Architectural Design*, vol.23, no.10, October 1953, pp.292–3; obituary by Maxwell Fry, *RIBA Journal*, vol.67, no.7, May 1960, pp.248–9. Watkins, Gray & Partners worked for Bata from the early 1950s and designed buildings for the parent and subsidiary companies in British Guiana (1953), Trinidad (1958), and Nigeria (1963, 1968 and 1973). *Architect and Building News*, vol.214, no.4, 23 July 1958, p.137; *The West African Builder and Architect*, vol.5, no.4, July-August 1965, p.76–8; Watkins Gray International Biography File, RIBA British Architecture Library.

25. *Grays and Tilbury Gazette*, no.2406, 16 July 1932, p.5.

26. *Grays and Tilbury Gazette*, no.2380, 12 January 1932, p.1.

27. ibid.

28. ibid.

29. Pavitt, *op.cit.*, p.38.

30. *Grays and Tilbury Gazette*, no.2406, 16 July 1932, r.5. It seems that Bata was not assured of sufficient markets for his goods in Essex and he could not get Northampton manufacturers to take the 'uppers' from his factory. Essex Records Office, cuttings: see also *Grays and Tilbury Gazette*, no. 2380, 16 January 1932, p.1; no.2387, 5 March 1932, p.8 (first steel arriving).

31. Essex Records Office, cuttings, ibid.

32. The barely legible signature on the plan could be that of Ant Vitek, who assisted Gahura in an ambitious plan for 'Great Zlín' in 1934. He also designed the layout for Ottmuth, Germany, and Best in the Netherlands, and the arrangement of the central axis and the form of the residential streets is very similar to that for Mohlin or Ottmuth. Cohen, *op.cit.*, p.42, Šlapeta, *op.cit.*, p.55.

33. *Bata Record*, no.816, 22 June 1956, p.2.

34. For example the formal axis concludes in a church rather than a sports stadium.

work, which provided a pool of semi-skilled labour. But the deciding factor may have been its transport connections: the site had a mile and a half frontage to the Thames, adjoined a railway line and had road access to Tilbury docks. Thomas Bata personally approved the site, visiting East Tilbury in December 1931, and it was acquired the following March.[25]

Bata's proposals were for nothing less than a 'gigantic new industrial centre which is to contain no fewer than forty different factories and the houses of the workpeople, together with a railway station, riverside jetty, shops, aerodrome, swimming baths, theatre, dance halls and cinemas'.[26] The intention was to manufacture not just boots and shoes but other leather and rubber goods (handbags, coats, toys etc.). The scheme also included a railway station, a siding from the railway line to the works, and a river jetty for small craft supplying coal and commodities to the factory (the docks at Tilbury were 'quite close enough' for exporting the finished goods).[27] Of these facilities, only the railway station was built.

Bata's vision for East Tilbury seems to have already been formed at the time of his visit, when he stood at the window of St Clere's Hall to show Mr Wilson 'how he intended to plan out the estate practically on the same lines as that at Zlín'.[28] A general plan for the settlement, defining its basic layout, would have been drawn up soon after. Responsibility for the scheme is usually attributed to Vladimir Karfik, although the original drawings do not seem to have survived.[29]

Work was due to start in March 1932 but did not; no reason was given to the press other than 'Mr Bata wanted to be sure of his markets before commencing work'.[30] Bata's death in July 1932 was a more potentially serious setback. However, assurances were given that the development would go ahead. Shiploads of rolled steelwork from Czechoslovakia were on site by July 1932 and construction commenced in January 1933.[31]

First to arise was a single-storey, welded steel-framed factory. More industrial buildings followed in 1934, including a boiler house and the first multi-storey block. Construction of the factory went hand-in-hand with the housing and some sports facilities, the first accommodation being completed between 1933 and 1935. The building work was carried out by local contractors Walsham Limited, working to blueprints from Zlín. Progress was steady; by 1935 the site comprised a factory of almost two acres, twenty semi-detached houses and two hostels.

That same year another general plan for the housing and civic areas was drawn up, possibly the work of another Bata architect, Antonin Vitek.[32] This scheme had housing radiating out across the marshes, with a formal central axis containing a 'Y'-shaped building, perhaps conceived along the same lines as Karfik's similarly shaped hotel at Bat'ov of 1933–36. This was a proposal of some ambition, albeit one that failed to incorporate all Bata's initial vision. It omitted, for example, the riverside jetty, railway siding and aerodrome. But in reality, little of this scheme was realised.

On the ground development continued at a modest pace, undertaken from the mid–1930s by British Bata's own building department. Construction of a new residential area was begun but the Second World War slowed the rate of progress, although houses continued to be built until 1941. The factory continued to expand and the social facilities were significantly increased by the completion in 1936 of the multi-storey 'Community House', which included shops as well as dormitory accommodation. The Community House was a key building in all Bata settlements, acting as a focus for public and social life and central to the many activities designed to engineer the company spirit in the workforce. Other facilities followed, including an outdoor swimming pool, tennis courts, a 350-seat cinema which opened in 1938 and, in the 1940s, a school and technical college. The different elements – residential, communal and industrial – were enhanced and unified by planting and landscaping, reflecting the company ethos that 'attractive surroundings form one of the most valuable incentives to successful work'.[34]

A revised plan for the settlement was produced in 1945, either in the head

Figure 9. A version of the 1945 plan of the Bata estate, dating from 1947. It shows the intended development with the existing buildings in solid black (Bata Limited).

Figure 10. Plan of the Bata housing estate, drawn by Andy Donald (English Heritage).

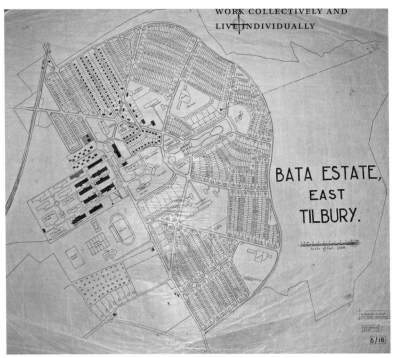

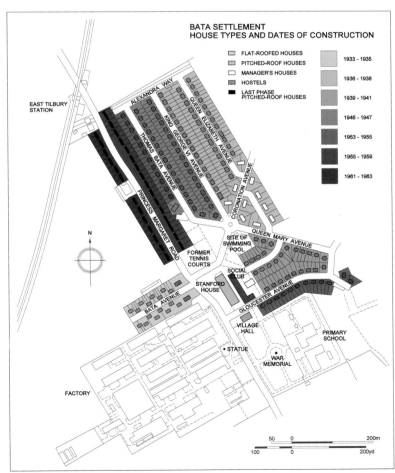

office, then in Canada, or within the building department at East Tilbury. The level of ambition remained high; the plan was designed on a scale comparable to the 1935 plan, although differing in street layout and some of the communal elements.[34] When the house building programme resumed after the war it initially continued to use pre-war models. These were only abandoned in the mid 1950s, when a new design was produced for what became the final phase of residential development. When this ended in 1966, the Bata estate comprised some 362 houses. This was never sufficient for the entire workforce and buses from the surrounding area had to be laid on. From 1950 development in the factory began to pick up, including a new boiler house, which opened in 1956, and continued until 1967 when the final building, a computer centre, was erected. The Community House underwent significant change, becoming the Bata Hotel in 1957–9, its provisions enlarged by the addition of a separate recreation and sports club, and an expresso bar in 1960.

By the 1960s plans were being drastically scaled down, although British Bata continued to produce modest proposals for future development. Land was earmarked for a residential expansion in 1962, but instead it was sold to the developers Fairview for a private housing scheme. This ended company involvement in the development of East Tilbury. Today the former company village remains a self-contained and relatively compact community, still divided broadly into residential, manufacturing and civic zones reflecting company planning tenets. On the west side of Princess Margaret Road is the industrial plant, the former factory now Thames Industrial Park, and a small area of housing. The bulk of the housing and the communal facilities lie on the east side. The grouping of the latter, which includes the remains of a park opposite the factory, derives from an intended town square, the symbolic axis of the settlement.

Figure 11. Bata Avenue viewed from the east (English Heritage).

Figure 12. The east side of King George VI Avenue (English Heritage).

BATA HOUSING

The company housing, uniform and regular in character, followed a modernist aesthetic (although mixing flat and pitched roofs). With street names derived from the company or from British royalty, it was laid out around two roads which meet at a rond point. There was one anomaly, Bata Avenue, a cul-de-sac on the west side of Princess Margaret Road built in 1933–5. This was the first housing to be constructed in East Tilbury and its position presumably reflects the initial thinking of the planners, modified for the later housing.

The two-storey, semi-detached, flat-roofed houses on Bata Avenue were arranged on a chequerboard plan pioneered by Raymond Unwin and Barry Parker at Letchworth, i.e. set at alternate ends of the plots to maximise the garden space between them. They were built of concrete and rendered brick; concrete was used for the flat roofs but a letter written by the Engineer and Surveyor of Orsett Rural District Council states that the houses were of brick construction.[35] This would be expected as brick was generally preferred in Zlín (and, subsequently, in East Tilbury). The entrances are at the sides, the usual arrangement in Zlín because Bata thought that entrances, rather than fences, made 'a good neighbour'.[36] Standardised fittings for the houses were brought from Czechoslovakia, hence the use of wood rather than metal for the window frames, unlike the later houses. The houses were designed as three-bedroom houses of a 'non-parlour' type (i.e. with only a single reception room) and a kitchen and bathroom on the ground floor. Attributed to Vladimir Karfik and Frantizek Gahura, the modernist handling of the Bata Avenue buildings is typical of company houses of this date. Their unadorned elevations are treated as flat planes, interrupted only by the straight lines and rectilinear forms of the downpipes, windows and door canopies, contained by the projecting eaves of the flat roofs. These houses, which are mostly listed, retain much of their original character and, although several houses were demolished in the 1980s, they were rebuilt as facsimiles.[37]

The great majority of the company houses were constructed in phases between 1936 and 1955 in two basic forms, flat-roofed and pitched roofed, and a variety of sizes, for managers and workers (with either two or three bedrooms). All were built of brick, usually rendered or painted. The combination of different

35. Orsett RDC Minutes, 22 November 1933, Thurrock Museum.

36. Cekota, *op.cit.*, p.232.

37. The original buildings can be identified by their bell-shaped rainwater hoppers rather than the simple box-shaped hoppers of the replacements. Some of the list descriptions describe these rendered houses as having concrete walls, but there is no documentary evidence to support this.

38. Pavitt, *op.cit.*, p.43. It was also present in Zlín and other satellite towns, see Moravciková, *op.cit.*

39. Company satellites were evidently allowed a degree of autonomy in matters of design, construction materials and detailing. For example, at Batovany, Slovakia, the local construction office was allowed to make improvements and alterations to projects – in 1941 it was claimed that they changed the housing types 'every year' drawing on their experience, and decided on the appearance of a broad range of family houses. Moravciková, *op.cit.*

types and finishes was not a concession to English building practice and conditions, but typical of Bata planning.[38] It seems likely that the design of the workers' houses, although possibly influenced by Czech models, was actually carried out by the building department at East Tilbury.[39] A simplified version of the chequerboard layout was used, with the houses placed near the front of the plots but not aligned with the opposite properties, allowing for views between the houses. Since their sale in 1980 there has been the inevitable loss of original features such as windows and doors although some brick garden walls (side fences were not allowed) and wrought-iron gates have survived.

More flat-roofed workers' houses are located to the north of Coronation Avenue, variations of a plan probably designed in 1936 that continued to be built until 1947. The original form was that of a 'parlour' house, with two reception rooms, and two or three bedrooms and a bathroom on the upper floor. Externally they differ from the Bata Avenue houses by having front entrances (with side doors) and simple detailing: a cornice band beneath the roof eaves and a projecting or recessed surround to front doors and windows. The pitched-roof type was used south of Coronation Avenue, several versions of which were erected between 1938 and 1955. These houses, which tend to be smaller and have less garden area, also came in two- or three-bedroom versions. The initial design was probably made in 1938, planned as a 'non-parlour' house.[40] Externally the main differences are their tiled roofs and tall brick chimneys, but also some houses have areas of exposed brickwork, presumably for variety.

40. An amended version of the plan exists from 1939, held at the Bata Reminiscence Centre, East Tilbury.

Figure 13. Plans of workers' houses; those of 1936 (left) have flat roofs while those of 1939 (right) have pitched roofs. Redrawn by Andy Donald from originals by the Building Department, British Bata Shoe Company Ltd. (English Heritage).

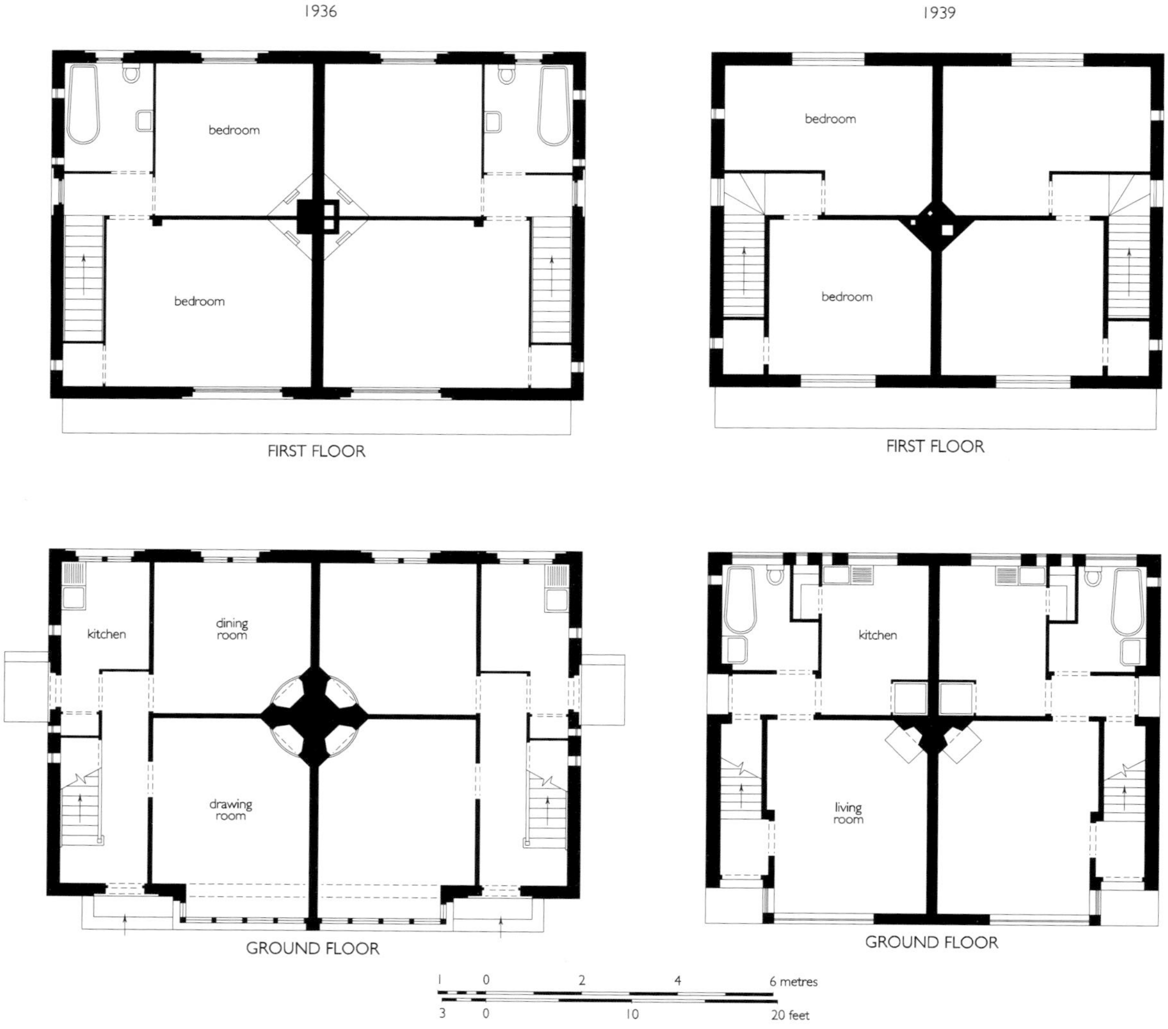

1936   1939

FIRST FLOOR   FIRST FLOOR

GROUND FLOOR   GROUND FLOOR

Figure 14. Houses on Gloucester Avenue (English Heritage).

Figure 15. Managers houses, Nos 1–2 Queen Mary Avenue (English Heritage).

Larger houses for managers were placed diagonally at the ends of the streets and along the southern end of Queen Elizabeth Avenue. Mostly built in 1938, they are more spacious versions of the flat-roofed workers' houses with, in addition, built-in garages with covered terraces above (this detail was omitted from the pair at the south-west end of Thomas Bata Avenue, built between 1946–7 incorporating a doctor's surgery). The most distinctive details are the square openings along the base of the terrace balustrades. Several different examples of managers' houses with garages were built in Zlín, some as a result of a competition held in 1935.[41] Although possibly adapted by the building department at East Tilbury, it seems likely that the design of these larger houses came from the head office. As they were intended for managers, it is also likely that many of the initial occupants were Czech.

The last phase of Bata housing, constructed in two stages – 1954–8 and 1959–66 – to either side of Princess Margaret Road, represents a clear break with the pre-war types. They were probably designed in-house by the building department, perhaps by Ralph Stanley Fraser, who joined British Bata in 1952.[42] These long but narrow two-storey houses, laid out mainly as semi-detached pairs, have brick exteriors with pitched roofs and small brick chimneys. The exteriors mix red and yellow brick, detailed with a wide band of render, concrete window boxes, a pattern of projecting headers to the ground floor and glass-block surrounds to the

41. The competition was international and received entries form 10 countries. The jury, which included Le Corbusier as well as prominent Czech architects, awarded prizes to four designs – including Erick Svedlund, Karfik and Vitek – which were then built in a model estate. A further 25 competition designs were also bought. Šlapeta, *op.cit.*, pp.59–67.

42. Ralph Stanley Fraser (b.1921) joined Bata as an architectural assistant after training at Southend Municipal College Department of Architecture and Building. It is his signature on a coloured perspective drawing of the houses but this may simply signify that he executed the drawings. ARIBA nomination papers, no.16092.

43. *Bata Record*, no.231, 25 November 1938, p.4.

44. *Bata Record*, no.816, 22 June 1956, p.2.

45. Michael Stratton and Barrie Trinder, *Twentieth Century Industrial Archaeology*, London, E. & F.N. Spon, 2000, pp.27, 131; Gillian Darley, *Factory*, London, Reaktion Books, 2003, p.172.

46. Tony Crosby, 'The Silver End Model Village for Crittall Manufacturing Co Ltd'. *Industrial Archaeology Review,* vol.20, 1998, pp.69–82.

front doors. There is some continuity with the earlier houses, including the use of steel-framed Crittall windows, flat canopies over the side entrances and front doors of dark wood and green margin glazing.

As well as family houses, dormitory accommodation for unmarried workers was provided. Two buildings at the east end of Bata Avenue dating from 1933–5 were constructed as separate hostels for single male and female workers. These were designed in a similar manner to the adjoining houses. The other principal residential building was the Community House, now Stanford House. When built in 1935–6 it accommodated a wide range of facilities, including ground-floor shop units, a ballroom, restaurant and works canteen, and a top-floor gymnasium as well as dormitories. The five-storey concrete-framed block was built to the same modular design as the multi-storey factory buildings, using a distinctive circular column form. At night the building was floodlit, becoming 'a landmark for miles', the yellow light of its windows 'contrasting with the bright red neon of the huge surmounting Bata sign'.[43] In 1957–9 the building was converted into the Bata Hotel by Bronek Katz. Further alterations occurred in 1982, when the block was converted to flats, but it remains easily recognisable as a 'Bata' building.

Because landscaping and planting were important to Bata, the company took great care with the open space around the estate and factory. This involved the creation of grassed areas and planting of flower beds, shrubs, privet hedges and trees (by 1955 over 100 trees, mainly Lombardy and Black Poplars, had been planted).[44] Company houses were provided with cherry trees, and annual competitions were held for the best garden in the estate and factory. A significant amount of this planting survives.

CONCLUSION

The Bata Settlement in East Tilbury is important, both internationally as one of an unparalleled global collection of functionalist satellites or colonies, and nationally as a rare example of an inter-war planned industrial village and an uncommon ensemble of modernist buildings. Zlín is acknowledged as an important centre of Czech Modern Movement architecture and a leading example of inter-war rational industrial planning. That this prototype was then used for the construction of industrial settlements on several continents was even more extraordinary. It appears to have no equivalent among other multi-national companies of the period.

A number of model or company villages were built in England in the inter-war years. These include Stewartby, Bedfordshire, built by the London Brick Company from 1927; Kemsley, Kent, for Bowater paper manufacturers, 1925–6; the Kent colliery villages Betteshanger and Aylsham from the 1920s; and Kirk Sandall, South Yorkshire, for Pilkingtons from 1922.[45] But the style of their housing was traditional. The only industrial village to combine Garden City planning and modernist design was Silver End, Essex. Built for the window manufacturer Francis Crittall between 1926 and 1932, the village was planned with separate zones and, like East Tilbury, was intended to be self-sufficient, with its own power supply, not-for-profit farm and communal facilities. It too had Modern Movement houses, designed by a team of architects that included Thomas Tait, C. H. B. Quennell and James Miller, although these only constitute one-third of the housing stock (the majority have pitched roofs and neo-Georgian detailing).[46] There are other points of difference: at Silver End the layout is centred on the recreation ground and village hall, the factory is less dominant (and its functionalism finds no equivalent in the community buildings) and the street pattern is more 'picturesque', with more curving roads and culs-de-sac. But, unlike East Tilbury, Silver End was unique, not one of a number of similarly planned satellites. Silver End has an essentially English sensibility, whereas East Tilbury has a middle-European one: here is garden-city planning, redone by the Czechoslovakians and brought back to England.

Although Modern Movement buildings were being built in England from the mid 1920s, they were not commonplace: the group of 150 houses at Silver End has been described as the 'most complete estate' of its type in the country.[47] Other buildings in this style in Essex include the seafront café at Canvey Island (1932–3) and a group of houses by Oliver Hill at Frinton on Sea. The number of modern houses designed by foreign architects (as opposed to émigré architects working in England) is even smaller, the most notable example being New Ways, No. 508 Wellingborough Road, Northampton, designed by the German architect Peter Behrens and built in 1925. The Bata Avenue housing at East Tilbury, whether designed by Karfik or another company architect, is therefore rare.

The long decline of the company inevitably had an impact on the settlement, including the loss of some its buildings such as the swimming pool, the school and technical college, as well as piecemeal changes to the houses and a decline in maintenance of the public realm. However, its status and importance was recognized in 1993 with the designation of a conservation area and the listing of the houses on Bata Avenue and one factory block. Public awareness has been sustained by the creation of a Reminiscence Centre in the Library and the fund-

47. ibid, p.80.

Figure 16. The former Community House, now Stanford House, in 1938 (NMR, Reproduction by permission of English Heritage).

48. Karen Guthrie and Nina Pope, writers and directors, *Bata-Ville: We are not Afraid of the Future*, a documentary of a coach trip to Zlín by workers from East Tilbury and Maryport.

49. John Tusa, 'Shoemakers to the world: The Bata estate on the Essex marshes, 1939-60', Burrows Lecture, University of Essex, 21 May 2003, transcript at http://www.essex.ac.uk.

ing of an art project in 2003, resulting in the film *Bata-Ville: We are not Afraid of the Future*.[48] Media coverage and a growing literature on Bata and its satellites have also contributed to a greater understanding of the unique character of this functionalist industrial village and the history it embodies.

But under ongoing planning initiatives for the Thames Gateway, the settlement of East Tilbury has been identified as a potential location for significant development. A draft master plan by a private development company, Thamesgate Regeneration Limited, was produced in June 2005. This proposed an extensive development, including 14,000 new homes, commercial and community facilities and a new town centre. This initiative would radically change the character of the place. But what its future planning deserves is imagination and vision to equal to that of its original founders. As the broadcaster and arts administrator John Tusa, son of the managing director of British Bata, observed: 'Today, the Bata Estate at East Tilbury survives, a physical reminder of the brave days of benign vision in the 1920s … embodying a community of responsibility, discipline, self respect, hard work and achievement. … It could yet form the twentieth-century core of a twenty-first century Thames New Town. If so, I hope that it is incorporated with a proper sense of history, the values, and the aesthetic that it once embodied.'[49]

ACKNOWLEDGEMENTS

This article is derived from an English Heritage report, 'East Tilbury, Essex: Historic Area Appraisal' (Research Department Report Series 21/2007). This, in turn, drew upon the article by Jane Pavitt, 'The Bata Project: a Social and Industrial Experiment' published in *Twentieth Century Architecture*, no.1, *Industrial Architecture*, 1994. Acknowledgement is made to English Heritage, Ladislava Hornakova and the State Gallery Zlín, Elain Harwood and to Mrs Sonja Bata and the Bata Corporation for permission to reproduce the illustrations.

5 Themes and Sources for Public Housing in Wales

JUDITH ALFREY

Themes and Sources for Public Housing in Wales

JUDITH ALFREY

Wales and England shared an architectural inheritance, and developed a common rhetoric suited to the new circumstances of the post-war era. But there was also a strong perception of designing for Wales, in recognition that it had its own character and identity. Some of the sources for that identity lay in the development of planning thought earlier in the century, and the power of these ideas imparted a distinctive quality to much of what was built in the early post-war years.

ARCHITECTURAL LANGUAGES

The architects of post-war reconstruction could draw on either modernism or traditionalism, and the best public housing estates built in its first flush include examples of both architectural languages. Large urban schemes like those of Johnson Blackett in Newport or Yorke, Rosenberg and Mardall in Brynmawr belong to a modernist aesthetic pioneered in Wales as early as 1901–5 with a factory by H. B. Cresswell on Deeside, but which was given its best expression in the remarkable Sully Hospital of 1932–6. This architecture of lines, planes and volumes, with flat roofs, strip windows, modular grids and (often) concrete, celebrated the expression of new materials and modes of construction. It was thought appropriate for new building types and programmes, and was most effectively used in the inter-war period for factories, schools and hospitals. When adopted for large-scale housing developments in urban areas stylistic purities were tempered by an awareness of the landscape. This made an important link between modern schemes and those that used quite a different architectural idiom.

Many notable housing schemes were worked in a romantic neo-vernacular style, allied to the picturesque. Perhaps the best exponent of this style was Sidney Colwyn Foulkes, working mainly in North Wales. This idiom had its own pedigree in earlier domestic work that stressed regionalism, rootedness and the *genius loci*. It looked to traditional vernacular forms, to local natural materials and above all to a relationship with landscape for its inspiration. These ideals sometimes produced strongly expressive buildings that demonstrated the power of tradition and symbol, but they were more often acknowledged in a modest neo-vernacular. This architectural language was very important in housing schemes throughout the twentieth century in Wales, not least because of its espousal by the Garden Village movement.

In the first half of the twentieth century Wales still defined itself as a rural nation, but the sense of tradition was given a new focus, a rural ideal was re-shaped, and fresh definition given to ideas of a Welsh landscape. After the Second World War this inheritance remained strong. There was a new confidence in specifically urban design, but traditional and modern styles of building alike were developed within ideas of place and landscape that had their roots in the preceding period, and which were given particular weight through the planning system.

PLANNING AND PERCEPTIONS OF PLACE

The early progress of planning, up to 1932, was shaped for an urban context,

Figure 1. Gaer Estate, Newport. Urban modernism by Johnson Blackett, late 1940s (author).

Figure 2. Seiriol Road housing, Bangor, by Herbert Luck North, 1927 (Elain Harwood).

1. E. Hall Williams, 'The Co-operative Housing Movement', *Welsh Housing and Development Year Book*, no.16, 1931, pp.95–103.

2. 'Public Utility Societies in Wales', *Welsh Housing and Development Year Book*, no.1, 1916, pp.58–60; T. Alwyn Lloyd, 'The Garden Village Method of Estate Development', ibid., pp.70–74; John Newman, *Buildings of Wales: Glamorgan*, Harmondsworth, Penguin, 1995, p.113.

3. Hall Williams *op.cit.*, p.103.

provoked by concerns over poor housing conditions and public health. The early housing and town planning Acts (chiefly those of 1909, 1919 and 1924) were principally concerned with providing and regulating schemes in urban areas. An important focus was the character and appearance of these places. Despite the urban context in which these ideas were developed, they were perceptibly drawn towards a rural ideal. An intellectual ambivalence towards the city had been inherent in the Gothic Revival and the Arts and Crafts Movement. This inheritance exerted a profound effect on planning and building design in the twentieth century, and its influence is clear in the Garden City movement and in the recommendations of the Tudor-Walters report (1917), the foundation for public housing in the inter-war years.

The housing and town planning acts helped to consolidate the role of public utility societies and other associations in housing provision. In Wales these organisations embraced the ideal of the Garden Village wholeheartedly. Foremost amongst them was the Welsh Town Planning and Housing Trust Ltd. established in 1913, under whose auspices several villages were developed. It had built 1,050 houses by 1932.[1] The Garden Village idea determined much suburban development in Wales as well as small-scale additions to country towns and villages. Rhiwbina was one of the first schemes, launched in 1912 and planned by Raymond Unwin for the Cardiff Workers' Co-operative Garden Village Society Ltd. Houses were designed by A. H. Mottram, with others by H. Avray-Tipping (better known for his books on historic houses) and, in 1920–23, by Thomas Alwyn Lloyd. Unwin was influential in the Welsh movement as consultant additionally at Barry and Sealand. Other Garden Villages at Barry, Wrexham, Machynlleth and Llanidloes followed, with Lloyd as architect, and more were established on their heels.[2] By 1930, Wales was 'in the forefront of the housing movement, and can show some of the best examples of Garden Village development on co-operative lines.'[3]

The Garden Village was not, however, the only model taken up by public housing schemes in the inter-war period. In Bangor, Herbert Luck North was the architect for a development in Seiriol Road on behalf of the Bangor branch of the Christian Order in Politics, Economics and Citizenship (COPEC). This organisation campaigned nationwide for improved housing conditions, and held a regional conference in Bangor in 1926. The local authority failed to take up the housing challenge, and COPEC acquired and developed its own site in 1927. It was a model of good practice, notable for its application of North's distinctive neo-vernacular style to the urban terraced street.[4] Where local authorities undertook building work themselves, it was more likely to be in an urbane neo-Georgian idiom and built to higher densities. Good examples include Acton Park, Wrexham – the work of Patrick Abercrombie – and housing at Llandudno Junction. A discussion of Acton Park in the *Architects' Journal* suggested that the site would not have justified the picturesque, and that brick could be used legitimately in a clay district such as this.[5]

Early planning legislation made no explicit strictures for the detail of individual house design. Its direct influence lay chiefly in housing layouts, where it did much to encourage good urban design. The 1919 *Housing Manual* noted that 'by so planning the lines of the roads and disposing of the spaces and the buildings as to develop the beauty of vista, arrangement and proportion, attractiveness may be added to the dwellings at little or no extra cost'. It advocated 'good exterior design in harmony with the surroundings and adapted to the site', and suggested that 'by the choice of suitable local materials, and the adoption of simple lines and good proportion and grouping of buildings, with well-considered variation in design and in the treatment of prominent parts, good appearance may be secured within the limits required by due economy.'[6] This is as good an exposition as any of the picturesque principles which were intended to underlie good practice, and which remained influential in the post-war period.

If public health and welfare was one prompt for the development of a planning system, another was the protection of the countryside. From the early years of the century, a growing lobby urged the proper protection of its character. The maintenance of clear demarcations between the country and the town called for regional planning and there were early moves, for instance on Deeside by 1922. But the first statutory interpretations of planning were urban in intent and reach, and the countryside was only explicitly introduced in the 1932 Town and Country Planning Act, which extended the principal of planning control to all types of land. Thereafter the recognition and management of a distinct town and country encouraged separate architectural languages.

In Wales a rural ideal had a campaigning edge and, despite its strong urban and industrial culture and way of life, national identity was more often defined in rural terms. Ideas about the relationship between a community and its land were highly influential in the campaign for Welsh Home Rule, *Cymru Fydd*, and in Plaid Cymru, founded in 1925, which saw peasant communities as preservers of Welsh cultural heritage.[7] The Honourable Society of Cymmrodorion espoused a similar cause, and was at times vehemently anti-urban – one of its members claimed in 1917 that urban civilisation was alien to the spirit of Wales, and that industrialisation had no values.[8] In the opinion of Daniel Lleufer Thomas, 'Wales, more than England, needs to rebuild a rural civilisation ... the country must be made attractive not just visually but as a place to live'.[9] As the author in 1896 of the *Report of the Royal Commission on Land*, he had already seen rural decay at first hand. Much later, Iorweth Peate dismissed the industrial areas of Wales with their towns as 'breaking away from the traditional peasant culture to become anglicized but deraciné areas'.[10] But perhaps the most passionate plea came from Clough Williams-Ellis, asserting that Wales is 'another country, with another people, another language, another culture – a land which not so long ago had its own architecture, plain and solid, yet answering to that wilder landscape, of which it formed a harmonious part'. He added, 'I want to see Wales keeping her own honest Welsh traditions, and not becoming an imitation England'.[11]

There were other articulate campaigners prepared to mount a defense of the countryside in the face not just of indiscriminate development (what Williams-Ellis termed the 'petrol pedlars and hedge caterers'), but also of deprivation and decay.[12] The Welsh Housing Development Association, founded in 1916 as an amalgamation

4. Rev. G. A. Edwards, 'A North Wales Housing Experiment', in *Welsh Outlook*, vol. 15, 1928, pp.36-7.

5. Lionel B.Budden, 'Recent Architecture in North Wales', *Architects' Journal*, vol.64, 20 October 1926, pp.475-82.

6. *Housing Manual*, 1919, quoted in John Burnett, *A Social History of Housing 1815–1970*, Cambridge, Methuen, 1978, p.221.

7. Kenneth O. Morgan, *Rebirth of a Nation: Wales 1880–1980*, Oxford University Press, 1981, pp.108-14, 206-7.

8. Robert Richards, 'Some Problems of Rural Reconstruction in Wales', *Transactions of the Honourable Society of Cymmrodorion*, Session 1917-18, pp.190-215.

9. Daniel Lleufer Thomas, 'The Housing Problem in Wales', *Welsh Housing Year Book* no.1, 1916, pp.24-31.

10. Iorwerth Peate, *The Welsh House*, (1940), Cribyn, Llanerch Publishers, 2004 edition, p.3.

11. Clough Williams Ellis, 'Wales and the Octopus', *Welsh Housing and Development Year Book*, no.1, 1930, pp.71-3.

12. ibid, p.71.

of two older bodies, urged the revival of rural communities by the improvement of housing, and the creation of amenities and institutions. It also campaigned for the development of towns, villages and suburbs on garden city lines, and for the preservation of scenery.[13] The Campaign for the Protection of Rural Wales, founded in 1928 under the auspices of the Honourable Society of Cymmrodorion, sought to protect the amenities of rural areas, and campaigned for suitable and harmonious development: the importance it accorded to new design and building is perhaps indicated in the fact that its first two chairmen were both architects, Clough Williams-Ellis and T. Alwyn Lloyd. Patrick Abercrombie was instrumental in its foundation, and a powerful advocate of the proper separation of town and country: 'let urbanism prevail and preponderate in the town, and let the country remain rural.'[14]

A celebration of rural values was not therefore just a romantic conceit, and the economic and social revival of the countryside came to be an important strand in planning and design. The Forestry Commission was a significant agent in rural revival and building; from 1924 it set up small forest holdings, and established 670 in Wales by 1930.[15] Its initiatives continued into the post-war period, including small groups of cottages designed by T. Alwyn Lloyd in Montgomeryshire.[16] Lloyd was also architect to the Welsh Land Settlement Society Limited, which was founded in 1936 to settle families from the South Wales Special Area on the land: it had established six settlements by 1938.[17] Another group seeking the re-population of the countryside was the smallholdings movement, using legislation of 1908, 1919 and 1926. New building in existing villages and the conservation or renovation of existing houses, though aimed at revitalising rural areas, had also to take heed of 'place'. The 1926 Housing Rural Workers Act required historical, architectural or artistic interest to be preserved, and its accompanying circular urged the importance of local materials and character.[18]

In both urban and rural areas, the imperative was to provide for a decent standard of life in congenial surroundings. The design agenda, however, held an implicit romanticism with its emphasis on fitness and harmony, and its espousal of a rural ideal. If the picturesque received new momentum in the post-war period, there was much in the preceding generations upon which it could draw.

DESIGN FOR PLACE

The design of a great deal of housing either side of the Second World War can be described as traditional, though this was rarely a literal local vernacular. Yet Wales was not without its vernacular scholars. One was the architect Herbert North, who with Harold Hughes published *The Old Cottages of Snowdonia* in 1908. They sang the praises of 'the white walls and lowly purple roofs' of humble dwellings that 'add to the beauty of the picture of which they form so integral a part'. Although North urged the importance of studying old buildings from a historical as well as an artistic point of view, the lessons he drew were above all aesthetic; 'it is still more important that we should not break into the beautiful harmony of the landscape with something quite out of tune with the district'. He noted that it was not age so much as the use of materials 'with nature's finger-marks still on them' that made the buildings integral to the scenery. Accepting the impossibility of reviving traditional craft techniques absolutely, he advocated using roughcast (for which he identified a pedigree) and a beautiful roof that demonstrated the broken colour of local slate.[19]

In 1940 Iorwerth Peate published *The Welsh House*. One of his aims was to influence modern building, seeking 'education in the value of the old tradition and in the methods of developing it to suit present social needs'. While recognising benefits from social progress and housing renewal he railed at council houses that replaced 'old cottages which were native to their environment'. The new houses 'seem too often to conform to a standardised pattern adopted indiscriminately by local authorities without thought for the particular requirements

13. *Building for the Future: How Wales is Tackling her Social Problems*, Welsh Housing and Development Association, 1917.

14. Patrick Abercrombie, 'The Preservation of Rural Wales', *Transactions of the Honourable Society of Cymmrodorion*, Session 1926–27, pp.156–61; *Welsh Housing and Development Year Book*, no.13, 1928, p.34.

15. R. C. McLean, 'Forest Holdings and Rural Settlement', *Welsh Housing and Development Yearbook*, no.15, 1930, pp.103–6.

16. Paul Mauger, *Buildings in the Country: a Mid-Century Assessment*, London, Batsford, 1959, p.210.

17. Pyrs Gruffyd, 'Battles for the Welsh Landscape 1920-1950', *Planning History*, vol.10, no.3, 1988, pp.17–19.

18. *Welsh Housing and Development Year Book*, no.12, 1927, p.34.

19. Harold Hughes and Herbert North, *The Old Cottages of Snowdonia* (1908), Snowdonia National Park Society, 1979, pp.69–70, 72.

of their own areas.'[20] What history taught above all was harmony with the land-scape, a tenet ultimately derived from romanticism. Clough Williams-Ellis was therefore not alone in asserting that rural buildings should be 'congruous with their setting, suitable to and harmonious with their surroundings, and ready and willing to be comfortably assimilated into the particular landscape of which they inevitably form a part.'[21]

Interpretation of the often-repeated mantra of harmony took several forms. Most frequently it fostered a free traditionalism with a widely applied vocabulary of white rough-cast, slate roofs with steep gables and high chimneys, casement windows and free, expressive planning. This is seen not only in North's work but in that of T. Alwyn Lloyd, and later of Herbert Carr in Montgomeryshire. Apart from its occasional emphasis on local materials this style was not regionally specific, but it could be built relatively cheaply and therefore suited the economics of public housing. Espoused by the Garden Village movement, it proved highly influential, with echoes in many post-war housing schemes.

Figure 3. The Close, Llanfairfechan, Snowdonia, by Herbert Luck North, 1910–40 (Elain Harwood).

20. Peate, *op.cit*. pp.1–2.

21. Clough Williams Ellis, *England and the Octopus*, London, Geoffrey Bles, 1928, p.133.

Herbert North had sought to place this architecture in the spirit of tradition. Half a century later, an outside commentator again advocated some of its features, but this time with an eye more to the pictorial qualities of the scenery than any nod at tradition. It was Paul Mauger's view that 'Wales did not develop the art of stone cottage building in the consummate manner achieved in the Cotswolds and it has left twentieth-century architects free to exploit the use of rendered or colourwashed finishes which is effective against the bright green of the lower hill country, the darker tones of the newly afforested mountains and the grey mountains beyond'.[22]

IDEAS OF THE WELSH LANDSCAPE: THE HILL VILLAGE

There was one over-riding feature of Welsh topography that caught the imagination and exercised the ingenuity of architects working in both rural and urban areas: its hills and slopes. The hillside was proclaimed as the essence of the Welsh landscape, and after World War II the problem of designing for steeply sloping sites was vigorously embraced. This was partly an invented tradition, since historically settlements occupied slightly more tractable land. In the South Wales valleys, where urban development in the nineteenth century had perforce to colonise steep slopes, ingenious arrangements had been made to step or slope terraces straight across the contours. Twentieth-century development adopted quite new design solutions, which were refined in the post-war period.

Several hill villages were built in the first part of the century. An early example was Fishguard Harbour village, built for Great Western Railway employees from c.1907. Commentators noted its hillside site, and that the beautiful situation needed controlled variety in design. 'In the result the main street of the new harbour village presents already that pleasing feature which is always begotten of different styles of architecture, confined within such limits as not to be aggressive or unsightly, and which tends to individualise buildings'. In another gesture towards its landscape, it used 'native stone' for walling.[23]

The hill village was also taken up by early municipal initiatives in Swansea. In 1910, the South Wales Cottage Exhibition was held at Mayhill. A competition was held for a Garden City, and several architects contributed designs for cottages. One of these was Charles T. Ruthen, who published several 'types of houses suitable for hilly sites' in the *Welsh Housing and Development Year Book* for 1917.[24] He noted the special need for planning in hilly districts, and the concomitant need for quite different methods of town planning in Wales. The theme was taken up in subsequent editions of the *Year Book*. The nearby hilltop site of Townhill was also developed as a Garden City by Swansea Corporation. Proposed in 1912, building did not begin until 1919. Raymond Unwin worked with the Borough Surveyor on the layout, which incorporated a novel switch-back road to cope with the gradient[25].

Other housing developments also took up the hill village. The patrons of several of these were colliery companies, favouring a village idiom for what was essentially industrial housing. Of these, Victoria Garden Suburb in Ebbw Vale, begun in 1913 for the Ebbw Vale Iron, Steel and Coal Co Ltd., has been described as 'one of the most successful attempts.... to create the appearance from afar of an informal rural hillside village'.[26] Others included Pontywaun Garden Suburb for the same company in c.1918, and Taff Merthyr Garden Village for the Taff Merthyr Colliery from c.1916.

The cumulative impression gained from these examples is of a strong rural – or pseudo-rural – perception of place in Wales before the Second World War. This vision helped to inform landscape sensibility in the post-war period, but whereas a rural ideal retained some of its hold, there was also a growing recognition of the value of an urban culture. Building in both rural and urban contexts in the post-war period nevertheless took up one of the strongest themes which had emerged earlier and shaped it to new purpose: the idea of the hill village.

22. Mauger, *op.cit*. p.28.

23. Simon Unwin, *Early Twentieth Century Planned Housing in Wales: An Inventory*, 1991.

24. *ibid*.; Charles T. Ruthen, 'The Town Planning Movement in Wales', *Welsh Housing and Development Year Book*, no.2, 1917, p.71.

25. Unwin, *op.cit*.; Prys Morgan, 'Art and Architecture', in Glanmor Williams, ed., *Swansea: an Illustrated History*, Swansea, Christopher Davies, 1990, p.210.

26. Unwin, *op.cit*.

While some existing themes continued in public housing after the war, circumstances had changed and there were new challenges. Not the least of these was the sheer scale of new building, and an agenda that sought housing for all. The need for new homes was seen as particularly acute in rural Wales, where housing conditions were held to be especially low, and where de-population was again considered a severe threat to the integrity of rural communities. Just as in the pre-war period, rural Wales carried the flame of national identity and culture. The Council for Wales and Monmouthshire set up a special Rural Depopulation Panel, later re-named the Rural Development Panel, whose brief was to consider the causes of rural depopulation, and identify practical measures that could be taken to improve living conditions in rural Wales consistent with its traditions and culture.[27]

Particular importance was attached to a series of pioneering schemes to develop new rural communities. The Forestry Commission was heralded as an important contributor to rural re-population and housing, which small local authorities could not always afford to tackle. The new settlement at Llwynygog, begun in the Hafren Forest of Montgomeryshire in 1950, was hailed as the first Welsh forest village.[28] Montgomeryshire also saw another pioneering rural building project, at Llanwddyn in 1948. This was the result of co-operation between Montgomery County Council and Liverpool Corporation, whose water supply came from the nearby Vyrnwy Reservoir. Creation of the reservoir in 1881–8 had seen the development of three related industries in the area – water supply, forestry and farming, mainly in smallholdings. As the forest matured, so more workers were needed, and with them came a demand for housing, education and community facilities. The centre-piece of the scheme was a new school, which, in line with the county's policy, was combined with a community centre. Within the village, fourteen houses and six bungalows were set aside for Liverpool Corporation's workers and pensioners.

The buildings are informally grouped in pairs around the school, in a spacious layout whose rural character is accentuated by large gardens and the modest neo-vernacular style earlier espoused by the Garden Village movement. Its architect was Herbert Carr, who, as County Architect from the early 1930s, had already developed this idiom in the smallholdings he had designed before the war. The scheme was deemed to have excellent picturesque credentials, Mauger admiring 'the good contrast which the stucco cottage-walls provide with the dark forest background', while the school used brown-grey Stamford bricks and hand-made plain roofing tile which 'in turn are a foil to the lighter cottages … these buildings are of a modest character and in such a landscape as Vyrnwy, this makes them the more fitting'.[29] Llanwddyn also addressed some of the perceived problems of the Welsh countryside, offering support to rural cultural and social life whilst fostering village-based education.

Outside the special circumstances of the rural areas, the need to provide houses in large numbers put the housing estate at centre stage. Local authorities were encouraged to use architects to design whole estates, their discipline intended to encompass all aspects of townscape and building design. Architects had designed the layouts as well as the individual buildings for earlier estates and villages, but the Garden Village ideal seemed outmoded and impractical by 1950. Instead, emphasis was placed on urbanism, and the creation of new urban spaces and communities. It is nevertheless striking how far this new urbanism adopted tenets from the earlier movement – in the openness and informality of many new estates, and in a continuing rhetorical appeal to local traditions and landscape.

Requirements for higher density encouraged a return to terraces while building for general housing need called for a greater mix of accommodation. These

27. *The Council for Wales and Monmouthshire, A Memorandum of its Activities*, October 1950.

28. *ibid.; Wales and Monmouthshire Report of Government Action for the Year Ended 30 June 1951.*

29. Mauger, *op.cit.*, p.213; The Council for Wales and Monmouthshire: a Memorandum of its Activities, 1950; *Architect and Building News*, vol.198, no.4269, 13 October, 1950, pp.411–13.

Figure 4 and 5. Cae Bricks, Beaumaris / Bryn Hyfryd, Anglesea: Sidney Colwyn Foulkes designing for topography and setting, 1948–54 (author).

necessities were turned to advantage in picturesque planning, since they encouraged harmonious composition and visual variety. Neither principle was new, but in their adaptation to changed circumstances they took new directions. This may be illustrated by the work of Sidney Colwyn Foulkes, who as an architect in private practice designed many housing estates for local authorities in North Wales. His scheme at Caer Felin, Llanrwst, won a Ministry of Health award for Welsh housing as the best urban scheme in Wales built between 1945 and 1949.[30]

Even better known – and more widely praised – was Foulkes's Cae Bricks estate in Beaumaris (now known as Bryn Hyfryd). It lies on sloping ground immediately north-west of the town, on a site crowned by a contemporary primary school. The estate was built between c.1949 and 1954, when it won a Ministry of Housing and Local Government medal. The estate is structured around a single through-road, with broad green spaces, lesser roads and culs-de-sac opening off it. It uses a planning principle of continuous terraces without rear access roads, and its design employs a range of picturesque devices to achieve a high degree of visual coherence. In many ways it epitomises best practice in public housing of the period, not least for the skill in which the whole terrace was treated as an architectural unit without sacrificing a small, domestic scale.[31]

The scheme was illustrated under the caption 'Harmonious Unity' by Clough Williams Ellis in *The Pleasures of Architecture*.[32] Mauger described it as 'an achievement of landscape design which should be a stimulating example for subsequent work. The curving terraces finishing at each end with an effective stop in the form of salient gables testify to the artist's impulse for unity between his work and the natural scene. It is only necessary to imagine the road down the hill as being straight to realise how good a scheme has been achieved.'[33]

Both estates feature long rows of terraced houses either curving across or following the contours, and they take up once again the theme of the hill village. Great play was made of this at the time. 'The Welsh necessity to build on hillsides' was noted by the *Architects' Journal*, a topographical fact which 'made conventional pairs of houses twelve feet apart very expensive, and a satisfactory grouping of pairs almost impossible.'[34] Colwyn Foulkes himself considered that a series of terraces was the best way of laying out an estate on a hilly site. In his report to the awards committee for Caer Felin, he reflected on 'our particular problem in Wales', and noted that the traditional council house might be suitable for the flat counties of England but not for Welsh conditions. He described the problems faced at Caer Felin as how to build foundations on a hill that cost little more than those on the flat; how best to keep the small houses warm, and how best to equip the kitchen within the price allowed. Houses built in a row were cheaper

30. Caer Felin is discussed in *Architects' Journal*, vol.112, no.2897, 17 August, 1950, p.158; *RIBA Journal*, vol.57, no.12, October 1951, p.431, and *Architect and Building News*, vol.198, no.4257, 21 July 1950, pp.445–7.

31. J. M. Richards, 'Buildings of the Year', *Architects' Journal*, vol.113, no.2916, 18 January 1951, p.75.

32. Clough and Amabel Williams-Ellis, *The Pleasures of Architecture*, London, Jonathan Cape, 1955, FIG.16.

33. Mauger, *op.cit.*, p.219.

34. *Architects' Journal*, vol.111, no.2879, 13 April 1950, pp.466–477.

and easier to heat, and the savings made allowed the installation of better kitchen equipment.[35] At the same time a harmonious composition was achieved across the site as a whole, in a simplified plan which eliminated any need for a back road or passage, or for tunnels between the houses. Conventionally, building in a row necessitated either a back road, or a back passage. Colwyn Foulkes came up with a solution which he believed to be used for the first time at Caer Felin: he set two doors in a covered porch at the front, one for the coalman and the other for the vicar and the visitor. The little dustbin stores adjacent to the front doors in Beaumaris became a strong, witty component of the design.[36]

Planning for a hilly site posed challenges of its own. Colwyn Foulkes described his compositions at Beaumaris and Caer Felin as accepting the contours absolutely, and he went on to say that 'the study of contours will reveal quite unexpected and exciting opportunities of composition, of contrasting the dynamic with the static.' Perhaps more significantly, he represented this as a strong connection between his new schemes and 'the Welsh tradition of building into hillsides. These early Welsh cottages snuggle into the hillside as naturally as a birds nest.... They constitute the only essential Welsh tradition: in this scheme, I have endeavoured to pick up that tradition and adapt it to the larger scale and modern needs of today. Our aim should be the evolution of an essentially Welsh house fitted completely to our physical conditions. It will be quite different to a house in Kent.'[37]

An important element in the composition was the judicious use of colour. At Beaumaris, Foulkes specified a pallet, and whilst there have been many changes there is still a strong sense of colour on the estate. This use of limewash was again felt to reflect a Welsh tradition. To what extent this was genuinely based on study of the vernacular is less clear, but Beaumaris is a town of limewash and render, exposed brick being relatively rare.

Similar themes were taken up in Colwyn Foulkes's larger scheme at Elwy Road, Rhos on Sea, of 1952–6. Again there were long rows of houses facing each

35. Reported in *Architects' Journal*, vol.112, no.2897, 17 August 1950, p158.

36. See, however, a comparable use of entry doors, and also of colour, contrasting end gables and linking walls, in the work of Tayler and Green in their contemporary terraces in Norfolk (Editors' note).

37. *Architect and Building News*, vol.196, no.4220, 4 November 1949, pp.445–7; vol.198, no.4257, 21 July 1950, p.78–80; vol.206, no.1, 1 July 1954, p.7; *Architects' Journal*, 13 April 1950, pp.466–467. Cae Bricks is discussed together with Elwy Road in *ABN*, vol.111, no.2879, 10 June 1959, p.754.

Figure 6. Elwy Road, Rhos-on-Sea: an appeal to romanticism and tradition in an urban setting, by Sidney Colwyn Foulkes, 1952–6 (author).

Figure 8. Elwy Road, Rhos-on-Sea, the
rhythm of contrasting doorcases (author).`

Figure 7. Elwy Road, Rhos-on-Sea, contrasting end blocks (author).

other across wide open spaces. The scheme adopted some of the principles of
Radburn planning (pioneered in Britain at Wrexham only slightly earlier), with
its careful separation of vehicle and pedestrian access. One critic felt that practical consideration may have given way to a Celtic romanticism, but though the
houses do have some whimsical decorative touches what impresses most is the
scheme's elegant practicality.[38] Like the earlier estates, Elwy Road demonstrates
a sympathetic relationship to its landscape, with long curved terraces following
the contours and stepped terraces set against the slopes. Harmonious composition is assisted by the use of end-stopped gabled blocks in a contrasting material
or colour, and by the use of yard walls to bind corners and link parallel terraces.
There is a strong rhythm of detail, for example with variations on a theme for
doorcases. Frank Lloyd Wright, who visited in 1956, thought it 'perfectly charming.'[39]

The large scale and mix of flats and houses gives Elwy Road a distinctly town
character, and its smooth curving terraces are also more urban than the stepped
cottage-like rows of Caer Felin and Cae Bricks. The terrace as a unit of building
was embraced for its suitability to a new urbanism. Elwy Road in some ways
exemplifies this, though the individual housing units draw on traditional architecture rather than modernism. The scheme shares with Colwyn Foulkes's other
schemes a sympathy to its landscape, and a careful, unifying picturesque.

Elsewhere, the gentle neo-vernacular which emerged from the garden village
did not seem appropriate for new developments in an urban context after the
Second World War. In Newport, Johnson Blackett was a self-confessed modernist
who had traveled widely in Europe and declared that 'it behoves architects… to
keep awake to the possibilities of logically using these mediums out of which a
new building art must arise.'[40] He designed several large housing estates, including Ringland, Always, and Saint Julians, but it was Gaer-Stelvio which was most
praised, and which won a Ministry of Housing and Local Government Bronze
Medal in 1950. It was planned to accommodate 3,900 people on 163 acres on
a prominent hillside on the west side of Newport, and combined terraces and
pairs of housing with small blocks of flats, with sites for community buildings,
shops and parkland.[41]

The scheme was featured in the *Architects' Journal* in January 1950 as exem-
plifying 'the sort of efforts that are being made by the more enlightened local

38. *Housing Review*, vol.7, no.6, November-
December 1958, p.176.

39. Borough of Colwyn Bay Minute Books,
BD/D/1/22, Clwyd Record Office, Ruthin.

40. Johnson Blackett, 'Continental
Architecture and Town Planning', *Welsh
Housing and Development Year Book*, no.13,
1928, pp.107–9.

41. *Architects' Journal*, vol.11, no.2875, 16
March 1950, pp.339–43; *Builder*, vol.180,
no.5654, 29 June 1951, pp.916–17.

42. J. M. Richards, 'Buildings of the Year', *Architects' Journal*, vol. 111, no.2867, 19 January 1950, p.73.

43. John Newman, *Buildings of Wales: Gwent*, Harmondsworth, Penguin, 2000, pp.76, 458.

Figure 9. An appeal to the picturesque, housing at Malpas by Johnson Blackett, early 1950s (author).

authorities'.[42] It was thoroughly modern in style, with brick walls, wide-span metal roof structures and slab porches, and metal windows projecting box-like from the walls. It was urban in the completeness of its provision (housing, shops and community buildings), and it achieved an accomplished urbanism apt for its landscape in the sinuous terraces following the contours and exploiting its hillside site.[43] In this respect, Blackett had much in common with the visually very different work of Sidney Colwyn Foulkes, since they were designing for a similar topography, and both produced schemes sympathetic to their setting. At Gaer, the use of flat roofs on parallel terraces helped to open out a view to all the houses. For all his modernist credentials, Blackett had a strong eye for pic-

Figure 10. Gaer-Stelvio, terraces by Johnson Blackett, *c.*1946–51 (author).

44. *Architects' Journal*, vol. 114, no.2965, 27 December 1951, pp.770–4; *Architectural Review*, vol.111, no.666, June 1952, pp.408–9.

45. F. R. S. Yorke, *The Modern House in England*, London, Architectural Press, 1944 edition, pp.92–3; *Architects' Journal*, vol.98 (no.26), 30 December 1945, p.485; Alan Powers, *In the Line of Development: F. R. S. Yorke, E. Rosenberg and C. S. Mardall to YRM, 1930–1992*, London, RIBA, pp.28–30.

turesque composition. A debt to the picturesque was also explicit at Malpas, an estate developed in a parkland setting, but it was not only in relationships with the landscape that this inspiration was manifest. Individual elements within each estate were carefully composed, and contained within a strong overall composition. At Gaer, for example, visual interest was provided by the varied materials – brown brick alternating with render – and in the moulding of boldly overhanging flat roofs. The blocks of flats that punctuate each estate were modelled with a sculptural flair.

Blackett was by no means alone in working in this modern-picturesque idiom. The first phase of Cwmbran new town was visually very similar, and a close kinship is also suggested in the Brynmawr scheme of Yorke, Rosenberg and Mardall.[44] Like Gaer, this was also built on a sloping site, with south-facing terraced houses in long linear blocks placed along the contours. The design contrasted rendered finishes with re-used local stone facing for end walls – another gesture in the direction of local context.[45]

CONCLUSIONS

Welsh public housing of the early post-war period was developed in a climate of thought that emphasised the newness of challenge, and the creativity of response. But underlying the work was also the legacy of an earlier period in which definitions of the character of Wales as essentially rural occupied a prime place in planning thought. Much of the best practice in the early post-war period took these ideas forward, scaling up the garden village idea to meet the larger scale of demand. In the immediate post-war period, urban and rural developments had much in common, for all their stylistic differences, since both drew on picturesque ideas, particularly those regarding the Welsh landscape. One of the most powerful ideas was that of the hill village, which was refreshed and adapted for both rural and urban contexts. This was a theme which would still be resonant, though stripped of its rural references, in later phases of post-war development. At the same time, however, there are clear signs of an emergent urbanism which would later find its expression in the development of Cwmbran and Newtown.

6 Neurath, Riley and Bilston, Pasmore and Peterlee

ELAIN HARWOOD

Neurath, Riley and Bilston, Pasmore and Peterlee

ELAIN HARWOOD

There is a loose thread linking social ideas that had their foundation in the 'Red Vienna' of the 1920s and the curious choice of the artist Victor Pasmore as the concept planner for a swathe of housing in the south-west quadrant of Peterlee new town. The limited literature on the building of Peterlee as a model town for the Durham coalfields has concentrated on the earlier unrealised schemes by Berthold Lubetkin, and his disputes with the first Chairman of the Development Corporation, Monica Felton.[1] But one other imaginative appointment had been made while the idealism behind the new miners' town held good, that of Vivian Williams, who served as General Manager from 1948 to 1974. It was Williams who invited Pasmore to revitalise the spirit of the town in the mid–1950s.[2] His earlier history of architectural patronage perhaps makes the initiative less surprising.

Arthur Vivian Williams (1909–93) was born in China, where his father was a professor of mining engineering, and grew up in Manchester. He studied history at Oxford and Manchester universities before turning to law, and in 1936 he became Assistant Solicitor to Holborn MB in London, progressing rapidly to become Deputy Town Clerk at Finchley in 1938 and Town Clerk to the small borough of Bilston in 1941 and to the larger County Borough of Dudley in 1946. He made his name not only because of his relative youth, but through his reputation as an active reformer with an appetite for town and country planning already developed by 1942–3 when Bilston began to consider its post-war reconstruction. He was highly ambitious, extremely aggressive and difficult to work with; he may possibly have been fortunate not to be drawn into the investigations leading to trials for corruption for T. Dan Smith (Chairman of Aycliffe and Peterlee Development Corporation 1968–70) and John Poulson, retiring quietly the next year. But there was no doubting his remarkable intelligence.[3] This article is about the talent he promoted.

Bilston was an ancient village on the London-Holyhead road east of Wolverhampton, where open-cast coal mining was first recorded in the fourteenth century. There were also seams of iron ore, and John Wilkinson produced pig iron there in 1767, built Boulton and Watt's first steam engines and launched the world's first iron boat on the local canal. By 1790, of 21 blast furnaces in the Black Country, fifteen were in Bilston. The town's heyday as the cradle of the Industrial Revolution was the 1820s, and by 1860 it was already in decline. Coal mining ceased by 1920, and while Stewart and Lloyd's steelworks, founded in the 1880s, remained the largest employer, it was contracting by mid-century. By then the town was characterised by acres of derelict land surrounding a small and unusually overcrowded centre, with workshops and factories packed into courtyards behind the houses. Redevelopment was further constrained by a girdle of roads, railways and canals, which isolated outlying communities. Although there was little male unemployment, the limited opportunities encouraged a perpetuation of poor conditions. When it was raised to the status of a Metropolitan Borough in 1933, Bilston began a vigorous slum clearance programme, and built a model health centre in 1938 following a public competition won by Lyons, Israel

Figure 1. Victor Pasmore, Apollo Pavilion, 1969 (English Heritage).

1. John Allan, *Berthold Lubetkin, Architecture and the Tradition of Progress*, London, RIBA Publications, 1992, pp.450–507. RIBA BAL Drawings Collection, PA 115/7 (13).

2. John Pasmore, lecture on Victor Pasmore, DoCoMoMo, 6 June 2002.

3. Tom Toward, Williams's Personal Assistant at Peterlee, in conversation January 2006.

4. *Discovery*, vol.8, no.8, August 1947, p.252.

5. CMB-BIL/14/1/Box 30, D59, Wolverhampton MB Archives.

6. Dr Robert Abbott, talk on BBC Midland Home Service, 7 November 1946, text in LB 3391(P), Wolverhampton MB Archives.

7. CMB-BIL/14/1/Box 30, C29, Wolverhampton MB Archives.

8. Christopher Long, *Josef Frank, Life and Work*, University of Chicago Press, 2002, pp.57–8; 1114–17. This excellent biography was the inspiration for the article.

and Elsom; plans for a new swimming baths were frustrated by the war. In 1946 the council recorded that there were 2,655 houses 'unfit for habitation' (a large number for a small town), while 1,176 more lacked sanitation, while all the plans for new housing were on derelict industrial land that first required extensive reclamation works.[4]

From 1942 Williams was an active member of the voluntary West Midlands Group on Post-War Reconstruction, and he argued vigorously that new house-building was impossible without proper town planning.[5] He was joined in his enthusiasm by Dr Robert Abbott, the 'very vital' Chairman of the Development and Reconstruction Committee. In a talk on the BBC's Home Service, Abbott explained how families in the 1930s had been moved from slums to new estates and expected to adapt to their new surroundings, but instead the new housing had rapidly degenerated to resemble the old. 'If these estates are to succeed as social experiments some preparation of the tenants must be undertaken ... people must be told how to make the best use of the houses – fullest use of the facilities provided – and they must be given some assistance and re-education so that they can undertake, as far as possible the management of these services.'[6] The council used the Bilston Corporation Act of 1943 to set up an information bureau, then a novel idea. T. Alwyn Lloyd, a Cardiff planner associated with the Town and Country Planning Association, was appointed in June 1943 to make a town plan in association with the Birmingham firm of Jackson and Edmonds. Even in a time when many cities were making 'civic surveys' – studies of their physical and social development, and commissioning post-war reconstruction plans, Bilston's work was remarkable. A Civic Survey Exhibition held in Bilston in the summer of 1944 included planning schemes by Lloyd and Jackson, and by Geoffrey Jellicoe, along with a study of atmospheric pollution by G. E. S. Sheldon. The exhibition emphasised public participation and education, and in 1945 Williams addressed the Town and Country Planning Association Summer School on the 'team spirit' of the Bilston Survey.[7]

To continue 'outreach' work among the residents, Councillor Abbott turned to an international expert, the Viennese economist, socialist and educator Otto Neurath, suggesting he organise an exhibition on 'housing and happiness'. Otto Neurath (1882–1945) was an empirical philosopher – huge and exuberant both physically and in a range of interests that extended from economics through housing management to the exposition of difficult concepts through pictorial means. All these endeavours were dedicated to the broader aim of improving the social and economic conditions of common humanity. His preliminary training was as an economist in Vienna, but it was in Leipzig during the First World War that he first sought to display complex economic ideas in a museum setting for a lay audience. He then set out a plan for the socialisation of the economy of the Bavarian Republic, declared in November 1918, claiming that normal economics did not look at issues like happiness. Neurath's alternative society included factory councils overseeing conditions and wages, and emphasised self-help and an economy in kind. This was a very personal, flexible and Epicurean view of socialism that owed little to Karl Marx, and which saw him arrested for high treason once the republic fell. Only the intercession of Max Weber and Austrian friends got him deported back to Vienna, where Neurath found himself among like thinkers in promoting education and improving housing conditions. He advocated the end of private kitchens, and worked with architects such as Margarete Lihotzky and Josef Frank. Frank was connected through his brother Philipp with Neurath's philosophical group, the Vienna Circle, and had an empirical approach to both architecture and politics. This included a questioning of pure functionalism and an interest in simple decoration as both cheerful and instructive.[8] Such a gentle, humane approach to architecture and emphasis on social commitment was well suited to post-war Britain.

From the late 1920s Neurath dedicated himself to promoting his pragmatic philosophy and anti-metaphysical stance through exhibition design. To illustrate complex issues he developed the 'Vienna Method' of pictorial statistics, using a flat figure of a man to represent, perhaps, several thousands of population, an image of a factory for a unit of production, and so on. In February 1934 his Museum of Economy and Society was closed by the Dollfuss regime. Neurath and his assistant Marie Reidemeister moved to The Hague, where they refined this picture language as a series of images, owing something to Egyptian murals and hieroglyphics, and was called 'Isotype', the International System of Typographic Picture Education, first published in 1936. But in 1940 Neurath and Reidemeister had to flee again, this time to Britain. Neurath lectured on logical empiricism and social sciences at All Soul's, Oxford, and in February 1941 founded the Isotype Institute for the continuing international promotion of visual education.[9] Isotype was used to illustrate a popular edition of the Beveridge Report.[10]

Neurath visited Bilston in the summer of 1945, and advised that maisonettes for pensioners should be scattered among other housing so that the tenants could share to the full in community life. 'Neurath insisted, as in Vienna, that no town planning is any use unless an attempt is made to approach the individual who is to be re-housed and to find out what he feels are his needs – to make him realise that the whole success of the venture depends on his taking his own part in its working.'[11] In November he was invited to co-operate with Lloyd and the Bilston staff, the Borough Architect Wallace G. Lofthouse and Borough Surveyor A. F. B. Sidwick, in the replanning of the town. Abbott's Health Committee agreed that the sociological aspect of Neurath's work was of 'paramount importance', as planning and reconstruction work should reflect the needs of the people. Neurath was formally engaged by the council at Abbott's instigation to advise on health education and the rehousing of slum dwellers on 27 December 1945. But by then he was dead, having had a fatal heart attack on 22 December.[12]

All should have been lost. But Williams then turned to an English architect and educator with a surprisingly similar stance on the importance of community life in planning, and who had evolved a similarly empirical approach to architectural style and an enthusiasm for decoration. Sir Charles Reilly, Emeritus Professor of Liverpool University, had been appointed Planning Consultant in February 1944 to the Borough of Birkenhead, to produce a civic survey and outline plan. In the course of this work he saw plans for a dormitory suburb on land recently purchased by the corporation at Woodchurch, an attractive valley 'which should have been left for farming'. Reilly did not like the conventional garden suburb proposed, 'with isolated pairs of houses mostly looking away from one another on curving roads behind hedges', and indeed the previous year he had resigned from the Town and Country Planning Association – 'those silly little suburban people' - because of their preference for garden suburbs over Forshaw and Abercrombie's *County of London Plan*.[13]

Now Reilly offered a radical design of his own. Hitherto his writings on town planning had concentrated on the need for tall buildings in undiluted city centres, but now he turned to low-rise, low density dormitory developments with a proposal for setting pairs and short terraces of two-storey houses and a few flats directly on to village greens, with limited 'one-way' road access round them and private gardens to the rear. Two or three of these greens, housing 500–1000 people, would be served by a 24-hour nursery and a community centre or club house, fulfilling many of the functions of the village inn, but including a laundry and 'a good cook'. Garaging, schools and other facilities were to be placed at the entrance to the development. Reilly was so keen that the residents should enjoy a delivery service of meals from the hotel (as 'happened in hotels in Vienna and Budapest before the war') that he petitioned Lord Listowel, the Paymaster General, for dispensation to install a private telephone system linking the houses with the club house, as normal telephones were beyond working-class means. In his words, the idea was 'to plan the houses round oval greens and these greens

9. Otto Neurath, *Basic by Isotype*, London, Kegan Paul Trench Truber and Co., 1937; J. A. Edwards and Michael Twyman, eds., *Graphic Communication through Isotype*, University of Reading, 1975; Elisabeth Nemeth, 'Otto Neurath's Utopias, the Will to Hope', in Thomas E. Uebel, ed., *Rediscovering the Forgotten Vienna Circle, Austrian Studies on Otto Neurath and the Vienna Circle*, Dordrecht, Kluwer, 1991, pp.285–92; Nancy Cartwright, Jordi Cal, Lola Fleck and Thomas E Uebel, *Otto Neurath, Philosophy Between Science and Politics*, Cambridge University Press, 1996, pp.29–86.

10. Sir Ronald Davison, *Social Security, the Story of British Social Progress and the Beveridge Plan, visualised by Isotype*, London, Harrap, 1943.

11. Derek Wragge Morley, 'The Bilston Experiment, a Problem in Social Engineering', in *Discovery*, vol.8, no.8, August 1947, p.250.

12. Bilston MB Council Minutes, Housing and Town Planning Committee, 18 September 1945; Health Committee, 13 November 1945; Main Council, 27 December 1945; Wolverhampton MB Archives.

13. Sir Charles Reilly, 'Bilston, its Problems and its way of Tackling them', 1947, partly published in *Discovery*, August 1947, in D207/4/4, Reilly Archive, University of Liverpool; *London Evening News*, and letter from Reilly, 23 November 1943, in D207/13/5, Reilly Archive, University of Liverpool.

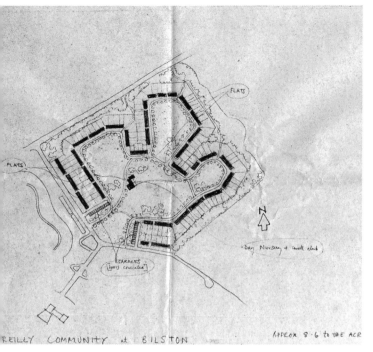

REILLY COMMUNITY at BILSTON   APPROX 8.6 to the ACR

Figure 2. 'A Reilly Community at Bilston', a set of three greens and a clubhouse, D207/4/14, Reilly Archive, University of Liverpool.

Figure 3. Scheme at Batman's Hill, Sedgley, for Bilston MB, by F. X. Velarde and G. G. Dobson, July 1947, D207/4/4, Reilly Archive, University of Liverpool.

14. Letter from Sir Charles Reilly to Lord Listowel, 10 June 1946, in D207/4/14, Reilly Archive, University of Liverpool.

15. Letter from Charles Reilly, *New Statesman and Nation*, vol.32, no.822, 23 November 1946, p.380.

16. Peter Richmond, *Marketing Modernism, the Architecture and Influence of Charles Reilly*, Liverpool University Press, 2001, p.186.

17. Lawrence Wolfe, *The Reilly Plan: A New Way of Life*, London, Nicholson and Watson, 1945. *Architects' Journal*, vol.100, no.2598, 9 November 1944, p.346.

18. Letter from Reilly to the Right Hon. Earl of Listowell, 10 June 1946, in D207/4/14, Reilly Archive, University of Liverpool.

19. RIBA Nomination Papers, Wallace George Lofthouse, ARIBA 1920. RIBA / V&A archives. Lofthouse had joined Bilston UDC in the First World War.

like the petals of a flower round a [community] centre'.[14] Reilly claimed to have 'heard very little of' Neurath, though he placed a similar emphasis on shared dining, facilities, art and drama.[15] But he had a nearer model in the design of Port Sunlight, the paternalistic community established by Lord Leverhulme for his workforce south of Birkenhead, which also featured clubhouses and village greens, especially in the earlier phases of its development.[16]

In Birkenhead, Reilly's greens were acclaimed by the Labour and Communist Parties, but were rejected by the council's Conservative majority, amid a provocative local campaign that led to an unsolicited book by Lawrence Wolfe, *The Reilly Plan: A New Way of Life*, and articles in the national dailies, *Picture Post* and the *Architects' Journal*.[17] This last was seen by Williams, who saw the similarities with Neurath's outline proposals and invited Reilly to Bilston. 'In spite of by accident my calling Bilston 'Belsen', they have asked me to lay out twelve of my little communities,' Reilly gleefully reported.[18] For Reilly the concept of what became known in correspondence as 'Reillyism' and 'Reilly Greens' became a crusade in the years before his death in February 1948. From his home in Twickenham he made outline plans from prepared surveys, which would then be worked up into detailed designs by other architects. Reilly would accept no fee for his work, but he insisted on approving the choice of architect and the final design. A site at Green Lanes, Stowlawn, had already been offered to the Viennese refugee Ella Briggs, to whom Reilly gave crits at the RIBA. The rest were mainly passed to his former Liverpool students, notably to his son-in-law Derek Bridgwater, but also to William Crabtree, F. X (Val) Velarde and Bernard Miller; other schemes went to Clough Williams-Ellis working in partnership with Lionel Brett and to W. G. Lofthouse, the long-serving Borough Architect.[19] Reilly's ex-students – even Bridgwater – wrote to him as 'Prof', and accepted his postal crits and directions to 'please see and report to me' without demur.[20]

Williams admitted, however, that legislation and planning could not determine the choice of inhabitant, and that the 'human factor' recognised by Neurath was 'the more complex end of it'. At Bilston he organised another exhibition, in

July 1946, which was opened by Reilly and attracted an enthusiastic notice from Alison Settle in the *Observer*.

> *Under the Reilly Plan for Bilston, Staffs, every form of service is to be made available to the housewife as an extension of her own home. If she does not choose to cook in her own kitchen, hot meals will be delivered: the meal over, she will put her used crockery into a basket to be collected, washed and returned duly sterilised.*
>
> *If women are to return to the labour market, schemes of this kind must be speeded up. The Bilston Plan includes both hobby rooms and homework rooms where children can be kept occupied until parents return from work. There will also be a staff of home helps – all men.*[21]

In April 1946 Vivian Williams moved to Dudley, a larger town five miles south where mining had been superseded by small-scale metalworking. Its role as a dormitory town for the smaller settlements around it meant that it had experienced exceptional levels of unemployment in the 1930s.[22] Reilly was initially disappointed, 'but Williams says it only means more "Reilly Greens", while his eventual successor at Bilston was an enthusiastic convert, confusingly named A. M. Williams. By July 1946, Reilly could claim fourteen schemes for greens in Bilston and Dudley, and brought in other ex-students for industrial areas and schools there.[23] Reilly Greens were also proposed at Southampton, where the Chief Architect, Leon Berger, was another ex-Liverpool man, and the Minister of Town and Country Planning, Lewis Silkin, commissioned a model of a Bilston scheme that was widely exhibited and published. For a scheme of two 'Reilly Greens' proposed by Miles Aircraft Ltd. for their workers at Woodley Green, outside Reading, he approved the appointment of Edric Neel and Raglan Squire of Arcon as architects.[24] Reilly also claimed that greens were being designed by Sven Markelius, town planner for Stockholm.

The system of greens had one advantage for Bilston, in that it was suited to the flat land left by reclamation. Reilly described

> *an angry sea of black shale with which the town is surrounded and penetrated. They level off this shale with bulldozers and then offer me a series of grand stretches of flat land covered with soil and grass they bring from Shropshire. The plateaux of c.30 acres each only cost £200 an acre so they should be able to make some inexpensive housing. The billiard tables are not always on the same level but for my rather separate little communities that makes no difference.*[25]

At Old Park Farm, Dudley, where Bridgwater and Peter Shepheard prepared two schemes in 1946–7, the 'petals' of the greens had to be adapted to a steeply sloping site on former farmland. The difficulty was the shortage of materials and

20. See especially a letter of 18 June 1947 from A. M. Williams to Reilly which has this annotation to Bernard Miller, D207/4/4, Reilly Archive, University of Liverpool.

21. The *Observer*, no.8093, 7 July 1946, p.7.

22. Department of Social Sciences, *Social Aspects of a Town Development Plan, A Study of the County Borough of Dudley*, University Press of Liverpool, 1951, pp.21–3.

23. Letter to Lewis Silkin, Minister of Town and Country Planning, 4 July 1946, in D207/4/13, Reilly Archive, University of Liverpool. At Dudley, Gordon Timmins was brought in to design the industrial area, and a school was commissioned from Derek Bridgwater and F. X. (Val) Velarde.

24. Letter to Miss Ellis, Miles Aircraft Ltd. 'I approve'. 7 January 1947, in D207/4/13, Reilly Archive, University of Liverpool.

25. Letter to Lord Listowel, 10 June 1945, in D207/4/14, Reilly Archive, University of Liverpool.

Figure 4. Flats (based on designs by William Crabtree), and houses, Park View Road, Bilston (author).

Figure 5. Church Green, Stowlawn, Bilston, by Ella Briggs, 1947 (author).

Figure 6. Oak Green, Dudley, based on designs by Bridgwater and Shepheard, c.1950 (author).

rising inflation that dogged all building in the late 1940s, and made the Ministry of Health unwilling to support any but the simplest housing proposals. There was also a problem that many of the schemes were on land owned by Bilston and Dudley outside their administrative areas, in the intervening districts of Sedgley and Coseley hostile to ingress from north and south. Today the whole area is a continuous sea of suburban housing.

With an average of 8.6 houses per acre because of the large village greens, Reilly's proposals had a density even lower than that of the garden suburbs. Only by combining them with flats were there adequate numbers for a club house, and the district heating and refuse systems he and Williams sought. Heating from a common estate boiler and a dustbin-free refuse system were ideals of high-density city flats from their first introduction at Quarry Hill, Leeds, in the late 1930s, but to propose them for a low-rise scheme was exceptional. Reilly believed that district heating would save coal, 'prevent rheumatism and bronchial trouble', and that it and a refuse system would make houses cleaner. Money for building district heating systems, granted on a case-by-case basis at Bilston from July 1947 and through a Bill in parliament at Dudley in 1947, was a rare success for the two Williams. Yet even Stowlawn, the first of the Bilston schemes, was eventually built with conventional chimneys.[26] Today, Briggs's work can still be recognised at Bilston, with three blocks of flats based on designs by William Crabtree giving

26. *Architects' Journal*, vol.105, no.2710, 2 January 1947, pp.15–16; *The Builder*, vol.177, no.5564, 7 October 1949, pp.448–51.

Figure 7. Mural by Hans Feibusch, Dudley Assembly Hall, 1948 (author).

added density, but many of the greens have been built over. Building by Dudley MB to 'modified Reilly Green lines' finally began at Old Park Farm in 1950, and this single large scheme survives much better. The Dudley Bill also permitted Vivian Williams to set up information bureaus with special staff, and to make 'libraries into cultural centres instead of just book borrowing stations'.[27] In some respects the Dudley Bill resembled that initiated by the London County Council in 1946 to extend its library powers to build the Royal Festival Hall, but Williams also included a clause permitting the council to supply food on the lines of Reilly's community centres.

After an exhibition at Dudley in January 1947 Williams brought in T. S. Simey, Charles Booth Professor of Social Science at Liverpool University, to advise on selection and resettlement. A social survey of Dudley was published by the university in 1951.[28] Another commission secured by Reilly and Williams was the appointment of the artist Hans Feibusch to decorate the rear stage of the assembly hall at Dudley, now the Concert Rooms, with a mural intended as a war memorial. Showing Sir Roger de Someries hunting in the Lickey Hills, it is a rare secular work in which his characteristic acid yellows and pinks are subdued in a greensward; the figures' faces are said to be drawn from those of local dignitaries.

PETERLEE

In November 1946 Stevenage had been declared the first new town, set up as a public corporation on the model proposed by Lord Reith in 1945–6 and inspired by his beloved BBC. Instead of a Town Clerk there was a General Manager, and Vivian Williams applied unsuccessfully for the job.[29] The first General Managers were all appointed from outside local government, from military or business backgrounds. But in 1948 Williams was appointed General Manager to a new town, albeit one very different from those founded around London.

In 1933 J. B. Priestley wrote in his *English Journey* that `Nobody ... goes to East Durham'. He described Shotton, one of the larger villages, as 'a few shops, a "public house", and a cluster of dirty little houses, all at the base of what looked at first like an active volcano. .. No doubt it was fortunate for England that you could dig down at Shotton and find coal. It did not seem to have been very fortunate for Shotton.'[30]

A new town for the Durham coalfield, to bring recreational and educational facilities and a wider range of employment opportunities was a local initiative. It was conceived in wartime reports by C. W. Clarke, Engineer and Surveyor to Easington Rural District Council, whose proposals extended to the site and the name. Peterlee, named after a local miners' leader, was duly designated as a new town by Lewis Silkin for the Labour Government in March 1948. Its subsequent history was less happy, for Clarke's site, a natural amphitheatre between Shotton Colliery and the coast from which views of the surrounding pits were concealed, and bounded to the south by the wooded gorge of Castle Eden Dene, had beneath it substantial coal reserves which had to be extracted before building could begin. The National Coal Board would give no timetable for this. Subsequent histories have focussed upon the frustrated negotiations between the NCB, the indomitable first Chairman of the Peterlee Development Corporation, Monica Felton, and the Corporation's architect, Berthold Lubetkin. Lubetkin and Williams had a poor relationship, 'aggravated by personal chemistry and shared frustration with external obstacles'; one of their arguments was over control of the social research department at Peterlee.[31] Both Felton and Lubetkin left Peterlee in early 1950, leaving the town to be built with conventional two-storey semis that would 'ride' the extraction and subsequent subsidence.

Lubetkin's departure made the Development Corporation more flexible. Moreover, a reduction in coal shortages weakened the NCB's power, and fear of compensation for subsidence made them more willing to negotiate. Lubetkin was succeeded by George Grenfell Baines, who had established good relations

27. Letter from Vivian Williams to Charles Reilly, 9 November 1946, in D207/4/15, Reilly Archive, University of Liverpool.

28. Department of Social Sciences, *Social Aspects of a Town Development Plan, A Study of the County Borough of Dudley*, *op.cit.*

29. Letter from Vivian Williams to Charles Reilly, 21 April 1947, in D207/4/15, Reilly Archive, University of Liverpool.

30. J. B. Priestley, *English Journey*, London, Heinemann, 1934.

31. Allan, *op.cit.*, p.495.

32. Co-Operative Wholesale Society. Vivian Williams to Grenfell Baines, 26 February 1951, in NT/PE/3/1/303, Durham County Archives.

Figure 8. Plan of Peterlee (Robert Reid).

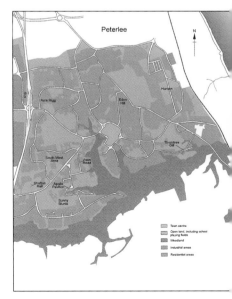

33. Garry Philipson, *Aycliffe and Peterlee, New Towns 1946–1988*, Cambridge, Publications for Companies, 1988, p.101.

34. Letter from Vivian Williams to R.T. Kennedy at MHLG, 13 October 1953, in NT/PE/3/1/303, Durham County Archives.

35. Report by Vivian Williams, in NT/PE/1/415.

36. King's College became the core of Newcastle University in 1964 but was then part of Durham University. Reports of the General Manager, 1955-6, NT/PE/1/4/5; Development Corporation Minutes, 26 October 1955, NT/PE/1/1/3; Durham County Archives.

37. Report by Victor Pasmore, n.d. c.1963, in NT/PE/3/1/98, Durham County Archives.

38. A. V. Williams, 'A symposium with Sir J.M. Richards, A.V. Williams, A.T.W. Marsden (Chief Architect) and Victor Pasmore, extract from BBC Radio, 22 Jan 1967', in Victor Pasmore, *Victor Pasmore*, London, Thames and Hudson 1980, p.255.

39. Geoffrey Jellicoe, 'Buildings in the Landscape', in *Studies in Landscape Design*, London, Oxford University Press, 1960, p.61, pp.103-4.

40. Report by Victor Pasmore, n.d. c.1963, in NT/PE/3/1/98, Durham County Archives.

with the NCB as consultant architect to the new town of Newton Aycliffe, and who was prepared to build conventionally. By the end of 1954 a considerable amount of housing had been built. Thorntree Gill was followed by the development of the north-east quadrant as Edenhill and Chapel Hill, with smaller houses to lower standards to achieve the highest possible numbers with limited building resources. The numbers were impressive, but the total effect was monotonous. Individual buildings were no better, Williams complaining to Baines in 1951 that the technical college by the County Architect looked 'like a CWS factory'.[32] Williams decided that something needed to be done.[33] A letter to the Ministry of Housing and Local Government in 1953 shows his disappointment with what was being produced, hoping that the scheme for Acre Rigg was 'a little more interesting' than previous efforts and promising 'more interesting layouts' for the future.[34] In October 1955 he reported that the need for almost daily consultations with the technicians of the NCB had precluded the use of freelance architects on an *ad hoc* basis, but suggested that the look of Peterlee might instead be improved by 'the employment of an artist capable of organising small units of building in terms of mass and colour.'[35]

At 11pm one evening in 1955 Williams telephoned Victor Pasmore, who had lately begun teaching at King's College, Newcastle. The Chief Architect, Wilfrid Scott, welcomed the suggestion, publicly at least, and the Chairman, Alderman F. C. Pette, agreed to Pasmore's part-time appointment at Peterlee on a salary of £1,000.[36] Pasmore later wrote that the 'constant subordination of the architectural staff to technical systemisation, statistical pressure and economic limitations had produced a state of fixation and sterility. Williams determined that the appointment of another specialised architect was not enough. What was needed was not merely an addition to the architectural staff but an extension of it.'[37]

Victor Pasmore had achieved some prominence in the 1930s as a landscape artist, but in 1948, inspired by an exhibition of Picasso's wartime paintings at the Victoria and Albert Museum, he shifted decisively to abstraction. Partly inspired by the American artist Charles Biederman and his work, *Art as the Evolution of Visual Knowledge*, with whom he corresponded for some years, Pasmore made a number of low reliefs in a bid to explore three-dimensional space. He also produced murals, the best known being that in ceramic at the Regatta Restaurant for the Festival of Britain, where he worked with Misha Black and Alexander Gibson of the Design Research Unit. But abstract art is hard to sell, and the teaching job at Newcastle was timely. Williams felt intuitively that 'if it were possible to bring him into collaboration with our own architects it might be possible to create against the larger canvas of an actual landscape of considerable beauty, forms and proportions in housing terms. It seemed to me, if he would embark on this venture, he could contribute to the aesthetics of the Town and help the architects to lift their eyes to a new horizon and bring in a fresh vision to New Town planning.'[38] Jellicoe had seen painterly qualities in Frederick Gibberd's master plan for Harlow; now, he remarked, was a unique occasion where a painter contributed directly to the planning. 'It is interesting to know that even when his work is flat on canvas, Pasmore walks in imagination round the spaces between his forms, the space between forms being as important as the forms themselves.'[39] Pasmore explained that Williams wanted to make an aesthetic use of space to encourage social participation. He himself saw in architecture and landscape a way of reaching a fourth dimension, or space-time continuum that he realised only imperfectly in his paintings and reliefs.[40] Pasmore stayed until control of housing passed from the Development Corporation to Easington District Council in 1978.

Pasmore's first impression of Peterlee was suppressed by Williams from an article intended for the local paper. 'As I approached the town I saw a vast mass of red brick housing encroaching over the countryside like lava from a volcano which nothing could stop. But if the impression from the distance was alarming, once inside I lost all sense of "place". Moreover there appeared not only nowhere to go, but also no way out.'[41]

Pasmore felt that his work 'was not about pioneering new forms of urban habitation or new building techniques, but simply to inject new life into an existing system. ... The new Peterlee does not do more than what it set out to do - to revitalise and redefine existing urban design in terms of modern spatial concepts, concepts that have become lost in the fog of overwhelming quantity and low cost building demands.'[42] Yet Pasmore's five principles, termed 'points' in the manner of Le Corbusier, made for a radical change to the environment. He sought a more modern architectural style, with a cross-wall construction whose use of timber cladding was honestly expressed and which was flat roofed. He substituted black brick for red and developed with his two young architectural assistants, Peter Daniels and Frank Dixon, a system where the principal windows were placed in the non load-bearing walls, the windows stained brown and the main panels painted white. Secondly, thirdly and fourthly, the layouts were to articulate the topography, to break down the multiplicity of repeated units and to reduce them to a pedestrian scale. Public space, private gardens and garaging were to be integrated into the overall scheme as 'positive' features. His net-like treatment of private spaces is important in understanding how Pasmore's abstract grids of broken lines - in his planning work and paintings alike - translated themselves into housing layouts. The fifth principle was one found in other new towns, yet it produced radical results in Pasmore's hands. That was to free the housing from the road system.[43]

From the first Pasmore was an integral part of the Housing Group, working directly with the architects and planners in providing a fresh eye; indeed, after the brief had been established, the site visited and the team had discussed their ideas, the first 'cartoon' or sketch lay-out was his. As Pasmore suggested in the first of two draft articles written in 1971,

the New Town seems to provide an ideal opportunity to revive, in a new form, the great tradition of the classical architects and the English parks. ...

41. Victor Pasmore, 'Urban Design as a Problem of Topology and Psychology', written for *Sunderland Industrial Review*, August 1971, unpublished; in NT/PE/3/1/386, Durham County Archives.

42. ibid.

43. ibid.

Figure 9. Housing in South West Area, Peterlee, as a drift in the landscape (Eric de Maré, English Heritage, NMR).

44. ibid; Pasmore, *Victor Pasmore, op.cit.,* p.259.

45. *Victor Pasmore,* ibid., p.261.

46. *Architects' Journal,* vol.133, no.3436, 23 February 1961, pp.291–8; *Concrete Quarterly,* no.49, April-June 1961, pp.26–7; *Architectural Review,* vol.129, no.768, February 1961, pp.88–96; vol.141, no.842, April 1967, pp.271–6.

Urban environment is an artificial landscape so that the process of cosn-structing it is not unlike making a pictorial compositon through which you move imaginatively; along the road, down the path, through the trees, round the corner, over the hill, always coming to a new place. In landscape painting you create an imaginary environment; in urban design you made a real one. It was not difficult, therefore, to get on the same wave-length as my architect colleagues.[44]

Pasmore's ambitions were realised in five developments for south-west Peterlee, a self-contained area between the proposed town centre and the old village of Shotton. To the south and east it was bordered by Blunts Dene, where a fault line determined changes to the topography and extraction programme. The first designs, based around the housing unit as a cube and using Pasmore's distinctive colour scheme, began to be built in 1957 as Avon and Thames Roads. At first he made models of his layouts, but abandoned this approach as he gained experience, as 'one is in danger of looking at the plan from the sky' rather than from within.[45] The actual house types were largely established in the first phase, and are seen well in Phase III, completed in 1967 south of Passfield Way and including the pedestrian Leven Walk.[46] His most freely designed schemes are huddles of houses and three- or four-storey blocks of flats that form drifts through the rolling greensward of the town, their manner imitated by corresponding tree planting. 'In the whole of the south-west area tree plantations and grass spaces have been considered as positive and integrated factors in the housing layout' to create distinct but related communities, as Pasmore declared in the second of

Figure 10. Housing and small courtyards in South West Area, Peterlee (Eric de Maré, English Heritage, NMR).

94

his two 1971 articles. The hard landscaping was also impressive, with small pram ramps and concrete bollards to define the pedestrian routes.

This unity of housing and landscape was most fully realised at Pasmore's fourth scheme, for Sunny Blunts, where a small stream runs along the fault line into the gorge of Blunts Dene. Here he was at last able to fulfil his ambition of separating the housing layout entirely from that of the road engineers over whom he had no control. Whereas the road layout followed the contorted topology and was 'curvilinear', the housing retained its 'cubic' form and featured a long continuous terrace which acted as a 'spine'. 'This confrontation not only allows house and road to function quite freely in terms of their own identity, it also produces a dynamic relationship in which one enhances the other.'[47]

The alarm roused by Pasmore's first proposals – termed 'nonsense' among architects at the Ministry of Housing and Local Government - indicates the radical nature of his thinking. P. L. Joseph of the Ministry described a meeting in Peterlee as 'a disturbing experience. Mr Pasmore clearly knows nothing whatever about the problems of designing local-authority layouts.'[48] Economics had determined many conventions for housing layouts, such as setting the roads along the contours and limiting the proportion of public open space. Pasmore flaunted these, while his house plans were thought too small and too radical for miners – they had first-floor living rooms to enjoy the views, and even the architectural magazines complained about the smallness of the patio gardens.[49] The Ministry's Chief Architect, J. H. Forshaw, co-author of the *County of London Plan* and responsible for the London County Council's first post-war estate at Woodberry Down, suggested that Pasmore visit housing at Sondergaard Park near Copenhagen. In October 1957, Colonel Peile, Chairman of Peterlee Development Corporation, sought adjudication from Lionel Brett, whose support for Pasmore prompted work to begin.[50]

Yet the novelty of the housing produced many problems. The novice architects had to work with inexperienced and overstretched builders, Milton Hindle, and when in 1960 this firm went into liquidation not only were there serious delays but it was found that the completed houses had been built badly. The MHLG also criticised the architects for specifying poor insulation, poor weathering details and using thin roofing felt, the money saved being used for expensive interior finishes. The scheme had started without Ministry sanction, and might not have gone through if there had been an opportunity for closer scrutiny.[51] Dixon resigned, and thenceforth Pasmore worked with a more experienced team, including Harry Durell, Chief Architect from 1962, Colin Gardham and a landscape architect, David Thirkettle. In 1973 it was realised that the houses could not stand up to the hard weather conditions of the exposed site, and within a decade all had been substantially rebuilt and given pitched roofs. Subsequent flat-roofed housing built by Crudens to the Skarne system, including the Mark II version used at Sunny Blunts, also had problems of water ingress and pitched roofs were added in the 1980s. The problems with the housing has led to the individuality of Pasmore's layout being overlooked, and prompted a hostile reaction to Pasmore's most personal contribution to the scheme, at Sunny Blunts.

Pasmore was concerned that 'the complete subordination of individuality to mass repetition' grew in part from the lack of local centres in Peterlee. He decided to create such a centre for Sunny Blunts, on a site where Grenfell Baines had proposed a primary school.[52] The idea of a lake at the point where the stream enters Blunts Dene was suggested by Williams, and Pasmore gave it dramatic emphasis.

> We enlarged the perspective scale of the lake by erecting across one end an architectonic feature large enough to dominate the scene. The function of this feature is not only optical, but also environmental and pedestrian, in other words a structure through which one can actually walk. For this reason the Sculpture takes the form of a full-scale architectural building of two storeys

47. Victor Pasmore, article submitted to *Sunderland Echo*, 1971, unpublished, NT/PE/3/1/96; Durham County Archives.

48. Memo, 21 September 1956, in PRO, HLG 91/685

49. *Concrete Quarterly*, no.49, April-June 1961, p.26.

50 . PRO, HLG 91/685.

51. Frank Shaffer, Ministry comments on 170 dwellings, SW Area, in NT/PE/3/1/63; Durham County Archives.

52. Grenfell Baines plan, 1951, in NT/PE/3/1/322, Durham County Archives.

53. Pasmore, *op.cit.*, in NT/PE/3/1/96, Durham County Archives.

54. Jellicoe, *op.cit.*, p.104.

55. Letter from Victor Pasmore to Garry Philipson, 24 October 1981, in NT/PE/3/1/96; NT/PE/3/1/63 discusses litter and vandalism in 1964.

56. NT/PE/3/1/80, Durham County Archives. One is still near the pub; the other sits in the lake next to the Pavilion.

57. Lloyd Rodwin, *The British New Towns Policy*, Cambridge, Harvard University Press, 1956, p.106.

58. John Pasmore, talk to DoCoMoMo UK, 20 June 2002

that bridges the lake at a point where the main footpaths converge. Thus, in its subsidiary function as a bridge or ford, the Sculpture is organically united to the lake. Lake and Sculpture therefore form a single composite work of art which by virtue of its unique image, gives to the neighbourhood not only a focal centre, but also an identity; an identity which is essentially qualitative and psychological.[53]

Pasmore felt that a church or chapel was inappropriate to the 1960s, but wanted something that would 'embrace the whole process of the human psyche'. The model for the pavilion closely resembles the wooden relief sculptures, in white or using a muted palette, which Pasmore had been designing since around 1950, and in particular a model for a memorial museum to the Italian physicist Enrico Fermi which he had made for a competition in 1955. The pavilion was designed to be architectural, with the cubic quality of the houses but expressed using reinforced concrete and cantilevers rather than simple cross-wall construction. 'In sculpture he would like to see persons passing around and through the forms, rather in the manner of children's concrete climbing sculpture in Sweden,' Jellicoe commented.[54] Its completion in 1969 coincided with the launch of Apollo XI for the moon, and so Pasmore always wanted to call it the Apollo Pavilion.[55] Pasmore and his son John designed two other sculptures for Peterlee, one for the town centre and the other to stand between the Heart of Oak public house and the shop in the centre of South West Area III (1963).[56]

Peterlee remains something of a Cinderella, of all the early new towns the one that promised most and achieved least, the most inaccessible, with problems of unemployment and lack of self belief. The market thrives, but the library has closed down and litter and graffitti problems identified by 1980 are worse than ever. But as Lloyd Rodwin observed back in 1954, 'the miners are tough-minded. They want what they like and no "fancy" experiments.'[57] At least the pavilion is beginning, finally, to be appreciated. Yet a fancy experiment was exactly what Peterlee was, and while stories of the town have been dominated by the frustrated idealism of Berthold Lubetkin, the General Manager was also a man of imagination – his role has been neglected because he and his first architect did not get on. John Pasmore, described Vivian Williams, whom he first met while studying at Newcastle in the 1960s, as 'a wise old bird', but he was also capable of considerable idealism.[58] His employment of Victor Pasmore as a landscape planner may seem as extraordinary to us as to the Ministry architects. But it makes more sense when set against the social and planning policies Williams encouraged in the West Midlands in the 1940s, with his employment of Otto Neurath and Sir Charles Reilly, and the artist Hans Feibusch.

7 Sense, sensibility and tower blocks: the Swedish influence on post-war housing in Britain

PETER CAROLIN

Sense, sensibility and tower blocks: the Swedish influence on post-war housing in Britain

PETER CAROLIN

Developments in Swedish housing were of immense interest to British architects in the immediate post-war period. But only a tiny minority of British schemes matched the landscape and place-making qualities of the Swedish exemplars. However, Swedish (and Danish) system building was to profoundly influence public housing in Britain after 1964.

Twice in the last century, Scandinavian – and, more particularly, Swedish – design swept the field in Britain. The most recent incursion, starting in 1987 and now expanding into the provision of prefabricated housing, is that of the all-conquering IKEA. But Swedish design also made an impact on British architects in the post-war period. Whereas IKEA responds to the far more affluent Europe of today, the Sweden of the 1940s was seen as an exemplar of what a welfare state could achieve. Studying journals of that period, visiting groups of buildings like the LCC's Alton East estate or one of Eric Lyons's earlier Span estates, remembering shops like Primarvera and Finmar, Dunn's of Bromley and Bowman's of Camden Town, or hearing architects of the time reminiscing, one could be forgiven for assuming that the Scandinavian impact on the great British post-war housing programme must have been profound.[1] There was apparently every reason why it might have been, for there was a sense and sensibility about the Scandinavian way of making things that had been admired in Britain since the 1920s.

Britain's historic links with architecture in Sweden had started much earlier and included Frederik Henrik af Chapman, Sir William Chambers and Thomas Telford. Chapman, an architect of both buildings and ships and Master Shipbuilder to the Swedish Navy, was the author of the great *Architectura Navalis Mercatoria*, published in 1768: the beautiful white-hulled, three-masted sailing ship that acts as a Stockholm youth hostel is named after him. Chambers was born in Sweden but the link ends there although Nikolaus Pevsner's essay on 'The Other Chambers' was, intriguingly, published alongside the *Architectural Review*'s first New Empiricism feature.[2] Telford, primarily an engineer but also an architect, designed and built the Gotha Canal linking Gothenburg with the Baltic. In recent times, Ralph Erskine spent his entire working life in Sweden – and hordes of British architects have visited that country.

1920–39: THE LURE OF STOCKHOLM

J. M. Richards, the long-standing Editor of the *Architectural Review* (*AR*), observed that vacation tours in the 1920s included 'the new buildings in Stockholm and Gothenburg that members of the Architectural Association (AA) staff admired most of all.'[3] Lionel Esher, writing about the 1930s, noted 'As was customary, one took a trip to the Continent, and first to Stockholm, where since 1923 Ostberg's romantic Town Hall had established itself as the realisation of all that the Arts and Crafts movement had struggled to achieve in Britain.'[4] Little wonder that, talking at the AA in May 1948, Hugh Casson remarked that 'by 1930 the traffic in architects to Stockholm was only rivalled by the traffic in old horses to [the knackers' yards in] Antwerp.'[5] In November 2006 Leonard Manasseh recounted that he had visited Sweden on his demobilisation leave in 1946, describing how

Figure 1. System-built tower blocks in Bellahøj, Denmark, made it to the pages of the *Architectural Review* in 1954. 38 towers using a variety of concrete systems (Strüwing Reklamefoto)

1. *Senior Architect Academicians: Evenings in Conversation* – part of the Royal Academy Architecture Programme, October 2006–January 2007.

2. Nikolaus Pevsner, 'The Other Chambers' and 'The New Empiricism: Sweden's Latest Style', *Architectural Review*, vol.101, no.606, June 1947, pp.195–8 and pp.199–204.

3. J. M. Richards, *Memoirs of an Unjust Fella*, London, Weidenfeld and Nicholson, 1981, p.43.

4. Lionel Esher, *A Broken Wave: the Rebuilding of England 1940–1980*, London, Allen Lane, 1981, p.21. (Esher was known as Lionel Brett, as in some other footnotes here, before acceding to a peerage.)

5. 'AA: Hugh Casson', *Architects' Journal*, vol.107, no.2784, 17 June 1948, p.560.

'the Scandinavians are the most civilised people on earth ... They have a grasp of everything – certainly architecture ... I am an admirer. Long live Scandinavia!' Trevor Dannatt similarly visited Stockholm in 1946.[6]

The Stockholm Exhibition of 1930 accelerated this flow of visitors and, twenty years later, was to have a profound impact on the design of the Festival of Britain's South Bank site. One of Gunnar Asplund's two major ventures into urban design, it developed the exhibition site as a series of *places* rather than a setting for *buildings*.[7] Housing formed a major element. And years later, in a recording for the British Library sound archive, Mary Medd recalled visiting Denmark and Sweden in 1930 in a large AA party. For her, the visit to Stockholm was a turning point. 'The Swedish thing was very good ... they never stopped making things ... delightful, simple, straight-forward things ... that influence goes right through architecture from [the building to] the washing-up bowl.' Asked about the mono-pitch roofs on the houses she designed (as Mary Crowley) at Tewin in 1936, she replied that 'I was Scandinavian by then'.[8]

Of all the pre-war visitors to Scandinavia, and Sweden in particular, F. R. Yerbury, architectural photographer and AA secretary, was the most influential. It was his photographs, initially in the *Architect and Building News*, that informed the profession on developments. In parallel with this, the AR, under the editorship (until 1935) of the 'blond, bland, partly Swedish' Christian Barman, broadened the spectrum through the writings of Morton Shand and J. M. Richards – both of whom had a particular interest in Finland and Alvar Aalto.[9] John Betjeman worked on the AR staff and, years later, wrote: 'We didn't like Cubsim but we liked what was pure and simple and Scandinavian like our nominal editor'.[10] This sounds a bit like a trailer for the struggles at the London County Council fifteen years later.

1940–45: PREPARING FOR PEACE

The onset of the Second World War temporarily severed the architectural connection to Scandinavia. Norway, which had never featured strongly architecturally, was occupied together with Denmark, while Finland found itself ground between the Russians and the Reich. Sweden, maintaining a precarious neutrality, remained untouched, but the only new construction permitted was for housing, factories and a few hotels. With steel, asphalt and the coal used in their production in short supply, timber, bricks and concrete became the principal materials.[11] And, as in Britain, architects and planners became involved in planning for peacetime.

As the fortunes of war changed for the allies, coverage in the AR, the *Architects' Journal* (AJ) and *Architectural Design and Construction* (ADC) turned more and more to those countries where building continued. Articles appeared on innovations in American emergency housing, on new building in Sweden and, rather exotically, on the flowering of modernism in Brazil. The link between these countries was the American architect and architectural photographer, G. E. Kidder Smith, whose photographs formed the backbone of the Museum of Modern Art's wartime *Stockholm Builds and Brazil Builds* exhibitions. Kidder Smith also provided most of the photographs in the September 1943 AR special issue, *Swedish Peace in War* – the editor for which was almost certainly Eric de Maré. Better known as an architectural photographer, de Maré, born in England of Swedish parents, had worked briefly as an architect in Stockholm before joining the Architectural Press and becoming Acting Editor of the AJ in 1943.[12]

The principal article in this AR issue was by William (later Lord) Holford, who had somehow managed to visit Sweden shortly before. The editorial introduction stated that:

> Professor Holford's eloquence should convince those who still believe that
> ... Swedish housing is the most progressive in Europe in its social organi-
> sation. The Co-operatives build better than anywhere else, and building

6. *Senior Architect Academicians, op.cit.,* Leonard Manasseh, 24 November 2006; Trevor Dannatt, 26 January 2007.

7. The other was the unbuilt Royal Chancellery scheme which Colin Rowe admired; Colin Rowe and Fred Koetter, *Collage City*, Cambridge, MIT Press, 1978, pp.71–77.

8. British Library, *NLSC: Architects' Lives: Mary Medd, 1907–2005*, recorded in 1998, tape 1B (F6745). (Tape 2A (F6749) also deals with Scandinavia.)

9. Bevis Hillier, *Young Betjeman*, London, John Murray, 1988, p.256.

10. John Betjeman, 'Mackay Hugh Baillie Scott', first published in *The Journal of the Manx Museum*, vol.7, no.84, 1968, and reproduced in Diane Haigh, *Baillie Scott, the Artistic House*, London, Academy Editions, 1995, pp.114.

11. Sven Backström,, 'A Swede looks at Sweden' in *Architectural Review*, vol.94, no.561, September 1943, p.80.

12. J. Makepeace, 'Eric de Maré' obituary, *Independent*, no.4768, 29 January 2002, p.6.

Figure 2. The nine pioneering 'punkt' or point-blocks in Backström and Renius' 1945 cluster at Danviksklippan. Brick construction, rendered and washed in a variety of light colours. (Unknown)

societies don't lag behind. Prefabrication is used more widely and sensibly than anywhere else ... Detail is as generally sensitive as any of the eighteenth century. And even where, as sometimes occurs even in Sweden, the design of buildings is not particularly distinguished, the way they are placed on the site and set off with rocks and conifers or silver birch – the way in fact they are landscaped – provides an object lesson for the English town-planner and architect.[13]

Included in this AR issue was the first British publication of Gunnar Asplund's great Woodland Crematorium, completed in 1940 shortly before his death. This building and landscape drew a stream of post-war architects from Britain. Also featured was an article, 'A Swede looks at Sweden', by Sven Backström, with Lief Renius the architect of the Stockholm housing schemes which, more than any others, would attract future visitors from Britain. Backström, after a year working for Le Corbusier, had been Asplund's principal teaching assistant at the Royal Institute of Technology in Stockholm.[14] His article describes the emergence of functionalism in Sweden, the gradual disenchantment with the 'new objectivity' and the shift towards something more humane. 'Today we have reached the point where all the elusive psychological factors have again begun to attract our attention. Man and his habits, reactions and needs are the focus of interest as never before.'[15] The echoes of Alvar Aalto's obituary of his friend, Asplund, 'the foremost among architects', come through loud and clear. 'A newer architecture has made its appearance, one that continues to employ the tools of the social sciences, but that also includes the study of psychological problems – the "unknown human" in his totality ... Within this ... architecture, Asplund has his place.'[16]

The AR was not to publish another major issue on Scandinavia until the first of 'The New Empiricism' issues, in June 1947. However, between 1943 and 1947, in

13. Editorial Introduction to 'Swedish Peace in War', *Architectural Review*, vol.94, no.561, September 1943, p.59.

14. Henrik O. Andersson, and Frederic Bedoire, *Swedish Architecture, Drawings 1640–1970*, Stockholm, Byggförlaget, 1986, p.242; Christina Engfors, E. G. *Asplund, Architect, Friend and Colleague*, Stockholm, Arkitektur Förlag, 1990, pp.85–6.

15. Backström, *op.cit.*, p.80.

16. Alvar Aalto, 'E.G. Asplund in Memoriam', first published in *Arkkitehti*, 1940, p.81, and reproduced in Göran Schildt, ed., *Sketches: Alvar Aalto*, Cambridge, MIT Press, 1985, pp.66–7.

17. 'Timber prefabricated houses designed by Cyril Sjöstrom' in *Architects' Journal*, vol.98, 30 December 1943, pp.485–6. See also editorial introduction to 'Swedish factory-produced timber houses' in *AJ*, vol.99, 3 February 1944, pp.101–5. The exhibition of Swedish timber houses was a subject of a leader in the same issue, pp.93–4, and also featured in *Architect, Design and Construction*, vol.14, no.2, February 1944, pp.25, 29–35. An earlier article by Sjöstrom had appeared in *Focus*, no.3, Spring 1939, pp.40–7. Sjöstrom taught at the AA and inspired David Medd and Bruce Martin to visit Sweden in 1938 to study prefabricated timber housing on allotment sites.

18. 'Swedish Sectional Timber Houses in Scotland', *Architectural Design and Construction*, ibid., p.36.

19. Charles A. Hellstrand, 'Co-operative Housing in Sweden', *Architectural Design and Construction*, vol.13, no.2, February 1943, pp.35–7.

20. Charles A. Hellstrand, 'Sweden: Standards of Planning and Building', *Architectural Design and Construction*, vol.13, no.5, May 1943, p.98.

21. H. Braddock, 'Flats', *Architectural Design and Construction*, vol.14, no.3, May 1944, p.55.

22. Lionel Esher, 'Sir Robert Matthew', *Oxford Dictionary of National Biography*, vol.37, Oxford University Press, 2004, p.343; 'Swedish timber houses' in *Architectural Design and Construction*, vol.15, no.12, December 1945, pp.305–10.

23. 'Swedish timber houses', ibid.; 'Building a Swedish pre-fab', *Architects' Journal*, vol.102, no.2654, 6 December 1945, p.410; 'Swedish timber houses at Abbots Langley', *AJ*, vol.103, no.2658, 24 January 1946, pp.87–92.

24. Esher, 'Sir Robert Matthew', *op.cit.*, p.343.

25. Eva Rudberg, *Sven Markelius, Architect*, Stockholm, Arkitektur Förlag, p.156.

26. ibid., p.156.

27. ibid., p.108.

both the *AR* and the *AJ,* Swedish buildings featured regularly. Danish buildings completed during the war started to appear in 1946. Finnish buildings followed in the early 1950s, and Norwegian buildings by mid decade. As the war drew to a close and the housing authorities started to grapple with the problems of actually constructing new housing, the *AJ* reported on Swedish timber-frame systems. The first wartime article on prefabricated timber-frame housing appeared in December 1943 and described a system designed by the Finnish-born Cyril Sjöstrom (later the C. S. Mardall of Yorke, Rosenberg and Mardall).[17] Sjöstrom had been consultant to the manufacturers of 200 similar Swedish houses in Scotland before the war – some of which were designed by William Kininmonth and Basil Spence.[18]

Meanwhile, *A*DC, under the energetic editorship of Monica Pidgeon, was publishing, from January 1943, a series called 'Housing Forum', 'in which all matters of housing interest are considered, in readiness for the post-war period ... chiefly concerned with technical information on house and flat planning, design and construction'. An article on 'Co-operative housing in Sweden' in February 1943 was followed by further articles on Swedish housing in May and June.[19] These were highly informative pieces, comparing, for example, LCC and Tudor Walters standards with the more generous Swedish ones.[20] The first article devoted to Swedish flats appeared in March 1945 with the Swedish answer to the question 'Should blocks of flats be narrow or wide, high or low?' The Swedes concluded that, although wide blocks were cheaper, narrower blocks 'can be used more satisfactorily and offer possibilities for such excellent planning that they usually prove the more economical and practical to live in', but that they should be '6 storeys or more, with 4 flats per floor, as such a block affords greater concentration [of collective amenities such as laundries, crèches and centralised kitchens] and yet provides good living quarters'.[21] It is at this point that one senses the chasm between Swedish aspirations and realities and those that were to pervade post-war Britain.

1946: LEARNING FROM SWEDEN

In December 1945, Robert Matthew, Chief Architect and Planner to the Department of Health for Scotland – and, later, Chief Architect to the LCC – paid his first visit to Sweden as part of a Government deputation involved in the purchase of 5,000 urgently needed prefabricated timber houses.[22] Samples designed by the Ministry of Works were erected at Abbots Langley and Tannockside.[23] According to Lionel Esher, Sweden made a significant impression on Matthew, 'who admired the half-modern, half-vernacular housing constructed in Stockholm'.[24]

The Swedes themselves had long admired the English garden cities and the work of the planner, Patrick Abercrombie. On his appointment in 1944, one of the first acts of Stockholm's City Planner, Sven Markelius, was to commission a report on British planning, including the neighbourhood and community centre ideas which came to characterise the development of the new towns.[25] In 1946, the British New Towns Committee – including its chairman, Lord Reith, with the Minister for Housing and Planning, Lewis Silkin, and Abercrombie – visited Stockholm.[26] They admired Stockholm's new housing areas and the way her emerging satellites were developing. Indeed, the city became a kind of Mecca for town planners wishing to meet Markelius. Eva Rudberg, his biographer, describes how his home, which he had designed as a prefabricated timber structure,

> *became a natural meeting point where Markelius ... received foreign guests. ... Le Corbusier ... Patrick Abercrombie and Clarence Stein were regaled here with such delicacies as nettle soup and turbot with horseradish and non-Swedes must have gaped at the crayfish parties and the ensuing dips in the pond.*[27]

Monica Pidgeon was the first of the British architectural editors to visit Sweden after the war, in the spring of 1946. She left England in warm weather – in sandals

– to discover snow and ice in Stockholm.[28] Undeterred, she had an exhilarating time, appointed a local correspondent and produced a special issue on Sweden in July of that year – eleven months ahead of the *AR*. *A*DC was the first to publish Backström and Renius's Danviksklippan point-blocks – a prominently sited and highly distinctive cluster of nine pyramidal-roofed square towers, eight to ten storeys high, each finished in a different shade of colour wash.[29] The issue also included the HSB co-operative's Reimersholme housing, a community of light blue-green towers and red and ochre walk-up flats sited on an island complete with social and work facilities, and the first of Backström and Renius's 'star block' projects, in which Y-shaped walk-up units were articulated as courts or small towers.[30] Simultaneously, the *AJ* also published an article on Swedish housing.[31]

Following the government delegations and the editors came the architects and planners – usually in groups, large and small. For many of these visitors, travelling to – or via – Denmark, the Scandinavian experience began at Harwich, when they boarded one of the Danish State Railway's elegant motor vessels such as the *Kronprinz Frederik* with its interiors by Kay Fisker.[32] As Trevor Dannatt observed, one attraction was the absence of food rationing in Sweden! True to form, one of the first group visits, in September 1946, was organised by the AA. Others who visited Sweden included, rather improbably, Peter Smithson (who had a letter of introduction to Markelius and greatly admired Asplund's law courts in Gothenburg), and, in 1947, a group of AA students, Oliver Cox, Graeme Shankland and Michael Ventris.[33] The latter, who was later to acquire international fame for deciphering the Minoan script Linear B, quietly mugged up a working knowledge of Swedish before the visit and was the only one to secure employment in an architect's office in Stockholm.[34] Cox and Shankland spent the time visiting architects and buildings.

Returning to England, Ventris contributed a remarkable article, 'Function and Arabesque', to the first issue of *Plan*, the legendary AA student magazine. He compared architecture in Britain (where, in the view of Swedish architects, 'the safe municipal level means the brick and stone lump') with Denmark and, particularly, Sweden. He cited Backström and Renius's work with its liveable plans, simple exteriors and imaginative use of colour and texture, as perhaps the best examples of current work. More fundamentally, he drew attention to the northern climate and spirit shared by Denmark, Sweden and Britain, 'which makes nonsense of Corbusier's "magnificent play of masses brought together in light"'. He also drew attention to the powerful sense of landscape in Denmark and Sweden, which he contrasted with the far more heavily worked landscape of Britain:

Building is not to cover the land as a solid blanket, but must preserve con-

Figure 3. One of Backström and Renius' 'star'-block estates: Grondal, Stockholm, 1946 photographed in 2007. Star blocks were either used individually as towers or linked to form courts. (Author)

Figure 4. Light touch on landscape. One of the star-shaped towers at Grondal, Stockholm, by Backström and Renius, 1946, photographed 60 years later. (Author)

28. Monica Pidgeon, interview, London, 2006.

29. Some of these distinctive Swedish colours were reproduced by David and Mary Medd in their schools for Herts CC.

30. *Architectural Design and Construction*, vol.16, no.7, July 1946, pp.80–2. All this excellent issue is devoted to Sweden.

31. Bertil Hultén, 'New Housing and Planning in Sweden', *Architects' Journal*, vol.104, no.2684, 4 July 1946, pp.2, 7–14.

32. 'M/S Kronprinz Frederik', *Architectural Review*, vol.101, no.602, February 1947, pp.51–56.

33. Peter Smithson, 'Reflections on Hunstanton', *arq (Architectural Research Quarterly)*, vol.2, no.4, Summer 97, p.34.

34. Andrew Robinson, *The Man who Deciphered Linear B*, London, Thames and Hudson, 2002, pp. 53–7. Ventris's period working in the Swedish Cooperative Union and Wholesale Society's Architects' Office is recorded – under the name Wentris – in *Swedish Cooperative and Wholesale*, Stockholm, 1949, p.8.

stantly the sense of topography, by exploiting the distant view, the secluding wood, and the orientation lines of parks, rivers, shores and downs. That sense varies in sun and snow, rain and fog; but not even the latter can make Stockholm flat and formless for us.[35]

Ventris's essay is amazingly perceptive. In it, with hindsight, one can begin to see how the British context was, with a few notable exceptions, so totally unsuited to the transplantation of social democracy's triumphs in 1940s Stockholm. The urban challenge differed; the attitude towards the public realm, planting and landscape was far less generous; and, as he pointed out, progressive clients and construction companies were common in Sweden but a rarity in Britain. Significantly, much of Backström and Renius's best work – in which the repetition of towers and of the basic 'Y'-form clustered in different ways was a significant factor – was commissioned by a builder-developer, Olle Engvist.[36]

There were to be many other visits – both collective and individual – to Denmark and Sweden and, increasingly, to Finland, in the 1950s. The former group included local authority housing committees visiting Danish housing, the latter, Scandinavian enthusiasts like David and Mary Medd who, like many architects, admired the economy, craftsmanship and sense of total design and brought this to their own work with schools, most notably at Amersham.[37]

1947: THE NEW EMPIRICISM

But, before turning to the *actual* impact of Sweden on post-war British housing, we must complete the scene-setting with a final look at the journals and books of this period. In the *AR* for June 1947 an unsigned article – almost certainly by J.M. Richards – entitled 'The New Empiricism: Sweden's latest style' formed an extended editorial introduction to three houses by Markelius, Stüre Frölen and Ralph Erskine. Asserting that the principles of functionalism were 'never more relevant than now', it continues:

The tendency is, rather, both to humanise the theory on its aesthetic side and to get back to the earlier rationalism on the technical side. … However, the effort to humanise the aesthetic of functionalism is open to many interpretations. The Swedish one … may, on the basis made by Swedish architects themselves, be called The New Empiricism. Briefly, they explain it as the attempt to be more objective than the functionalists, and to bring back another science, that of psychology, into the picture.[38]

Three months after Richards's *AR* article, CIAM 6 was held in Britain, at Bridgwater. Richards, as a member of the MARS Group, was one of the hosts and the struggle between Siegfried Giedion's New Monumentality and Richards's New Empiricism (or Humanism) began.[39] But that is not part of this story. In January 1948 the *Review* published its second New Empiricism issue. This included an introductory article by Eric de Maré, outlining 'the antecedents and origins of Sweden's latest style' and another, on 'Housing and technical developments in Sweden', by Lars Giertz.[40] The latter provides probably the best summary as to why Sweden was of such great interest to those involved in new housing in Britain. For several decades, as Sweden industrialised, and its countryside emptied and its cities and towns grew, building activity had centred on the provision of flats. Before the war, construction – of a generally high standard – was mainly by private owner-builders. During the war, as building costs and rates of interest escalated – and the flight to the cities continued – the state, though the State Building Loan Office and the co-operatives, took over. Construction was no longer of individual flats but of groups of flats, often as many as a thousand. Although costs had risen, improvements in technology and construction, together with an element of subsidy, had kept rents down and raised standards, particularly at the lower levels. Because of their climate and need to import coal and oil, the Swedes were far ahead in both insulation (leading to economies in heating) and in the energy-efficient production of building materials. There had been a programme

35. Michael Ventris, 'Function and Arabesque', *Plan*, no.1, 1948, pp.7–12. Ventris also contributed a revealing book review, on contemporary Swedish architecture, to the *Architectural Review*, vol.99, no.594, June 1946, p.183.

36. Andersson and Bedoire, *op.cit.*, p.242.

37. David Medd, interview, Welwyn, 2006.

38. 'The New Empiricism', *Architectural Review*, vol.101, no.606, June 1947, pp.199–204.

39. Seigfried Giedion, 'MARS & ICA', *Architects' Journal*, vol.108, no.2794, 26 August 1948, pp.206–7; no.2796, 9 September 1948, pp.251–2.

40. Eric de Maré, *The New Empiricism*; Lars M. Giertz, 'Housing and Technical developments in Sweden', *Architectural Review*, vol.103, no.613, January 1948, pp.9–11.

of component standardisation (in which Markelius played a major role) and, because of the pressure to export home-grown timber, the Swedes became adept at making very high quality timber components – such as windows – economically.[41] To co-ordinate these components and materials in construction, the 10cm (4 inch) module had been adopted. In other words, the Swedes were not only adept at designing attractive housing (and landscaping) but, by 1946, they were way ahead on technical and quality issues. Ten months later, in November 1948, the *AR* was to publish a similar, special issue on Denmark, which had a strong emphasis on domestic architecture and garden design.

Besides the journals there was one annual, Trevor Dannatt's *Architects' Year Book*, that should be mentioned. Scandinavia first featured in the 1947 edition.[42] The introduction to Swedish architecture was by Bertil Hultén, later the author of a well-illustrated Penguin book on *Building Modern Sweden*, whose publication indicated the widespread post-war lay interest in the achievements of Swedish social democracy.[43] The annual also contained features on Backström and Renius's Danvikslippan 'punkt' (point) blocks, Lewerentz's funeral chapels at Malmo, and Lauritzen's elegant Copenhagen airport terminal. Scandinavia also featured in the next, 1949, annual but thereafter had no prominence.

Finally, there was Kidder Smith's book, *Sweden Builds*, first published in 1950 by the Architectural Press. His extensive introduction provides an excellent summary to the country's architecture and people. On the latter, he remarks:

> *Their ability to run machines has convinced them that they can run themselves on their own ball bearings as so many controlled, mechanical units. The State increasingly considers its citizens as so many children … One cannot dance in Sweden after twelve o'clock; one cannot have a cocktail without having something to eat; one cannot do this; one cannot do that. If this continues, the atmosphere (and this includes the architecture) will become an unbearable norm of colourless mediocrity.*[44]

As if in confirmation, he later adds:

> *the architecturally mediocre has become the easiest. State controls and investigations have become almost unbearable. There is waiting, waiting, waiting … too much architecture is becoming rubber-stamped, stiff, dry, unexciting, sterile and ingrown, or to use one word – bureaucratic. … Swedish architects today are better than their government will let them be; that there is more in them than the law allows.*[45]

As Aalto, a close observer of trends in contemporary Swedish architecture, said (in another context), 'the architectural revolution is still going on, but it is like all revolutions: it starts with enthusiasm and stops with some sort of dictatorship. It runs off the track'.[46] The bureaucrats and the big contractors were taking over Swedish housing.

So, given the great British interest in Swedish housing – and, to a lesser extent, Danish – what impact did it have on Britain's post-war housing programme? Did we adopt the Swedes' extraordinarily high technical standards and level of pre-fabrication? Were the point-block clusters replicated here? Was our new housing noted for the quality of the open space around it?

LCC BATTLEGROUND

By far the most interesting post-war housing in Britain was constructed by local authorities. Initially, in much of this, the design of housing came under the Borough Engineer and Surveyor – responsible not just for the design of housing but also, critically, the roads that so affected its layout. Even in the greatest authority of all, the LCC, housing came under the Valuer. For four years after the war, the LCC built a mass of totally uninspired housing such as the Minerva Estate, which could have been completed at any time in the 1930s. It took a major campaign by the *AJ* – involving several very senior public sector architects – to wrest that control away from the Valuer and to the Architect, Robert Matthew.[47] And, though

41. Rudberg, *op.cit.* p.23.

42. Jane Drew and Trevor Dannatt, eds., *The Architects' Year Book*, 2, London, Elek, 1947.

43. Bertil Hultén, *Building Modern Sweden*, Harmondsworth, Penguin Books, 1951.

44. G. E. Kidder Smith, *Sweden Builds*, London, Architectural Press, 1950, p.13. This splendid summary of the Swedish character was quoted by Eric de Maré in *Scandinavia*, London, Batsford, 1952, pp.251–2.

45. ibid., pp.18–19.

46. 'Alvar Aalto gives first RIBA "Discourse"', *Architects' Journal*, vol.125, no.3243, 25 April 1957, p.602.

47. 'LCC Housing: the Need for a Critical Assessment', *Architects' Journal*, vol.109, no.2823, 17 March 1949, pp.251–4; 'LCC Housing: a Special Announcement', no.2830, 5 May 1949, pp.401–2; 'LCC Housing', no.2833, 27 May 1949, pp.474–83; 'Recommended Change of Responsibilities', vol.110, no.2864, 29 December 1949, p.725.

48. 'Why architects are Not Necessary', *Architects' Journal*, vol.117, no.3021, 22 January 1953, pp.119–20.

49. H.J. Whitfield Lewis in 'Men of the Year, *Architects' Journal,* vol.123, no.3177, 19 January 1956, pp.78–9; Esher, 'Sir Robert Matthew', *op.cit.*p.343.

50. Rayner Banham, *The New Brutalism, Ethic or Aesthetic?*, London, Architectural Press, 1966, pp.10–13, 89; Nicholas Bullock, *Building the Post-War World: Modern Architecture and Reconstruction in Britain*, London, Routledge, 2002, pp.83–129 (for the battle for the control of housing in the LCC see pp.199–218); Oliver Cox, interview, London, 2007 – Cox also objected to being described as a 'New Empiricist' by J. M. Richards.

51. 'High Wimbledon', *Architects' Journal*, vol.119, no.3095, 24 June 1954, pp.756, 762–8; 'The LCC Housing Division's Triumph', ibid., pp.757–8.

52. 'The LCC Keeps in Keeping', *Architects' Journal*, vol.122, no.3160, 22 September 1955, p.378; 'Flats on the Fitzhugh Estate', vol.124, no.3222, 29 November 1956, pp.795–806.

Figure 5. Robert Matthew and J. H. Whitfield Lewis with a model of a point-block for the first Swedish-influenced LCC estate: Ackroydon, Wimbledon, 1954. (Barratts Photo Press)

Figure 6. A cluster of towers on the Stockholm model. The LCC's Fitzhugh estate, Wandsworth. Full advantage was taken of the mature landscape setting. (London Metropolitan Archive)

that particular battle was won in 1949, the *AJ* was still fulminating four years later about the failure of other local authorities to follow the LCC example.[48]

Under Matthew, the LCC rapidly became the largest architectural office in the world. He strengthened group working and, with private practices struggling, attracted the best and brightest graduates (many of whom were ex-servicemen) emerging from the architecture schools. Within the Housing Division, under the direction of the Markelius and Aalto-admiring H. J. Whitfield Lewis, battle was joined between the 'softs' who adopted the Swedish approach and the 'hards' who, seeking something more rigorous, were inspired by Le Corbusier's great Unité then nearing completion in Marseilles.[49] The story of this epic encounter has been well described both by Reyner Banham and by Nicholas Bullock (although some of the participants consider the terms 'hard' and 'soft' to be misleading).[50] The initial outcome, on the one hand, were the Ackroydon, Fitzhugh and Alton East estates set among mature trees and, on the other, the mini-Unités set in the rather arid urban settings of Bentham and Loughborough Roads.

Ackroydon, completed in 1954, was a mixed development of T-shaped eleven and eight-storey point-blocks together with five, four and three-storey flats, four-storey maisonettes and two-storey houses, all flat-roofed.[51] Fitzhugh, completed in 1955, had square eleven-storey point-blocks and replicated the form of a typical Swedish all-tower cluster – there were no lower buildings.[52] In contrast, Alton East**,** also completed in 1955 and the most outstanding of the estates designed by the 'softs', was a mixed development of square eleven-storey point blocks with four-storey maisonettes and two-storey houses, the latter two types with pitched roofs.[53] Loughborough Road, completed in 1961, was also a mixed development, but here the largest buildings were not towers but mini-Unités designed by the 'hards', in the form of eleven-storey slabs containing balcony-access maisonettes, combined with medium and low-rise buildings, all flat-roofed.[54]

Alton West, completed in 1959 and designed by a group of 'hards', incorporated both eleven-storey mini-Unités and two rare groups of twelve-storey point blocks clustered (as on the Fitzhugh Estate) in the Swedish manner. Its setting was spectacular, but in the tradition not of modern Sweden but, as Pevsner observed, of eighteenth-century English landscape.[55] There was another startling

difference between Alton East and West: the former utilised colour and traditional materials in the Swedish manner while the latter was mainly monochrome grey pre-cast concrete. Years later, Lionel Esher suggested that one of the factors in Matthew's decision to resign from the LCC was the 'final victory' of the 'modernist intellectuals' (the 'hards') over the empiricists (the 'softs') in the Housing Division. Once back in Scotland, 'his first significant job was Turnhouse Airport (1956), whose human scale and unaffected use of timber again showed Scandinavian influence'.[56]

Scattered around the metropolis and built during the late 1950s and early 1960s, there were other LCC estates embodying 'soft' characteristics. The largest was the Brandon Estate.[57] Smaller estates, sometimes set in mature suburban settings, were built in Lewisham, Wandsworth and elsewhere. Inner London boroughs occasionally built what might be described as Scandinavian-inspired housing. Some of the most successful – in Chelsea, Kensington and Marylebone – were designed by Edward Armstrong and his partner Frederick MacManus.[58] But by far the most convincing of the inner London 'Scandinavian' estates was the LCC's Lawson Street estate in Southwark (1953–6). For Ian Nairn,

> *This is a real place itself, not a hash of stale opinion served up for 'them' with skin-deep humanitarianism. All the utilitarian bits look honest and well built, all the views run out through friendly alleys to other courtyards. You are never in a desert … All yellow brick, beautifully laid. The effect is rather Danish, and this estate is up to the best in Copenhagen.*[59]

The long serrated block across Great Dover Street is a *tour de force*. The unnamed architect was an Australian, Bill Yuille of Sir John Burnet, Tait and Partners.[60]

NEW TOWN BLUES

Outside the capital, the obvious place to start looking for a Swedish influence is Harlow, the master planner and architect of most of the key buildings of which was Frederick Gibberd – assisted on landscape aspects by Sylvia Crowe. There is undoubtedly a sense of landscape in the town and Gibberd's tower at The Lawn has been described as 'Scandinavian'.[61] But it is, like so much of his work, very English. The extravagant plan form, the lack of prefabrication, the composition of each elevation and the window proportions are all distinctly un-Scandinavian. Even more telling, the Swedish point blocks were almost always built in groups

Figure 7. The high point of Swedish influence in the LCC, 1955. Alton East, Roehampton was a mixed development which has worn exceptionally well. (London Metropolitan Archive)

Figure 8. 'The triumph of the hards'. The LCC's Alton West estate of 1959 incorporated both mini-Unités and clusters of towers in monochrome grey concrete. (London Metropolitan Archive)

53. Nikolaus Pevsner, 'Roehampton: LCC Housing and the Picturesque Tradition' in *Architectural Review*, vol.126, no.750, July 1959, pp.21–35. Oliver Cox, one of the architects of Alton East, recalls that the use of both low-rise housing and colour was directly inspired by Backström and Renius's work. The introduction of central heating on LCC estates was also based on the Swedish model.

54. Robert Furneaux Jordan, 'LCC: new standards in official architecture' in *Architectural Review*, vol.120, no.718, November 1956, pp.314–15.

55. Pevsner, 'Roehampton', *op.cit.*, p.35.

56. Esher, 'Sir Robert Matthew', *op.cit.*

57. 'Housing at Brandon Estate, Southwark', *Architects' Journal*, vol.134, no.18, 1 November 1961, pp.825–42.

58. The later parts of the Cremorne Estate in Chelsea and the Boundary Road flats in St John's Wood.

59. Ian Nairn, *Modern Buildings in London*, London Transport, 1964, pp.65–6.

60. Information from Gavin Tait and Ken Jack, 2007.

Figure 9. Copenhagen in Southwark. Burnet Tait's LCC Lawson estate of 1956. Celebrated for its humane characteristics by Ian Nairn. (London Metropolitan Archive)

61. Elain Harwood, *England: a Guide to Post-War Listed Buildings*, London, Batsford, 2003, p.224; Miles Glendenning and Stefan Muthesius, *Tower Block: Modern Public Housing in England, Scotland and Northern Ireland*, London, Yale University Press, 1994, p.54; John Summerson, introduction, *Ten Years of British Architecture '45–55*, London, Arts Council, 1956, p.45.

62. Frederick Gibberd, *Town Design*, London, Architectural Press, 1953.

63. F. R. S. Yorke and Frederick Gibberd, *The Modern Flat*, London, Architectural Press, 1948.

64. From a later period, some might point to Michael Neylan's competition-winning courtyard scheme at Bishopsfield in Harlow (*Architects' Journal*, vol.133, no.3449, 25 May 1961, pp.765–7) – but this anticipates the 1970s housing casbahs rather than evoking the memory of Utzon's far more freely planned courtyard housing in Denmark. Erskine's housing at Milton Keynes and that at Newmarket for Bovis Homes seem now forgotten; Byker, in Newcastle, was, like Clare Hall in Cambridge, a 'one-off'.

65. J. M. Richards, 'Failure of the New Towns', *Architectural Review*, vol.114, no.680, August 1953, p.29.

66. Gordon Cullen, 'Prairie Planning in the New Towns', ibid., pp.33–36.

67. Lionel Brett, 'Post-war Housing Estates' in *Architectural Review*, vol.110, no.655, July 1951, pp.17–26.

68. Walter Manthorpe, 'The Machinery of Sprawl', *Architectural Review*, vol.120, no.719, December 1956, pp.409–26.

(reaping the benefits of repetition), rather than as an isolated 'townscape' feature as here. Similarly, the best of Gibberd's other Harlow housing, the gently curving crescent at Orchard Croft, is distinctly English and was inspired by a nineteenth-century terrace in Sidmouth. There is no evidence that Gibberd ever visited Scandinavia – one imagines this elegant moustachioed, art-collecting *bon viveur* more at home in Italy. He was the author of *Town Design*, a book that went through many editions between 1953 and 1970.[62] Backström and Renius's Grondal estate appeared (juxtaposed with Harlow) as a case study in the first edition and Vällingby featured in later editions, but the main text contains few references to Scandinavia and a lot on a very English picturesque approach to town design. Indeed, Gibberd claimed that the English School of landscape design was probably this country's greatest contribution to art. Nor was Scandinavia given undue emphasis in *The Modern Flat*, which he co-authored with F. R. S. Yorke in 1948; this contained just three Swedish examples as against fourteen from Britain (mainly pre-war), seven from Germany, six from France, and four each from Denmark and the USA.[63]

There was little approaching Scandinavian form and quality in the housing areas of our new towns.[64] Indeed, in 1953, when the early phases of Stevenage, Harlow, Hemel Hempstead, Crawley and Hatfield were largely completed, the editors of the AR were so troubled that they devoted part of the July issue to 'The Failure of the New Towns'. They regarded them as failed 'socially, economically and architecturally'.[65] Gordon Cullen contributed a piece entitled 'Prairie Planning in the New Towns', in which he castigated the appalling relationship between the buildings and the space between them where, almost always, roads dominated and divided.[66]

Back in 1951, the *AR* had published Lionel Brett's critique, 'Post-War Housing Estates'.[67] It was the time of the Festival of Britain and Brett did his best to be encouraging, showing examples both bad and good (the latter almost all by Tayler and Green or Gibberd). But, by December 1956, all the evidence was that 'it is practically impossible to build towns; only garden suburbs are permitted' and the *AR* launched its 'Counter-Attack' special issue, attacking 'sprawl'. Perhaps the most devastating article was by an LCC planner, Walter Manthorpe, who demonstrated in great detail how central government legislation and guidance were at the bottom of the dreary, land-guzzling, road-dominated layouts of vast tracts of new housing.[68]

Nearly thirty years later, Brett – now Lord Esher, a past president of the RIBA and himself the master-planner of Hatfield – looked back on housing of the period. He observed that the Ministry of Health's 1944 *Housing Manual* defined neighbourhood sizes, forms and densities and the use of terrace houses.

> *Indeed,' he wrote, 'by the late forties a serviceable brick-and-tile vernacular had evolved ... which was to become the hallmark of the first-generation New Towns. It was not Georgian; it was not Modern: given the standard components and the standard layouts without which cost targets could not be hit, it designed itself. ... Only an occasional group of walk-up flats broke the horizontal lines of 2-storey terraces, which had to be brick with concrete roof tiles because no amount of rationality would persuade contractors to price dry prefabricated systems, such as schools were using, as low. When the target was the £1,000 house, every pound counted. Trees were reserved and liberally planted and would soon, as at Welwyn, blot out the architecture. A tiny majority of the 1,434 housing authorities in England and Wales handled this vernacular with sensibility, among them the little rural district of Loddon in Norfolk, whose cottages by Tayler and Green were among the best and most characteristic products of the forties. For those few one-off institutional buildings for which licences could be obtained a prettier version, with a few feminine accessories, the architectural equivalent of the New Look, was available from the same source, and given the cachet of capital letters in the Architectural Review (June 1947) – the New Empiricism. Impeccable modernist personalities of the thirties, like Oud and Dudok in Holland, Markelius and Linström in Sweden, Fry, Spence and Gibberd in England' had switched to it, for the psychological need was manifest. After the rigours of warfare in foreign parts, people had had enough concrete to be going on with.*[69]

But concrete was to return – with a vengeance.

But there were other reasons why, in the first stage of the post-war housing boom (up to 1963), the Swedish influence was so very small – indeed, in the total scope of things, insignificant. The first was that the new areas around Stockholm, themselves inspired by war-time British planning ideas, were extensions to an *existing* high-density city with a well-developed transport system rather than self-sufficient new towns. And Stockholm itself was far, far smaller than London. The second was that, whereas the Swedes were building on largely virgin sites the British cities were invariably re-using bomb-damaged and slum clearance sites: with the exception of Ackroydon, Fitzhugh and Roehampton, very few London sites had the landscape potential of the Swedish ones. Third, the Swedes had two preferred housing forms – the free-standing detached house (prefabricated and built over the short summer) and the well-serviced urban flat, while the British preference was for cottages (invariably semi-detached) and terrace houses: by 1950, 90% of all new dwellings were in the form of three-bedroom cottages.[70] Extending the period to 1979, 64% of total housing output in Britain between 1945 and 1979 comprised cottages, 20% were flats up to five storeys and the remaining 16% multi-storey flats.[71]

But there were other more fundamental differences – such as the very different origins of the British and Swedish welfare states. In Britain, a long class struggle had dominated. In Sweden, industrialisation had come late and, initially, within a rather paternalistic framework. The labour movement was powerfully entrenched and represented politically by a Social Democratic party formed out of an alliance of disparate groups whose interests extended beyond narrow class issues.[72] With such an inclusive political outlook, Swedish housing – even when it became highly rationalised in the 1960s campaign for a million new homes – was never reduced to a mere political numbers game as in Britain, although standards did drop. Nor was it to define class location in an often literally concrete way.

With the exception of some LCC estates and others by Tayler and Green,

69. Esher, *A Broken Wave, op.cit.*, pp.46–8.

70. Kidder Smith, op.cit, pp.30–31, 62.

71. Glendenning and Muthesius, *op.cit.*, p.2.

72. Jim Kemeny, *Housing and Social Theory*, London, Routledge, 1992, pp.129–134. Chapter 8 of this book – 'The Political Construction of Collective Residence: the Case of Sweden' – is central to an understanding of Swedish housing provision.

73. See also Elain Harwood, 'Post-War Landscape and Public Housing', *Garden History*, vol.28, no.1, pp.102–116. This article summarises the paucity of well-designed landscape settings in post-war British housing: set against the few, often architect-designed settings identified by Harwood ('a tiny part of the whole') the vast majority of such housing never had the benefit of a landscape input.

74. Kidder Smith, *op.cit.*, pp.17–18.

75. Ian C. McHarg, 'Can we afford open space? A Survey of Landscaping Costs', *Architects' Journal*, vol.123, no.3184/5, 8/15 March 1956, pp.260–75.

76. Ivor Cunningham, interviewed by Elain Harwood, February 2006.

77. Robert Maguire, 'Techniques: Double Glazing', *Architectural Review*, vol.117, no.700, April 1955, p.282. Frederick McManus of Armstrong and McManus was architect to the English Joinery Manufacturers Association and, working with Oliver Cox, played a major part in the introduction of an economic and effective version of this type of window to Britain, where it was pioneered on the first wave of LCC architect-designed estates, replacing the Crittall metal window type.

78. Cox supplied this and following information on Alton East and the LCC in interviews, London 2006 and 2007.

79. Glendenning and Muthesius, *op.cit.* p.78.

80. Jurgen Varming and the Architects' Co-operative Partnership, 'The End of the Smoke Age', *Architectural Review*, vol.101, no.604, April 1947, pp.139–40, Yorke, Rosenberg and Mardall and Jurgen Varming, 'District Heating for a New Housing Scheme', ibid., pp.142–3.

Gibberd, Bridgwater and Shepheard, and a few others, perhaps the most glaring gap – indeed, the *fundamental difference* – between Swedish and Danish housing and that in Britain was in their landscape setting.[73] For the Scandinavians, this was something upon which they spent both care and money – whether in a high density urban scheme or in a woodland setting. Kidder Smith emphasised this point. 'Stockholm represents the ultimate union of architecture, planning and landscaping, each working for the fullest expression of resources and needs. But architecture everywhere in Sweden is almost always interpenetrated by and subordinate to nature. There is no question here of calling in a landscape architect to coordinate things with a few bushes after the buildings are complete. He was there before the architect!'[74] Provision for children's play and its supervision was also an integral part of Swedish and Danish landscaping and an inspiration to those, like Lady Allen of Hurtwood, who sought to make similar provision in Britain.

Despite the British passion for gardening, our shaping of the public realm has always had a very low priority – and photographs of post-war housing prove the point. Indeed, so awful was the position by 1956 that the *AJ* commissioned the young Ian McHarg (shortly to move to America where he developed the concept of ecological planning) to conduct a substantial survey of British landscaping costs in an article entitled 'Can we afford open space?' One of the picture captions observed that in Scandinavian housing 'it is the site plan and the development of open space rather than the buildings as exercises in architecture which explains their distinction.'[75]

Eric Lyons, both in his work for Span and for local authorities, was outstanding for his commitment to the space between houses. He and his landscape architect partner, Ivor Cunningham, who worked in Stockholm before joining Lyons, admired Scandinavian work by Erskine, Jacobsen and Utzon.[76] Indeed, one of their landscape architects was the Dane, Preben Jakobsen. But, set against the total output of the housing sector, Lyons's output was minute.

MATERIALS, MEN, MISCELLANEA – AND TOWER BLOCKS

There were, of course, other ways in which the Swedes influenced aspects of post-war British housing. There was the use of Swedish-developed Stramit compressed straw slabs for roofing and partitioning, which led to the establishment of a factory in the East Anglian grain-growing area and the use of these slabs in much Span housing. There was also the use of Scandinavian-designed high-performance, double-glazed pivoting windows, which permitted window cleaning from inside blocks of flats.[77]

Then there were the people themselves. During this period the LCC housing teams included many young Swedish and Danish architects. Oliver Cox recalls that, of the two, it was the Danes who, designing and building for the first time since 1940, made the greatest impression.[78] In structural engineering, the British-born Dane, Ove Arup, made a major contribution both on Tecton's Finsbury flats (where he used the Danish-developed box frame system) and (learning from his experience on Tecton's Highpoint flats) on the design of the structure for Alton East.[79] In services engineering, yet another Dane, Jurgen Värming (one of the founders of the Steensen Varming Mulcahy consultancy), contributed two *AR* articles on heating.[80] And there were others, including energetic manufacturers and entrepreneurs like Torsten Mosessen of TOMO windows and trading.

Within the LCC, Oliver Cox used the *Information Bulletin* to promote ideas based on the Swedish experience and devised a colour range which owed much to the Swedish Munsell system. Swedish user studies and ergonomic research also had a profound impact on kitchen fitting and furniture design (the latter mainly in schools) – even if the Swedish self-assembly furniture brought back by architecture students in the late 1940s had to wait another forty years before it became, through IKEA, common in British homes.

But there were two Scandinavian-originated developments which were to be profoundly influential. The first was relatively harmless. It concerned the process of design and affected virtually every architect practising in Britain in the 1960s and 1970s. This was the Swedish SfB system adopted, together with the European A-range of paper sizes, first by the *AJ* and then by the entire building materials and components industries to classify architectural and construction information.[81] It was a period when, at the start of the information age, it was becoming increasingly important to be able to access information in an organised manner. Housing articles were always filed under SfB (98). The system started to wither under its own weight in the early 1980s but nothing has ever entirely replaced it.

The second development was fundamental and related to the construction and *very form* of public sector housing. In September 1952 the *AJ* published three articles on Swedish building techniques for housing.[82] The first, on building organisation and efficiency, was followed by articles on the use of a portal crane for flat building and on productivity. In April the following year, an article followed on building with large concrete units.[83] These articles were the first of many, often by engineers such as Peter Dunican, Ove Arup's associate on Alton East, on Swedish and Danish developments in the construction of prefabricated high- and medium-rise housing. The first British equivalent to be published by the *AJ* was the LCC's Picton Street development in November 1956.[84] Even the *AR* covered technical developments in Scandinavian prefabricated high-rise housing as at Bellahøj in Denmark[85] – the outcome of which was good enough to be appreciated as architecture of quality.

Up to 1964, British architects were, in the words (again) of Lionel Esher,

> *looking for a kit from which a humane variety of low-rise types could be assembled faster and cheaper than bricks and mortar could do it. They never succeeded. But what were available, mainly from France, Denmark and Sweden, were patented systems for the rapid building of multi-storey flats, which met the demand in continental countries. For the Ministers and for housing committees seeking to beat all productivity records for new dwellings, this had to be the answer. A National Building Agency managed by … Cleeve Barr, was set up to help the urban housing authorities … to find their way among the multiplicity of systems … As early as 1961 Barr himself had warned of the dangers of monotony and an inhuman scale, but to no avail. Additional subsidies took care of the extra cost of tall buildings and of the far higher cost of inner-city compared with green field sites. Indeed, successive Ministers provided that the higher the tower, the higher the subsidy per flat.*[86]

81. Dargan Bullivant, 'A New System of Classification', *Architects' Journal*, vol.10, no.3361, 17 September 1959, p.189.

82. Technical Section, *Architects' Journal*, vol.116, no.3002, 11 September 1952, pp.321–9.

83. Peter Dunican, 'Economics of Multi-Storey Flats', *Architects' Journal*, vol.115, no.2988, 5 June 1952, pp.703–9.

84. 'Construction: Complete Structures, the LCC's Picton Street Development', *Architects' Journal*, vol.122, no.3167, 10 November 1955, pp.637–45.

85. G. Anthony Atkinson, 'Recent Developments in Danish Building', *Architectural Review*, vol.115, no.687, March 1954, p.215.

86. Lionel Esher, *A Broken Wave, op.cit.*, p.57. Oliver Cox states that point-blocks were often misunderstood and used on very restricted sites as an imposed form of excessive height – as at Red Road in Glasgow where 4 bed flats were located in 24-storey towers.

Figure 10. Tower blocks at Clever Road, London, built with a Scandinavian but British modified system. One – Ronan Point – was demolished, following partial collapse, before this 1988 photograph. (Unknown)

Figures 11 & 12. Borough Engineer's Contemporary, 1954. The flats in Hounslow which the Ministry of Housing selected for the King of Sweden's visit. (*Architects' Journal*)

Set against the vast amount of post-war housing constructed in Britain, the Scandinavian influence was infinitesimal. We tend to blank out from our awareness the thousands of acres of two-storey cottage and three storey flats estates encircling so many of our towns – the *Housing Manuals* from 1949 onwards illustrate the better examples and it is striking how similar they are in design to those of the mid–1930s. But there was one exception to this minimal Scandinavian influence: the enthusiasm for the idea of the tower block – which can be traced straight back, particularly in the LCC (as Pevsner demonstrated in his *AR* critique of Roehampton and as John Summerson observed in his extended introduction to the catalogue for the Arts Council's 'Ten Years of British Architecture' exhibition in 1956), not to European precedents of the 1930s – but to the war-time tower clusters of Stockholm.[87] And from there, it was a short trip down the same route – foretold by Kidder Smith – to the widely adopted Scandinavian tower block systems such as Jespersen (adopted by Laings), Skarne (by Crudens) and Larsen Nielsen, which, marketed by Taylor-Woodrow-Anglian and modified by British engineers, was used for both the ill-fated Ronan Point block of flats and the once infamous Broadwater Farm estate. The Swedes – in their 1960s Million Dwellings in Ten Years programme – suffered too, but, working from a far higher level of standards, the consequences were nothing like as disastrous as in Britain.[88]

But let us end this account not with the tragedy of Ronan Point but with a tragi-comedy from the *AJ*'s Astragal in the 1 July 1954 issue. Under the heading 'Fit for a King', Astragal wrote:

> *The King and Queen of Sweden, who had asked to be shown a housing scheme during their brief visit to this country, were taken to the Butts Farm Estate, Hanworth. Why was this typical example of Borough Engineer's Contemporary chosen? "Nothing to do with us," said Buckingham Palace, "try the Swedish Embassy." The Embassy was unwilling to take the blame, but it did say, reassuringly: "The King knows that you can't judge by external appearances." Wincingly, Astragal telephoned the Lord Chamberlain's which cheerfully put the blame on to the Ministry of Housing and Local Government. "I don't know much about it," said the girl at the Ministry, "but I was told that if anyone asked I was to say it was on the rota." Exeunt brooding Astragal, smiting brow with trembling fist, and wondering why the Royal visitors could not have been taken to the LCC's point-block estate at Wimbledon, for which the Ministry has just awarded a housing medal.[89]*

That Wimbledon estate was the Ackroydon estate – the first of a most distinguished series of Swedish-influenced LCC estates. All the realities, doubts and disappointments about post-war public housing in Britain were encapsulated in the Ministry's response to the royal request.

87. Pevsner, 'Roehampton', *op.cit.*, p.35; Summerson, *op.cit.*, pp.44–5.

88. Jöran Lindvall, ed., *The Swedish Art of Building*, Stockholm, The Swedish Institute and Swedish Museum of Architecture, 1992, pp.136, 230–2.

89. Astragal, 'Fit for a King?', *Architects' Journal*, vol.120, no.3096, 1 July 1954, p.3.

8 Roehampton Housing

JOHN PARTRIDGE

Roehampton Housing

JOHN PARTRIDGE

Figure 1. Eleven-storey point blocks, containing two 2-bedroom and two 1-bedroom flats per floor (all photographs from the author).

Enthusiasm and excitement are not characteristics normally associated with local authority offices. Yet in the early 1950s as the newly established London County Council Housing Division of the Architect's Department began to get underway there was a buzz of expectation in the air and sense of mission that fired the work and gave it a new dimension. As one of the very first to arrive in this new organisation, I was able to observe it grow, gather strength and impetus and to compare it with what had gone before in the name of local authority housing.

I had done my training in the LCC under a scheme set up by John Forshaw in the war, whereby architectural students worked in the Architect's Department and studied by a joint arrangement with the School of Architecture of Regent Street Polytechnic who provided the lectures and studio teaching. There was another intake to a scheme tied in to Brixton School of Building.

I had started in the Schools Division, where at the end of the war they were looking at 3,000 pupil multi-lateral schools on the American and Canadian models. Thank goodness these were never built, but they were the forerunner of the 1,000 plus comprehensives of the 1950s. Life in the Architect's Department came to an abrupt end when one day most of us were transferred, much against our will, to the Valuer's Department to work on housing schemes, the responsibility for which had been wrested from Forshaw. The training scheme continued for a few years but was finally absorbed into the Regent Street evening school organisation.

I qualified at about the same time as housing, through the force of professional lobbying and informed public opinion, was returned to the Architect's Department in 1950 under Robert Matthew. The work of the Valuer's Department was totally dedicated to quantity and pre-war designs were hauled out of the drawer to be repeated with minimal alteration. I was the first of the then Valuer's staff to move across to the new Housing Division, probably because I had been such a nuisance and had persuaded my boss to let me design a modern building albeit, at that time, as yet unbuilt. I joined Colin Lucas and was excited to work with him and Michael Powell in what was called the Development Group. In the first few months I drew up Colin's back-of-the-envelope sketches of the eleven-storey T-shaped point block he had designed for the Ackroydon Estate. It had three flats per floor and very characteristic strip windows in a similar mould to his pre-war houses as Connell, Ward and Lucas.

The new organisation grew very quickly and many young newly qualified architects, together with those of more experience, joined the ranks. There was an immensely influential and talented influx, particularly from the Hertfordshire schools programme, whence came Cleeve Barr, Oliver Cox, 'Beak' Adams and Anthony Garrod. Under Whitfield Lewis, who as Chief Housing Architect arrived later in the year, the department was organised into groups with specific projects and tasks. When the Roehampton Lane site (later to be called Alton West) was brought into the programme Colin Lucas was put in charge of a team of four and I was teamed up with Bill Howell, John Killick and Stan Amis, all of whom had qualified that year at the Architectural Association. The chemistry seemed to work and we carried the scheme through, and the four of us joined together after 1959 to form the very successful private practice of Howell Killick Partridge and Amis (HKPA) which continued until 1995.

During the 1950s a large number of newly qualified architects regarded the LCC as their first stop after leaving formal education. It would be invidious to mention the names that come readily to my mind and impossible for me to recollect all of them. They had an unparalleled influence on the architectural work in housing, schools and general public buildings. There can be little doubt that the new set-up for housing in the Architect's Department and the inspiration of the 1951 Festival of Britain, with its new concert hall designed by the LCC, enthused

Figure 2. Aerial view of Roehampton Lane (Alton West) from above Richmond Park.

the young professionals to gravitate to County Hall.

The work in the Housing Division went on apace, particularly in the early years, and the architecture was debated and analysed in an atmosphere more like a postgraduate school than a local authority office. There were vehemently held views and intense architectural discussions took place about design issues and the social appropriateness of the buildings we were providing for London. The contrast with the low morale that existed amongst the architects working in the Valuer's Department was extraordinary. It was not just that they were unhappy working there, it was more that they were expected to do unimaginative schemes and to repeat some of the boring designs of the pre-war era. Many of them were well-qualified and experienced architects working hard in adverse circumstances and waiting for the time when they would return to the Architect's Department. There were, however, one or two time-servers. One in particular I remember, because he spent at least one day a week drawing out a chart for the football pools syndicate for which he was the prime mover.

The architectural debate in the new Housing Division soon became polarised into two opposing philosophies. In simplistic terms it became a battle between those looking to Scandinavia for inspiration from its recent examples of socially advanced housing, who liked to be called New Humanists, and those like my group who followed the teachings of Le Corbusier. The label of New Brutalism was not in evidence at the time but came into use much later to coincide with the general disillusionment with concrete buildings. For us a trip to the Unité d'Habitation in Marseilles was almost mandatory and Stan Amis and I duly made this pilgrimage (in a pre-war Morris with a leaking petrol tank stopped up with chewing gum), returning in total awe of the great master. In the office both camps existed side by side and debated the issues informally as well as at more struc- tured meetings. One particularly famous meeting organised by Colin St John Wilson took place in a local public house and attracted a gathering of at least a hundred members of the department. I have little doubt that the hothouse of ar- gument and the competitive spirit spurred everyone on to attempt the best pos- sible social architecture and, although at the time we would have been horrified to admit it, much of the polarity of view was concerned with architectural style.

Bill Howell had an intense interest in Le Corbusier's *Modulor* and we contin- ued his previous work in devising a more simple system of preferred dimensions based on the Fibonacci series. This assumed greater importance at Alton West as it enabled us to relate the proportions of buildings erected in brick with those

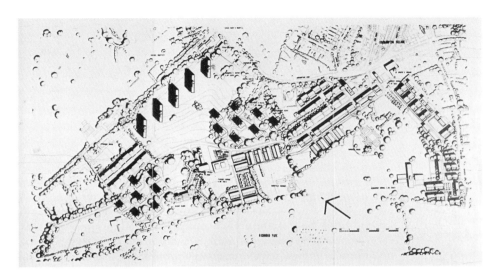

Figure 3. Plan of Alton West. Maisonettes to the north. (Author)

using pre-cast concrete, where the material itself has no scale other than that imposed on it by the designer. These dimensional developments were frowned upon from above but we carried on with the work. After all, we were putting the dimensions on the drawings. The harmonious relationship of the proportions of different elements has unified the scheme and given it consistency.

The Architect's Department had enormous resources. It had its own materials section, and facilities for testing engineering and chemical products in the Engi- neer's Department and the Public Health Department. Answers to questions and advice on building technology were available from in-house experts. There was also a very skilful model making group. The Roehampton layout was designed on a large-scale model which not only had all the contours but every tree to scale with its correct position and spread. Never subsequently have I experienced such a design tool at hand. Computers have of course made virtual reality a design tool but in the 1950s these expensive accurate models were remarkable. If there was a weakness at the LCC it was the lack of research into living experience in housing estates, particularly in new types of dwellings. The first sociologist in the depart- ment (Margaret Willis) was appointed in 1950, but it was to take considerable time before research findings were validated and had any major contribution to the housing types and layout designs that were on the drawing board.

Roehampton Lane (Alton West) was extremely fortunate in having a uniquely landscaped site with a mile-long southern frontage to Richmond. It was a hun- dred acres of mature landscape and the site of four historic houses on to which we were required to provide at least 2,000 dwellings, together with three schools, a community centre, library and shops. From the start we knew that the quality and scale of the landscape was a major factor in setting an approach to the layout

Figure 4. Ten-storey maisonettes on pilotis (two bedrooms), with eleven-storey point blocks in the distance.

design that made it different from that used on more urban sites. There was a valley running east-west through the length of the site. This meant that the ground in front of Mount Clare, a villa near the boundary with Richmond Park, sloped northwards away from the park until it reached this valley. It then rose up again more steeply towards Downshire House on Roehampton Lane. We aimed to use the complexity in the ground to enclose a very large open space linking the two historic houses. The backdrop to the landscape would be the eleven-storey slab blocks of maisonettes looking out over the Downshire field towards the park, and these would be flanked by two clusters of point blocks set in amongst the trees. The upper floors of the high buildings would have spectacular views for about ten miles over the Royal Park. The Downshire field was to be remodelled so that there was a slight valley rising against the hill towards the north and a new copse planted in the centre of gravity of the space aiming at a feeling of endlessness to the grass carpet. This spatial device has been destroyed in more recent years by indiscriminate planting by the local authority who have peppered the field with trees.

In housing schemes the design of the dwellings and the buildings of which they form part needs to be progressed at the same time as the layout. The LCC committees were used to the notion of standard type plans and in order to break new ground designs had to be approved and given the status of type plans. The eleven-storey point block had committee approval following the Colin Lucas 'T'-shaped block at the Ackroydon Estate, and the Portsmouth Road scheme (later to be called Alton East) was designed with points having four flats per floor and dotted amongst the trees on a steeply sloping site. Lower buildings, four-storey maisonettes and two-storey houses, were cleverly interwoven into the layout.

The eleven-storey slab block of maisonettes used at Alton West was a new type developed for more urban sites by Colin St John Wilson's group. This provided a much better response to the scale of Downshire Field than point blocks would have done and the proposed line of five gave all the dwellings magnificent views. Objections at planning stage to this proposed 'wall of building' resulted in the scheme being called in by the Minister of Housing and Local Government and being delayed by about a year, during which time we worked on other schemes. When finally given approval some changes had to be made. The most significant of these was to turn the slab blocks through ninety degrees so that they presented a minimum effect of mass when seen from Richmond Park. Although the dwellings had less panoramic views there were benefits from the change which set

Figure 5. Plan of Roehampton Lane (Alton West).

the buildings against the contours of Downshire Field. The ground floor *pilotis* increased in height as they stepped down the hill and we now decided to allow the pile caps to show as bases to the columns. This was not only an economic solution but it gave a very special character to the ground design which we considered a mini 'Giant's Causeway'. Robert Clatworthy, whose bronze sculpture of a bull stands to the east of Downshire Field with a backdrop of point blocks, originally wanted to site his work amongst the forest of *pilotis*. In the end he talked himself out of this and I think made the right decision.

The layout of the eastern part of the site emerged relatively unscathed from the planning procedures. It was designed with a more formalised series of streets and squares and had a preponderance of four-storey maisonettes with gardens for the ground-floor dwellings. Family houses of two and three storeys were incorporated into the scheme. Mixed development of different size and heights of dwellings was the policy adopted in all new housing estates and this fitted with the financial subsidies of the time. At the junction of the main spine road through the site and Roehampton Lane we planned two rows of shops with maisonettes above and allocated a site for a library. This was designed later and included a

Figure 6. Ten-storey maisonettes, each block containing 75 dwellings, with pram stalls at pilotis level.

Figure 7. Four-storey, 3-bedroomed maisonettes.

high maisonette 'marker' block to be built in a later phase of the scheme. I was to work on this with Roy Stout much later but left the LCC before the building contract started.

Towards the end of my time at the LCC I found myself showing many visitors around the scheme, which had become widely publicised. At the peak time there were two or three thousand visitors a year from many different countries. The Alton estates were also very popular with tenants and aspiring tenants on the waiting list, and this interest did not wane until well into the 1960s.

Looking back on this period, what stands out is the extraordinary design freedom that we were allowed. Control of our work was exerted by laid down cost limits and space standards rather than by instruction from senior members of staff. During the whole time my group was working on the largest housing scheme in the programme we never met the Housing Committee. Colin Lucas was very occasionally brought into contact with members, but generally all the liaison was done by the very senior architects and the results relayed to us later.

One of the kindest appraisals of Alton West was made by the broadcaster Alistair Cooke. He wrote in 1980 that 'the Roehampton Estate is the most elegant and harmonious housing estate to go up since the Second World War. At first glance it could be mistaken for an extension of Hollywood's Century City.'[1] I hope he experienced it at ground level as well as from the air.

1. Robert Cameron and Alistair Cooke, *Above London*, San Francisco, Cameron and Co., 1980.

9 The Water Gardens, 'An Underrated Corner of the Capital'

CHRIS WHITTAKER

The Water Gardens,
'An Underrated Corner of the Capital'

CHRIS WHITTAKER

CHRIS WHITTAKER

This corner is a short way up the Edgware road from Marble Arch, at the junction with Sussex Gardens.[1] It is also the northern corner of the Church Commissioners' Hyde Park Estate. It was redeveloped in the early 1960s by the Commissioners themselves as their first major step in transforming the estate from its previous down-at-heel state. They, and their predecessors, had owned the large triangle of land bounded by Edgware Road, Bayswater Road and Sussex Gardens since the Reformation, and developed it in the 1830s to a layout by George Gutch on 99-year leases. These had mostly run out during the inter-war period, when some 21-year renewals had been granted. In the Second World War many leases were not renewed and there were many requisitions, by the military and by Paddington Borough Council. By the mid–1950s the Estate was in a poor state of repair, with the dwellings in the houses badly converted and not self-contained.

In 1954 management of the estate was transferred to Chestertons, who recommended substantial redevelopment. Anthony Minoprio, of Minioprio and Spencely, was appointed, and his plan was approved by the Commissioners and the London County Council in 1956. Chestertons started to rehouse the tenants and licensees by finding alternative accommodation on the estate or their other holdings, by purchasing houses in the Kilburn area, and by making some grants for tenants to buy their own homes.

Redevelopment of the estate started in a comparatively small way in the late 1950s. The Commissioners went into partnership with Wates, and first used Wates's own architect, Ken Bland, to design and build terraced houses on the east side of Hyde Park Street and on Clarendon Place nearby. Following from this, the north side of Sussex Square was rebuilt as 'luxurious accommodation' in 63 flats, with Trehearne and Norman, Preston and Partners as architects. They also designed Clifton Place, next to Sussex Square, while Fry, Drew and Partners designed Chelwood House on the north side of Gloucester Square. All these schemes followed the grain of the original layout of the estate. By the time they were under way, Chestertons had completed the demolition of the northern part of the estate, between Sussex Gardens and the Edgware Road, resulting in five large sites.

Meanwhile, it had become apparent to the Commissioners that property values were rising rapidly. The average Sussex Square flat which had sold for £8,000 was changing hands for £11,000 or £12,000 two years later. The partnership with Wates was reconsidered, and Henry Wells, a senior partner in Chestertons, recommended that the Commissioners assume sole responsibility for the redevelopment of the northernmost corner of the Estate.[2] The Burwood Place Development Company was formed, its name taken from the street on the south-eastern edge of the site. The chairman was Douglas Overall, formerly senior partner of Hillier, Parker, May and Rowden and with expertise on shops and offices, while Henry Wells was the leading director and Donald Colenette, Estates Secretary to the Commissions was the third director. John Hollamby, a partner in Chestertons, was Company Secretary and Project Manager.[3] The Board

Figure 1. Under the cantilevered central tower, southern tower beyond (author, 1966).

1. *Guardian Weekend* (with *The Guardian* no.49,450), 3 September 2005, p.63.

2. Henry Wells later became Chairman of Hemel Hempstead new town, President of the Royal Institute of Chartered Surveyors and, under Harold Wilson, Chairman of the Land Commission.

3. I am grateful to John Hollamby for the early history of the Hyde Park Estate.

Figure 2. End of tower facing on to the landscaping (Tony Cook).

of the company appointed Trehearne and Norman as architects, G. D. Walford and Partners as quantity surveyors and T. C. Durley, Hill and Partners as structural engineers. Subsequently they nominated Wates as contractors.

There was a meeting with Leslie Lane of the Planning Division of the LCC, early in 1961, to discuss the Burwood part of the Minoprio development plan. Lane supported the scheme of three storeys of shops, showrooms and offices along Edgware Road, five storeys of flats along Sussex Gardens with a nine-storey block at right angles to it on Porchester Street, but he surprised everyone by suggesting that the proposed towers over the Edgware Road frontage be seventeen storeys high, rather than the twelve in the plan. This, of course, was accepted for its potentially greater economic return. Chestertons advised that the flats in these towers be spacious so as to be readily saleable, with the Sussex Gardens and adjoining flats to be smaller and so rentable. By the time they were built, the 1965 Rent Act ensured that they would provide the Commissioners with a rapidly increasing income.

So by the time that I came to be asked, by the partner under whom I was working, George Gneditch, to begin the detailed design of Burwood Place, the main lines of the scheme had already been laid down. One might think now that this would have robbed a young architect of much of the enjoyment to be gained from the project. But I had been with the practice long enough, nearly a year, to know that this was not necessarily so. At the LCC, from 1954 to 1960, I had been engaged in very satisfying work, mainly on the Brandon Estate in Southwark – firstly in the Planning Division under Leslie Lane and Geoffrey Clothier be-fore, with great difficulty, I had moved to the Housing Division of the Architect's Department so that I could go on working on the project with Ted Hollamby.[4] A major impression had been the always long sequence of securing go-aheads, from the Group Leader, then from the Head of Division, then from the Housing Committee, each more distant from the realities on the ground. Such sequences could take months. At Trehearnes it was 'Have you got everything ready? Right, we'll get a taxi', and within half an hour I was face-to-face with the client, explain-ing my own design.

In three major ways, Burwood Place produced its own excitements. First came the name. The practice had set up the team working on the scheme in a small vacant house more or less overlooking the site. On a lunchtime stroll to Wigmore Street I bumped into Philip Hicks, whom I had not seen since we left the Architectural Association ten years before. He had a small office round the corner, in Duke Street. 'Well, if you're into landscaping now, we have this large basement car park – if you'd like to do a sketch for the slab over it, I'll show it to the client' – and it was treated with acclaim. 'We'll call it the Water Gardens!'

Hicks had previously designed the small garden in the forecourt of Sander-sons in Berners Street. The building is now Sandersons Hotel, but the garden was meticulously recorded and remade in a courtyard behind the bar – a successful transplanting from the 'sixties to the 'nineties. His eponymous scheme for the Water Gardens integrated the open areas needed to ventilate the garage below the roofs of the shops, and the garage roof itself a storey below, by stairs and intermediate walkways. It looked well, both from the private balconies above and as one emerged from the foyer at ground level. It also made it possible to

4. John and Ted Hollamby were not related. For the Brandon Estate see Rosalind Bay-ley, *Celebrating Special Buildings: the Case for Conserving Post-War Public Housing*, Twentieth Century Society, 2002, pp.26–7.

Figure 3. Promotional perspective of 1963 by E. J. Thring.

Figure 4. The landscaping today (Tony Cook).

Figure 5. The landscaping from above, showing vents to basement car park (Tony Cook).

Figure 6. From the Edgware Road, looking north (author).

5. Colin Buchanan et al, *Traffic in Towns, a Study of the long term problems of Traffic in Urban Areas*, Reports of the Steering Group and Working Group appointed by the Minister of Transport, London, HMSO, 1963.

6. The Water Gardens is not gated, though this may happen following incidents of residents being bothered by outsiders.

7. Sherban Cantacuzino, *Wells Coates*, London, Gordon Fraser, 1978.

move about within the site without crossing its access road: this a year before the publication of the Buchanan Report, *Traffic in Towns*.[5] And, thanks to excellent and far-sighted maintenance, it looks even better today. This urban benefit is of course primarily for the lessees and occupiers: it is part of what they have paid for. But it is not gated away from passers-by, and is well worth a small detour.[6]

The second big excitement again came from a walk in the middle of the working day. Edmund Lucey, who had joined me to form the design team, and I had got as far as Green Park. Just as we needed to turn back, we glimpsed Denys Lasdun's flats in St James's Place. Back in the office, we had already settled on the long rectangular form of the towers and on the white tiles which were to form the external upstand beams around the perimeter of each floor. Here before us was this clear three-into-two statement of floor levels using not dissimilar elements. Lasdun had just four large flats in which three storeys of smaller rooms to the north are set against two floors of high-ceiling living rooms facing the park. Supposing…? We had a card model to show how 'three into two' would work for us: the fifteen upper floors of the towers would give ten large living rooms in each stack multiplied by the four corners of each block and the three towers: $10 \times 4 \times 3 = 120$. This would give a sufficiency of spaciousness, and, after a costing and valuation comparison of the height-and-a-half rooms with a conventional plan, it was approved at the next meeting.

We realised our debt to Lasdun. What we and everyone else had forgotten was an earlier stricture from John Hollamby: 'Don't let it look like the Hallfield Estate!' This was Lasdun's large scheme for Paddington Metropolitan Borough, three-quarters of a mile from Chestertons' office and the epitome of local authority housing at the time. Even further back in our memories, quite crusted over for me, was 10 Palace Gate by Wells Coates, completed in 1939: sixteen flats in a notable building, but the expression of 'three-into-two' is not very visible from the road. It was only when I picked up a copy of Sherban Cantacuzino's book on Wells Coates years later that I learned that Lasdun had worked for Coates at that time, and that the idea had first been realised by Mosei Ginsburg in the Narkomfin building in Moscow in the late 1920s, whence the news was brought to central London by Berthold Lubetkin.[7]

We did make our own contribution. For the residents of the Water Gardens and for anyone who does it again, three-into-two where one steps down into the living room should not have the floor at the mid-point in the section. It is too far down. We realised that three feet or 900mm were enough. So the end elevation of the towers, which expresses these floor levels, shows the floors paired rather than at constant intervals vertically.

Figure 7. The height-and-a-half living rooms at all four corners of each tower (Elain Harwood).

The third excitement at the Water Gardens, for us then and for the occupiers today, is due to the structural engineers, Durley, Hill and Partners. There was a dilemma within the design: the long, thin rectangle of each tower's plan meant that it was a considerable distance from the entrance at one end to the central lift foyer. Would it be possible, we asked, to bring the internal access road under the end of each block and to make a large opening at the end of the central spine walls? We had produced the card model to make things clear. The reply, by Tom Durley, was on the instant. 'Well, the spine wall is like a beam 150ft deep – there's no problem cantilevering 20ft out over the road, if that's what you want.' A pair of scissors was quickly produced. 'You mean, like this?' (*Snip, snip.*) The walk through the foyer was instantly reduced and the dramatic structural expression was cast. The internal access road itself was necessitated by another stricture of John Hollamby's: that the flats in the towers must not have an Edgware Road address; anyway, access from Edgware Road would have punctuated, three times, the continuity of the shopping frontage, and that would have been bad practice.

The engineer also quickly realised that the curtailed middle floor of each tier of three ended in a cross wall which again could act as a balanced cantilever beam projecting from each side of the central spine wall, and this beam could give support to the perimeter upstand beams which carried the floors. Michael Bunn, the partner in Durley Hill, appreciated being brought in at what he called 'the charcoal stage' when the elevations were being sketched and debated. They were debated to the extent that at one point there was an internal competition organised by the practice. It was a 'home win' for Edmund Lucey: two other attempts to 'elevate' the complexities of the plans which changed floor by floor gained little support in the office.

Figure 8. Isometric showing structure of cantilevered spine wall (author).

The importance of the cross beam is shown by the joining of the two middle floor beams in their white-tiled cladding – a structural justification. There is a more important aesthetic one, however. These 'U-on-its-side' elements of the elevation concentrate the eye on the central parts of the façade, making it seem narrower and so taller. Without this the almost square elevations could have looked squat. (I grew up at County Hall overlooking Howard Robertson's Shell Centre being perpetrated, an overnight betrayal of Graeme Shankland's slim tower into an obese form.) This post-hoc argument is also the answer to the present partner in Trehearnes who wrote to me recently that 'my only misgiving about the design of the Water Gardens is the certain lack of integrity in the principal elevations of the towers, where the white expressed structure is not an entirely honest reflection of the structural solution'. This observation is valuable for a number of reasons. At the LCC, 45 years ago, one walked a daily cross-fire of this sort of argument between truth and art (it was another reason why things took such a long time). Moving to Trehearne and Norman, the implied stress was to get on with it, architectural aesthetics being left for the hindmost. It is good to know now that the debate has been going on in this practice, especially

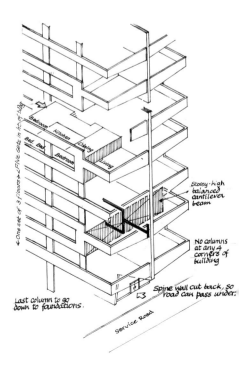

Figure 9. Living room with dining room beyond (Elain Harwood).

when a tacit submission of this article is that here is a scheme which deserves a wider discussion.

Once the main structural ideas were defined, it soon became clear that these could best be expressed by tile cladding, contrasting the upstand beams on the facades with the verticals. Langleys of London were the keenest supplier and – after a trip to the manufacturers in Lübeck – the white 2 inch by 2 inch square tile was chosen. Rather than apply all these in situ, it was decided to form pre-cast units to enclose the upstand beams, with the tiles already in place within the shuttering for the units. These were made by Trent and Hoveringham in Nottingham. This process went well, but it required the engineer to determine the width of each panel so that when they were abutted the joints did not show, and furthermore to set out the overall length of each floor to an accuracy of one thirty-second of an inch.

Whatever the external treatment of 'three-into-two', it fulfilled Chestertons' schedule for a wide range of accommodation. The curtailed middle floor could be joined to the upper floor with an internal stair flight, to give a three- or four-bedroom duplex – with a wide entrance hall, since the internal stair descended and so did not break the view through to the lofty living room – or it could be a separate one-bedroomed flat. The bottom floor of the three-floor sandwich was planned as a two-bed flat. These varying layouts, one on top of another, each needed their own fenestration, which we accepted without resorting to the extremity of placing the window in the corner of the room. Silux horizontally pivoted windows were placed where most sensible, with matching western red cedar boarding in between. That the windows keep moving about on elevation is not readily apparent.

The same windows, with cedar boarding between, were used on the Sussex Gardens block and its nine-storey neighbour. They were designed, under great pressure, by Max Honigsfield and David Goldhill, who joined the team from British Rail. The windows provided a unifying theme with the whole development. The blocks were built as a further stage of the same contract with Wates: the pressure came from their needing the drawings in three weeks from a standing start. Max and David decided to concentrate on the detailing of corners and junctions of materials and to standardise these and avoid exceptions, so reducing the number of drawings needed. David recalls that one of the site workers asked for a detail at a column to be checked: he had found an exception to the standardising discipline. In spite of the pressure, they both recall it as one of their happiest jobs, where decisions could be given on the spot, before a costing exercise or client corroboration.

In the middle of the long elevations of each tower, every floor had a black hole, the eight square feet of permanent ventilation leading to the lift foyers, from which short passages led out to the further side of the building where a short balcony gave on to the escape stairway. These ducts formed the 'pneumonia lobbies', an unavoidable feature of every tall block of housing, whether luxurious or not. Here, however, the day was saved by John Hollamby. He proposed, and it was accepted by the LCC, that there be louvers across the ducts, held by electro-magnets, which would be released by smoke alarms in the foyers. Luxury in the common parts was maintained.

Philip Hicks was not the only external designer that I was lucky enough to introduce to the practice. Aileen Boatman, a friend, designed mosaics and a lin-ocut floor when it was decided to make one of the upper foyers into a children's playroom, and Janet Semmens designed and made a two-storey silk screen hanging to go behind the porter's desk in the first of the foyers. This had just been prepared when Wilton Carpets, who quoted for all the common parts, said, 'if you need that quantity, we could make up your own design', so Janet designed the carpets too.

The shops, 22 units along the Edgware Road, provided their own occasional excitements, even though they were essentially unadorned voids. When Safeways decided to take six units, it was a catch not to be allowed to slip off the hook. But Edgware Road is on a very slight rise at this point, and each unit had a floor at a different level from the next one. For Safeways to have their letting with a level floor meant dashing across to the site and speaking to Len, the foreman of the concreting gang, with the laden skip overhead, before – well before – the variation was advised to the agent or the Q. S., so that today's new work would not have to be hacked up tomorrow. Architecture of the moment rather than of the century, but, since that time, memorable for us.

By the time I left the practice, at the end of 1965, all but six of the shops were spoken for, and the flats in the second tower were already on offer, at £26,000 for a 75-year lease of a four-bed duplex. The project was a success. The first of the lessees was perhaps among the most keen. This couple had been referred to Trehearnes' office in Kingsway and had later called at the firm's site office. Later, they had taken a flat in Park West, on the other side of Burwood Place, so they had an ideal vantage point from which to watch the Water Gardens grow. They were at the head of the queue on the day that the show flat opened.

Recently, someone who lives in a duplex in the centre tower wrote,
I adore living in the Water Gardens. The flats are all bright and spacious and serene. They are very well designed for living – no wasted space, no dark, poky corners that you find in conversions. The split-level sitting and dining rooms are great for entertaining. The tall windows on to the balcony give views from the new developments at Paddington round to the park with Battersea beyond. The two bigger bedrooms are spacious enough to take six-foot beds, almost uniquely in Central London flats and houses; and, most jealousy-inducing of all, there is plenty of storage space. The Water Gardens themselves are an unusually and ingenious use of a small and fairly tricky triangular shape. The ponds are home to several species of fish and waterfowl – koi carp, a heron and a few families of moorhen. Fountains in the ponds give a reassuring sound of running water as a counterpoint to the murmur of traffic and commerce from the Edgware Road. The gardens are an unusual feature in London, or in any English city. Lawns extending to parkland beyond, yes, an urban garden is a more difficult concept. But here, clearly inspired by a Japanese aesthetic, we have various tableaux of plants, stones, mosses and grasses contained in geometric shapes that are almost like a private conversation with those in the flats above, from which they appear like an abstract work of art.[8]
For those of us who worked on the Water Gardens forty years ago, this song of

8. Margaret Doyle, Westminster Council-lor and Water Gardens resident, letter to author 2006.

praise is a delight, making the silence of the interim not quite the shame it had seemed. It is also a compliment to the Commissioners' management and maintenance, and particularly to Tony Heywood who looks after the gardens.

The half dozen colleagues I have managed to contact recently (including one in Malta and another in Newfoundland) all remember more than anything else the camaraderie we shared and the way in which Trehearne and Norman, Preston & Partners provided the framework and the readiness to allow a team to grow, and to welcome their ideas. This must be one of the reasons that a practice founded on 1 January 1900 is still trading. It has been unlucky with some other projects. Although its name survives on Africa House in Kingsway, which was put through a century ago, State House around the corner in High Holborn has gone, and with it a small piazza with a large bronze by Barbara Hepworth. The Paternoster scheme north of St Paul's was never highly regarded, in spite of having Lord Holford as consultant planner, and was replaced in 2003–5.

I left to join UPD5, the Urban Planning Directorate of the Ministry of Housing, to work on Deeplish in Rochdale and later at Barnsbury in Islington: two more underrated corners and another story …

THE WATER GARDENS, BURWOOD PLACE, LONDON W2

Client: Burwood Place Development Co., a wholly owned subsidiary of the Church Commissioners.

Project Management: Chestertons. Project Manager *John Hollamby*

Architect: Trehearne & Norman, Preston & Partners.
Partner in charge: *George Gneditch FRIBA (d.1999)*
Associate in charge: *Chris Whittaker*
Design Architect: *Ed Lucey*
Architects for Sussex Gardens and adjoining block: *Max Honigsfeld & David Goldhill*
Assistants: *Alex Lane, Peter Wood, Bob Burchett* et al.

Landscape Architect: *Philip Hicks*

Quantity Surveyor: G.D. Walford & Partners.

Acting Partner *Geoffrey Armstrong*

Structural Engineer: T.C. Durley, Hill & Partners. Acting Partner *Michael Bunn*

General Contractor: Wates Ltd

Heating & Ventilating: Young, Austen & Young

Electrical: Rashleigh Phipps

Plumbing and Drainage: Ellis (Kensington)

Windows: Cawood Wharton (Silux windows)

External tiling: Langleys of London (Villeroy & Boch)

Pre-cast concrete with tiles as permanent shuttering: Trent & Hoveringham

Cills: Ajax Aluminium

10 Cluster Homes Planning and Housing in Cumbernauld New Town

MILES GLENDINNING

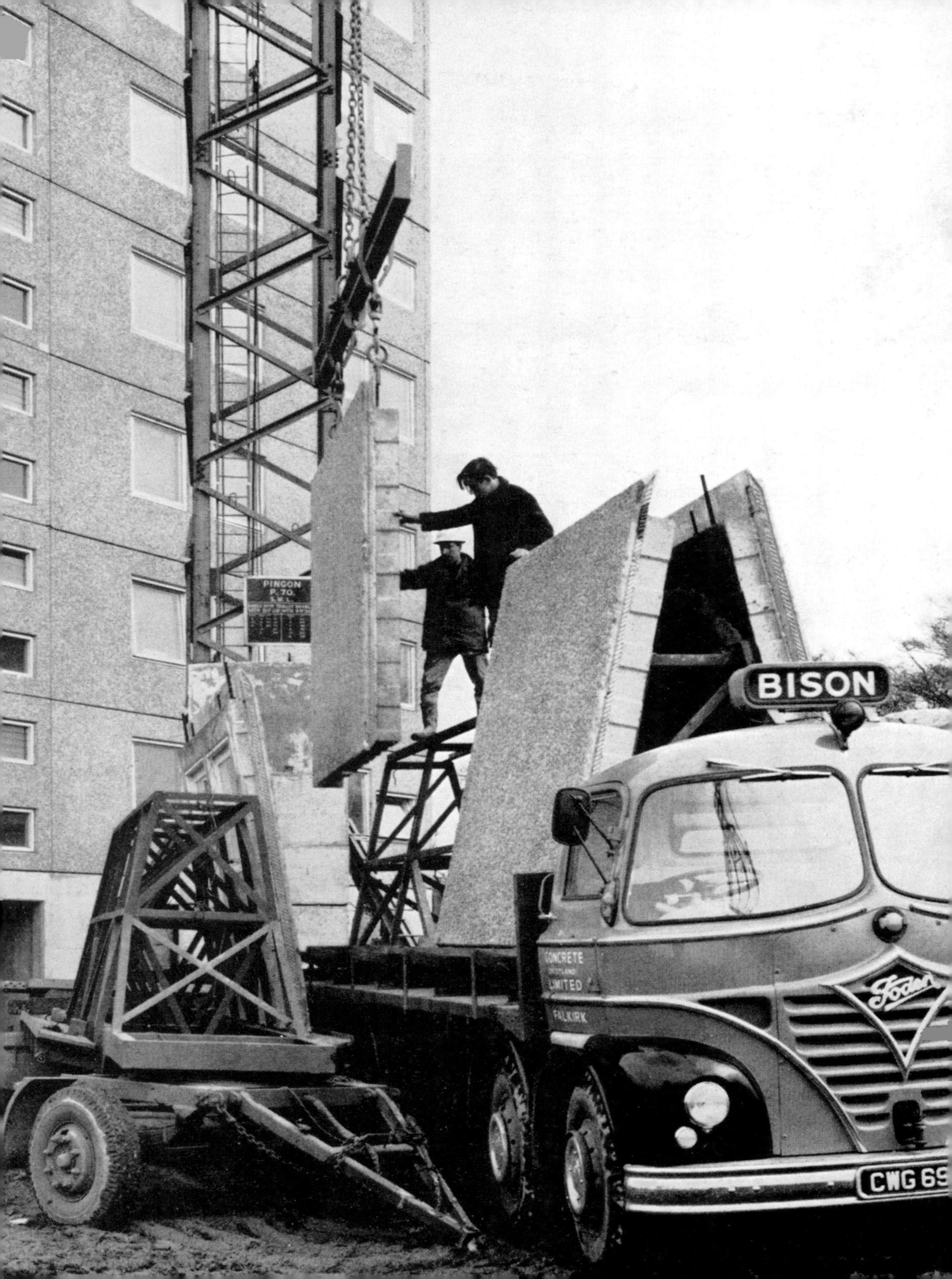
BISON
PINGON
P.70.
S.W.L.
CONCRETE
LIMITED
FALKIRK
Foden
CWG 69

Cluster Homes: Planning and Housing in Cumbernauld New Town

MILES GLENDINNING

H ousing in the new towns of Britain was both typical and exceptional. It was typical in the broad architectural-planning context of the Modern Movement, in the sense that that the completely new, planned town was one of the central symbols of international modernism in the mid-twentieth century. Leafing through the 1,200-page *Encyclopaedia of Urban Planning* compendium published by McGraw-Hill in 1974, written by a vast, multi-national authorial team, one finds country after country proudly presenting projects for new settlements laid out on rationalist Modern Movement lines with plentiful light and air, zoned segregation of uses, and *Zeilenbau* layouts of slab blocks of mass housing and offices in free-space parallel or rectilinear arrangements.[1] These settlements varied in size, prestige and politico-economic context from the new capital of Brasilia down to the more mundane industrial towns built by communist regimes, but they all had in common a recognisably Modern Movement spatial form, and a special focus on the building of 'community' as an aspect of the wider pursuit of progress through provision of housing and other social building programmes.

But the new towns were also exceptional, in the specifically British context of the organisation and patronage of twentieth-century mass housing. The powerful local political leaders who dominated municipal public housing looked on the new town programme with suspicion if not outright hostility, as a creation of central government and an outgrowth of the regional planning movement, calculated to siphon off their population and undermine their status. In this polarised context, the housing architects of the new towns saw their work in implicitly political terms, in opposition to the supposedly utilitarian, coarse, engineer-dominated dwellings built by most municipalities. Part of that assumed superiority, of course, stemmed from the fact that new town housing was not designed in isolation but, in each case, formed an integral part of an overall plan and community vision of the town. In the first or 'Mark I' new towns inaugurated by the 1946 New Towns Act, such as East Kilbride, Harlow or Stevenage, such integration was a rather loose affair, for the prevailing garden city planning paradigm structured them in a zoned, segregated pattern of 'neighbourhood units', each separated by greenery from each other and from the town centre. The overwhelming necessity seemed to be to contrast the new planned, spacious communities with the evils of the old, dense mixed-together *laissez-faire* city. But after the 1950s' revolt against this ideology, and the swing towards concepts of higher-density 'urbanity', the situation changed fundamentally.[2] If any fresh new towns were to be designated, they would be designed on far more tightly integrated lines, less strongly polarised against the 'urban'. So when, for reasons connected with the forceful regional planning movement in West Central Scotland, the Scottish Office decided in 1955 to designate a new town at Cumbernauld, fifteen miles north-east of Glasgow, the project immediately became the focus of intense interest among 'urban' minded architects and planners, especially in the south of England.[3]

The parallel, more practical narrative of reconstruction within Scottish and

1. Arnold Whittick, ed., *Encyclopedia of Urban Planning*, New York, McGraw-Hill, 1974.

2. J.M. Richards, 'Failure of the New Towns', *Architectural Review*, vol.114, no.679, July 1953, pp.28–32.

3. Ian Levitt, 'New Towns, New Scotland, New Ideology', *Scottish Historical Review*, vol.76, no.202, October 1997, pp.222–38.

Figure 1. Erecting cladding panel, Bison blocks, north-west Cumbernauld.

British culture goes back to the eighteenth-century beginnings of 'Improve-ment', a long-term strategy which bifurcated during the twentieth century into violently competing strands of activity between the municipalities and the new towns. Within Scotland, this narrative took a semi-autonomous form, with Cumbernauld forming the third of a post-war series of five completely new planned towns: East Kilbride, begun in 1947, Glenrothes from 1948, Cumbernauld from 1955, Livingston from 1962, and Irvine from 1966.[4]

This article traces the ideas that drove the initial conception of Cumbernauld New Town, and especially of its housing zone. This was above all a rather intel-lectual architectural-planning discourse, carried on at a national or international level, both through the public rhetoric of international mid-twentieth century Modern Movement planning and order, as well as the more individualistic avant-garde new groupings like Team 10 and the Independent Group. This was seen, for example, when in 1967 the American Institute of Architects awarded Cumbernauld the prestigious R. S. Reynolds Memorial Award for Community Archi-tecture, preferring it to Tapiola in Finland, and Stockholm – both themselves renowned centres of modernist planning – and hailing it as 'the most significant current contribution to the art and science of urban design in the western world'. Cumbernauld, the jury proclaimed, was designed 'for the millennium'... 'the dreams of the 1920s and 1930s are being built on a hill near Glasgow'.[5]

At Cumbernauld the housing areas of a new town were related to the overall town concept, making the overall town-plan as important as the housing itself. Despite the pervasive concept of dense integration, for organisational reasons the town was still quite strongly polarised between its different components.

FROM 'FUNCTIONAL PLANNING' TO 'URBANITY'

The intellectual context from which Cumbernauld New Town sprang was the long-running post-war conflict over the question of what constituted the best physical setting for urban life. Following the tradition first established by Pugin in the 1830s, this conflict took the form of successive, mutually opposed visions, or Utopias, each establishing itself by attacking its predecessors. During the as-cendancy of modern architecture in Britain – from c.1940 to c.1970 – there were two broad phases of this kind: the first 'heroic' period up to the early 1950s, and a later, more complex period centred on the early 1960s and lasting until the rejec-tion of modern design by avant-gardists in the late 1960s and 1970s. Cumbernauld is one of the key monuments of the latter. The well-spread, geometrical planning principles of the first period, the International Modern, were grounded in appar-ently simple, slogan-like ideas, some of which were rationalistic ('functional' or 'need-fit' planning) and others social or moral in orientation (the ideal of 'com-munity').[6] The second phase of modern architecture was more complicated and more abstruse. Some Utopian catchwords remained in use from the earlier pe-riod, such as 'community' or 'urbanity', but their stylistic and theoretical associa-tions changed completely. The Reynolds Memorial Award jury may have selected Cumbernauld as the world's most outstanding example of 'community architec-ture', yet its planning conception and style contrasted utterly with anything that International Modern architects would have understood by that term.

What, then, were the key values and theories of this second phase of modern urbanism? The idea of 'urbanity' received much greater stress, and was elabo-rated into a Utopia of dense agglomeration and urban life by those high priests of the new movement, Alison and Peter Smithson, and labelled as 'Cluster City'. Even the new town movement was influenced by these innovations.[7] From the end of the 1950s, the emphasis on dense 'urbanity' was complemented by a fur-ther utopian idea, 'mobility', which sprang from the unprecedented affluence of those years, above all from the suddenly increasing levels of private car owner-ship. American consumerism, with its ethos of freedom, was the inspiration.[8] The potential conflict between these two demands – concentration and mobility

4. David Cowling, *An Essay for Today, The Scottish New Towns, 1947–1997*, Edinburgh, Rutland Press, 1997, pp.48–70.

5. 'Stockholm, Tapiola, Cumbernauld – from Three emerged One', *American Insti-tute of Architects Journal*, vol.48, no.1, July 1967, pp.36–58.

6. Le Corbusier, *La Charte d'Athènes*, Paris, Editions de Minuit, 1957; Eric Mumford, *The CIAM Discourse of Urbanism*, Cam-bridge, MIT, 2000; Nicholas Bullock, *Build-ing the Postwar World*, London, Routledge, 2002; Dennis Sharp, ed., *The Rationalists*, London, Architectural Press, 1978; Alan Colquhoun, *Modern Architecture*, London, Oxford University Press, 2002.

7. Lionel Esher, 'The Environmentalists (SPUR)', *Architectural Review*, vol.125, no.748, 1959, pp.303–5.

8. Ian McCallum, ed., 'Machine Made America', *Architectural Review*, vol.121, no.724, May 1957, pp.293–394; Alison and Peter Smithson, 'Mobility', *Architectural De-sign*, vol.28, no.10, October 1958, pp.385–8.

Figure 2. Visit to Cumbernauld of the Right
Hon. Richard Crossman, MP, Minister of
Housing and Local Government, accompanied by General Sir Gordon H. A. Macmil-
lan and L. Hugh Wilson, 13 February 1965.

– provided the designers of these years with their greatest challenge and stimulus.
Naturally, there were underlying issues of power and status at stake. Just as the
architects of the 1960s (unsuccessfully) contested control of prefabricated building with the contractors, so, too, it seemed vital to them that traffic and circulation
should be secured as the province of the designer rather than the engineer, and
of the architect as well as (or even instead of) the planner. Yet the new movement was also bound up with its own, compelling set of Utopian values: to the
Smithsons, the 'identity' of a town depended partly on the proper expression of
the different experiences of vehicle users and pedestrians.[9]

How could one reconcile density and mobility? To the designers of the late
1950s and early 1960s, there seemed only one way: by complete segregation of ve-
hicles and pedestrians. And, in some ways, it was the Mark II New Town projects
– beginning with Cumbernauld and the London County Council's Hook New
Town, Hampshire (designed in 1957–60 largely by Hugh Morris, with Graeme
Shankland and Oliver Cox), that provided the most unfettered opportunities
for designers to put this separation into practice. Although Hook was never
built, it was widely recognised by contemporary commentators, both in Britain and abroad, as 'profoundly influenced' by Cumbernauld: in January 1963
L'Architecture d'Aujourd'hui pointed to the two projects, together, as spearheads
of ' la nouvelle doctrine anglaise d'urbanisme'.[10] In the residential areas of Mark
II New Towns, this was not difficult to achieve, as the density (although higher
than the likes of Harlow) was still sufficiently low to allow horizontal segregation,
through 'Radburn' layouts of separate pedestrian ways and vehicular routes. The
only significant vertical elements were grade separated junctions and – at Runcorn – elevated busways. These features were incorporated in all the later Mark
II New Towns – Skelmersdale or Irvine as much as pioneering Cumbernauld.
But Cumbernauld attempted to combine residential areas and centre into one
dramatic image – that of a hilltop city, with a town-centre acropolis ringed by
terraced tiers of housing and outcrops of slender point blocks.

Owing to the fervent expectations aroused by the project among younger,
'urbanist'-minded architects in London and the south of England, and the ability of a New Town Development Corporation to operate autonomously from the
local context, virtually the entire initial design staff of Cumbernauld comprised
young and somewhat avant-garde English architects and architect-planners.

9. Miles Glendinning and Stephan Muthesius, *Tower Block, Modern Public Housing
in England, Scotland, Wales and Northern
Ireland*, London, Yale University Press,
1994, esp. pp.121–31.

10. 'Une Importante Expérience Anglaise:
La Nouvelle Ville de Cumbernauld', *Archi-
tecture d'Aujourd'hui*, no.106, February-
March 1963, pp.13–15. Oliver Cox confirmed
the Hook connection in conversation with
Elain Harwood, 25 September 2002.

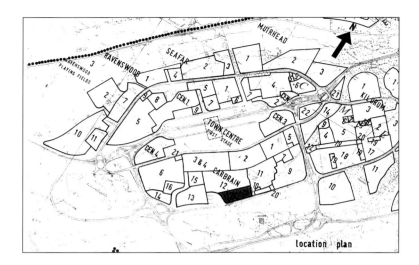

location plan

Figure 3. Plan of Cumbernauld housing areas.

They were led by L. Hugh Wilson, previously City Architect of Canterbury. While essentially of the late 1940s' 'picturesque' generation, he was determined, in the manner first established by Robert Matthew at the LCC, to use his department's autonomy, armed with 'the awesome powers presented by new towns legislation,' to nurture radicals of the next generation and make Cumbernauld a testbed of international standing for the new ideas of urban design.[11] By 1962, the *Architects' Journal* was duly able to talk confidently of 'the reputation Cumbernauld has earned as a fundamental advance on the Mark I new towns'. As was usual in a new town, a local small country house – in this case, William Adam's classical Cumbernauld House of c.1742 – was taken over as the Development Corporation headquarters. At first all the staff worked in this house, and Wilson recalled in 1963 the 'heady atmosphere... [with] all the chaps working in one large room'.[12] As the town grew, the Corporation expanded into a small village of system-built extensions, laid out to form a landscaped rear courtyard, and built on the Vic Hallam 'Derwent' system originally developed for school construction.

Wilson's team set out to show that it would be possible to build a new settlement that conformed to the demand for much lower densities than old, overcrowded Glasgow, yet denser and more monumental than the Mark I new towns, evoking urban vitality. Due to mineral and farming restrictions and local-political pressures, the site selected was a low, ridge-like hill, with the small existing village of Cumbernauld just to its north. In their preliminary planning proposals of April 1958, responding to this site, they chose to go for a concentrated plan. There would be no separated-out neighbourhoods, but a single wide band of housing ringing the hill. This would be arranged in low but quite dense groups, many in rows rather like nineteenth-century industrial housing, but this density would be offset by the broad incisions of a full grade-separated highway system, with pedestrians catered for by a fully segregated footpath system. And in contrast to the Mark I towns, with their blurred junction between residential units and surrounding countryside, there would be a very sharp separation at Cumbernauld, with dramatic forest landscaping designed by the staff of the corporation's young landscape architect, Bill Gillespie.

Most dramatically of all, not without argument, it was decided to set the town centre right on the top of the ridge. From this decision, doubtless taken with the popular late–1950s Italian hilltop city image in mind, stemmed a number of important planning and architectural consequences. Unlike all previous new towns, vehicle-pedestrian segregation would need to be designed right into the centre, in a fitting way for this post-war age of 'urbanity' and 'mobility'. This brought to the fore a conflict inherent in the new planning ideas. If the town was

11. Geoffrey Copcutt, 'Cumbernauld New Town Centre in Retrospect' (1995), in Miles Glendinning, ed., *Rebuilding Scotland, The Postwar Vision 1945–1975*, East Linton, Tuckwell Press, 1997, pp.89–92; Glendinning and Muthesius, *op.cit*, pp.13–14, 55–60.

12. L. Hugh Wilson, 'New Town Design – Cumbernauld and After', *RIBA Journal*, vol.71, no.5, May 1964, pp.191–206.

to be more dense, and not split up into neighbourhoods with local services, then the town centre structures must themselves become very large and dominant – aspiring to a grandeur not seen since the heroic classical projects produced by the Schools of Architecture under Albert Richardson and Charles Reilly in the inter-war years. Simultaneously, they had to accommodate the unprecedented demands of the motor vehicle, so that horizontal segregation was irrelevant. Wilson's team concluded that the only possible solution was vertical separation with, at the same time, an integration of functions – including housing – within 'a single envelope'. By spring 1959, Wilson could say in a journal article that the centre 'will probably be multi-level in character'.[13] His team was able to draw on a lively architectural debate that was already well under way – and, with their solution, to make a powerful contribution to that debate.

Wilson's desire to foster an LCC-style diversity of group-working, in conjunction with the interruptions of the 'cluster' plan by the highway system, encouraged a sharp architectural polarisation between the different elements of the town. In 1959, he appointed two deputy architect-planners – Derek Lyddon and Geoffrey Copcutt – both fervent urbanists, as group leaders, with Lyddon in charge of the housing zone and the flamboyant and eccentric Copcutt taking the town centre. In 1995, Copcutt recalled that, 'reporting on the same day, Derek Lyddon and I cordially agreed (Sir Hugh refereeing) to toss for duties. Derek had the pipe, the coin and the call, I had the beard and the prayer. ... Those to whom it may seem that the toss was a poor deal for the centre can be consoled that the rest of the town was spared my attentions.'[14] From that division stemmed the radical diversity that followed. The low-rise industrial estates and the fairly monumental secondary schools, ringing the outside of the housing area, effectively formed a further layer of zoned functions.

'A CANONICAL MEGASTRUCTURE'? CUMBERNAULD TOWN CENTRE AND THE NEW BRUTALISM

How would Copcutt's team set about planning their multi-level town centre? Before the problems posed by the motor car became fully evident, a series of unbuilt projects in the 1950s had responded to the demand for greater density in central areas by advocating the building of single large structures into which all functions could be incorporated, with traffic and services on lower levels, and residential, commercial and administrative uses above. Perhaps the most influential of these studies was Sergei Kadleigh's High Paddington project of 1952, which proposed the construction of massive towers, containing a great variety of uses, above railway yards at Paddington Station. But only in the early 1960s,

13 . L. Hugh Wilson, 'Cumbernauld', *Prospect* (RIAS Journal), no.13, Spring 1959, pp.12–17.

14. Geoffrey Copcutt, 'Cumbernauld New Town Centre in Retrospect' (1995), Miles Glendinning, ed., *Rebuilding Scotland, the Postwar Vision*, East Linton, Tuckwell Press, 1997, p.92.

15. Alison and Peter Smithson, 'Cluster City, A New Shape for the Community', *Architectural Review*, vol.122, no.730, November 1957, pp.333–6.

Figure 4. Cumbernauld Town Centre (model).

Figure 5. An aerial view of the town centre with the Phase Two newly completed on the left (1971). The surrounding empty space was intended for future expansion of the centre.

Figure 6. A sketch of the town centre in use.

Figure 7. Cumbernauld Town Centre (Phase One) in 1977, from the south-east, showing the bridges linking the now-demolished podium and the main 'megastructure'.

under the stimulus of the motor age, was this new multi-purpose urban building concept fully developed, and given its definitive name, 'megastructure'.

The notion of architectural design of traffic-separated structures had been pioneered on paper several decades before by Antonio Sant-Elia, and more recently by Le Corbusier.[15] 'Deck-access' housing, incorporating pedestrian streets at upper levels, had been devised by the Smithsons in their Golden Lane competition project of 1952 – partly inspired by Le Corbusier's Unité d'Habitation, Marseilles, and had been built on a large scale from 1957 at Park Hill, designed by Ivor Smith and Jack Lynn of the Sheffield City Architect's Department. These projects found a visual stimulus in the vertical stratification of circulation routes, and the incorporation of some commercial functions into essentially residential

buildings. Also in Sheffield, megastructural planning ideas were embodied in a multi-storey market built in 1958–9 in the city centre, designed by Andrew Derbyshire of the City Architect's Department.[16]

The ideas that eventually coalesced into megastructures were also much debated in the mid- and late 1950s by 'Team 10', an international group of young architects. Team 10, with the Smithsons at its literary fore, was partly responsible for the undermining of the original modern architectural establishment and the propagation of New Brutalist ideas. In 1958–9, Ralph Erskine, a young Stockholm-based member of the group, put forward designs for an 'Arctic City', which in some ways presaged Cumbernauld Town Centre in its conception of a fortified outer shell protecting from the elements a huddle of interpenetrating indoor-outdoor spaces. Megastructural thinking also influenced the design of the partly enclosed, layered centre, with flying bridges and jutting balconies, that Erskine had built at Luleå in 1954. Other cosmopolitan avant-garde groups, such as the French-based Situationists and the Japanese Metabolists, were working on parallel lines.[17]

However, it was only at Cumbernauld that a complete vision of a megastructure was to be realised. A few other dramatic agglomeration-buildings were completed in other countries around 1967, but were limited to a smaller range of functions: commercial, transport and a hotel in the case of Montréal's Place Bonaventure, and purely residential in the same city's 'Habitat' for Expo 67. The megastructure was not just a planning concept. It responded to more general architectural demands, bound up with the wildly fluctuating fashions of urban

16. Glendinning and Muthesius, *op.cit*, pp.121–31; Alison and Peter Smithson, *The Charged Void: Architecture*, New York, Monacelli Press, 2001; Dirk van den Huevel and Max Risselada, eds., *Alison and Peter Smithson, from the House of the Future to a House of Today*, Rotterdam, 010 Publishers, 2004.

17. Yona Friedman, 'Résumé du Programme de 'Urbanisme mobile (1957), in Friedman, *L'Architecture Mobile, vers une Cité Conçue par ses Habitants*, Tournai, Casterman, 1970, pp.62–4; Mark Wigley, *Constant's New Babylon*, Rotterdam, 010 Publishers, 1998; Libero Andreotti and Xavier Costa eds, *Situationists*, Barcelona, Museu d'Art Contemporani, 1996.

mass-housing design. The most avant-garde 1950s designers rejected the simple unified forms and the straightforward rectangular blocks favoured by the International Moderns either on their own or in juxtaposed 'mixed developments', where various household types were expressed in contrasting housing types from point block to terraced house.[18] Instead they demanded large complex structures, made of clusters of individually distinct but subordinate parts. Such structures typically took the form of ruggedly-modelled pyramids rather than clean rectangular towers or slabs. The almost geological or biological concept of megastructure culminated in attempts by some architects to create an artificial 'terrain' for housing or multi-function complexes through multi-level podiums, for instance at the Barbican, at Thamesmead, and in Michael Neylan's pioneering 'low-rise, high-density' scheme at Bishopsfield, Harlow. Another variation on this idea was that of terracing or inverted terracing (the so-called 'stadium' section), as built by Lasdun at Christ's College, Cambridge, and the University of East Anglia, or by Camden architect Neave Brown at Alexandra Road, Hampstead.

The New Brutalists' repudiation of simplicity in favour of complication did not imply any kind of wholesale rejection of architectural 'image-making' in its own right, rather the opposite. The late '50s and '60s saw architects' images and rhetoric attaining unprecedented levels of confidence, and prefiguring aspects of today's metaphor-laden 'Iconic Modernism'. Copcutt hailed his creation at Cumbernauld as a 'single citadel-like structure'. This bold new architectural trend fitted in very well with the planning ideal of megastructure. Just as in public housing the tall point or slab block were rejected in favour of medium-height deck-access groups, so the field of town centre redevelopment projects witnessed a move from the tall, gleaming towers of High Paddington to jagged mound-like or linear structures, a tendency which reached its climax at Cumbernauld Town Centre. In 1977, the *Architects' Journal* recalled the startling impact of the first phase on its completion: it had 'looked as if it was by Corb out of Sant'Elia'.[19] In fact the Centre's squatting bulk was very different to the relative verticality of Sant'Elia's and Corbusier's multi-level proposals, harking back to other early-modern precedents: even, in some ways, to the massive, sprawling *Stadtkrone* proposed by Bruno Taut.[20]

Among realisations of New Brutalist 'terrain' building, the rugged heaping up of Cumbernauld Centre on its south side was one of the boldest of all. In keeping with the Brutalist insistence on sharp separation of frame and infill, its main structure was a massive reinforced concrete skeleton, built in ruggedly shuttered form, with a bewildering range of infill structures including shops, a library and civic offices. As Copcutt said in 1995, it was 'a central infrastructure of highways and walkways, layers and ledges promising shelter, warmth and family freedom'.[21] In a further, flamboyant element of structural differentiation, the 'penthouse' executive housing which crowned the whole mound was supported by a separate line of six slab columns, punching their way up through the rest, rather in the manner of Rudolph Schindler's Lovell Beach House in Los Angeles; the penthouse range was proudly exposed at either end in hammer-head cross-section form, and bristled at the top with grey concrete protuberances. In a piece Copcutt wrote in a special issue of *Architectural Design* devoted to Cumbernauld in May 1963, he made clear the 'iconic' role of the penthouses in defining the building as an acropolis or *Stadtkrone*. The Centre was to be 'a single citadel-like structure nearly half a mile long ... a drive-in town centre ... a vast terminal facility [within which] all decks are perforated and interpenetrating, resulting in relatively narrow bands of development with continually changing views out of and through the centre. Within the centre all planes are inhabited both above and below until the final statement is made by long terraces of penthouses.'[22]

The move towards more irregular horizontal groupings had one further implication – although it would have been hotly denied at the time, amounting to another reformulation of the British Picturesque tradition. The earlier Moderns

18. Alison and Peter Smithson, 'House in Soho', *Architectural Design*, vol.23, no.12, December 1953, p.342; 'The New Brutalism', *AD*, vol.25, no.1, January 1955, p.1; 'The New Brutalism', *AD*, vol.27, no.4, April 1957, p.113; Reyner Banham, 'The New Brutalism', *Architectural Review*, vol.118, no.708, December 1955, pp.355–61; *The New Brutalism*, London, Architectural Press, 1966; *Megastructure, Urban Futures of the Recent Past*, London, Architectural Press, 1976; Bullock, *op.cit*, pp.151–67.

19. *Architects' Journal*, vol.166, no.40, 5 October 1977, 637–649.

20. Jim and Krystyna Johnson, 'Cumbernauld Revisited', *Architects' Journal*, vol.40, no.166, 5 October 1977, p.644; Banham, *Megastructure, op.cit*., pp.167–72.

21. Copcutt, *op.cit.*, p.89.

22. L. Hugh Wilson, D. R. Leader and Geoffrey Copcutt, 'Cumbernauld New Town Central Area', *Architectural Design*, vol.33, no.5, May 1963, pp.210–25.

Figure 8. Cumbernauld from the air, mid-1960s, from the west. Seafar is to the left (the further group of tower blocks).

had espoused asymmetry, but within the finite framework of closed compositions. The new cry was for 'open-ended' designs, for buildings looking as if they
could be extended or adapted. The end facades (to east and west) of Cumbernauld Town Centre Phase One are paradigms of 'extensible' design: almost every
feature, no matter how elaborate on section, is starkly chopped off at right-angles
at either end – in order, theoretically, to allow for future extension. The choice of
this linear model of expansion, however, meant that the town centre zone was
dominated for many years by gaping unbuilt sites at either end.

THE HOUSING CARPET: AN ARCHITECTURE OF 'SETTLEMENT'

Paradoxically, given the strong affinities between Cumbernauld Town Centre and
contemporary high-density housing design, the housing zone expressed 'density'
in a very different way. In its complex overlaying of functional and infrastructural
elements, the concept of the entire town expressed the growing fascination of
architects in the late 1950s and 1960s such as Constantinos Doxiadis and Kenzo
Tange with 'network' planning, a concept of the built environment in biological,
even prosthetic terms that pointed forward to today's concepts of dematerialised,
digital architecture and global internet communication. Although Buckminster
Fuller and others welcomed the implicit possibility of complete dissolution of
conventional architecture in favour of a 'formless' hyper-mobility, and a move
from 'settlement' to 'unsettlement', British architecture of the Brutalist era, with
its strong love of the gritty industrial city, was not prepared to countenance any
such radical disembedding formula.[23]

    At Cumbernauld, therefore, the primadonna cosmopolitanism of the Centre
contrasts strongly with the surrounding belt of housing designed by Lyddon's
team. This was treated, in effect, as a muted backdrop to the fireworks in the

23. Mark Wigley, 'Network Fever', *Grey Room*, no.4, Summer 2001, pp.82–122

middle, firmly anchoring the town while protecting its provocative, unsettling character. Its general concept related not to the stacked forms of medium-rise high-density but to the different, but parallel, patterns of 'low-rise high-density' housing. The layout was a typical early 1960s continuous 'carpet' or 'mesh', low in overall height, but deliberately denser than Garden City or inter-war CIAM patterns. The governing concept of space was one of enclosed space in the manner of Camillo Sitte rather than open or flowing space. The relatively muted character of the housing areas was emphasised by the collective way in which they were designed by various 'teams' within the Development Corporation architects' department – a sharp contrast with the individualistic work of Copcutt within the same office. That contrast, in turn, reflected the polarisation within Modernism between extreme artistic individualism and self-effacing concern with 'programme'. But the muted character was relative at most. The group system set up by J. H. Forshaw at the London County Council's Architect's Department in 1944 was meant to encourage highly varied solutions for public housing within an overall urban framework, and Cumbernauld's diversity was a resounding example of this principle in action. Writing in his diary following a 1965 visit to Cumbernauld, the (English) Housing Minister, Richard Crossman, reported his enthusiasm, and that of his Permanent Secretary, Dame Evelyn Sharp, for its 'tremendously austere, exhilarating, uncomfortable' concept: 'This is the kind of thing which Dame Evelyn and I are excited about, in contrast to the cosy, garden-suburb atmosphere of Stevenage or Harlow or Basildon, [about which] the Dame, of course, was contemptuous. She loves Cumbernauld.'[24]

Knitting this controlled diversity together were the two unifying elements of the infrastructure and the landscaping. Post-CIAM Modernists were no different to their Functionalist predecessors in taking a major practical requirement, in this case, the demand for total pedestrian-vehicle segregation, making it into a symbolic *leitmotif* and 'artistically' extrapolating it into a complex design solution. The grade separated hierarchy of paths and roads, and the Radburn system of segregated pedestrian/car access to dwellings, was interwoven by Bill Gillespie's team into the *genius loci* of the site, and its potentially disorientating 'network' character was embedded into a natural and built landscaping scheme intended to accentuate the 'localisation' of Cumbernauld's new housing. The south-east side was treated as hard and urban, with paved squares and streets, while the north-west was dealt with in a manner inspired by Scandinavian landscaping, intended to express the contrast between the town and the open country: a new 'forest' was interwoven with the dwellings, together with wild features like clumps of rocks. This pervasiveness of 'design', with landscape architecture the essential lubricant, marked the town at every turn from what was seen as the

24. Richard Crossman, *The Diaries of a Cabinet Minister*, vol.1, 1975, 1976 edition, London, Hamish Hamilton, pp.158–9.

Figure 9. Seafar 1, plans and evaluations by Cumbernauld Development Corporation.

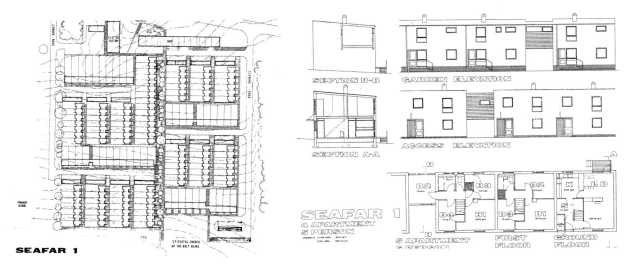

Figure 10. Kildrum 17 and 18, plans and elevations by Cumbernauld Development Corporation.

Figure 11. Seafar 3, Cumbernauld.

tastelessly discordant regimentation of municipal housing controlled by engineers. However, the housing zone also had another, less satisfactory border, the 'inner' one with the town centre, whose raggedly half-built expanses incongruously confronted the tightly planned housing.

As mere dwellings, Cumbernauld's housing types – terraced cottages and low flats, with some high blocks – were not dissimilar to the Mark I new-town housing of places like East Kilbride or Harlow; but their architectural form and layout were treated in a far more dense and place-specific way. Paradoxically, their 'advanced' character lay partly in their move away from the standardised solutions formerly thought to be an essential aspect of modernity, towards more complex forms partly influenced by 'tradition'. The oval-doughnut shaped housing zone was divided into a north-west side, facing over a steep escarpment across to the Campsie Fells, and a flatter south-east side, sloping gently away from the town centre. Accordingly, the south-east side was given a more homogeneous and more overtly modern treatment: many of its terraces of houses were flat-roofed with elements of *Zeilenbau* planning and strong rectilinear design. In the Carbrain area, for example, there were grid-like layouts of straight, boxy terraces somewhat reminiscent of J.J.P. Oud's Kiefhoek housing, but finished in grey rather than white render. What was consistently avoided, though, in the Radburn layouts, was anything smacking of 'front and back' facades along 'streets'.

The steeper north-west side was given a more abrupt and even picturesque layout. Here, much of the low housing is laid out in densely irregular rows along lanes with steep, swept-down roofs and lines of repetitive outshots, in an artistic, Sittesque reworking of nineteenth-century industrial patterns – following the terraced miners' housing found in nearby areas of Lanarkshire or West Lothian, or the older housing of small Scottish industrial towns. Along with some of the housing interventions in historic towns designed by practices like Wheeler and Sproson, these could almost be seen as harbingers of the 1970s movement towards 'neo-vernacular' architecture, especially in the 'pend' openings and steep steps that linked the different levels. Other groups of houses, especially in the sharply contoured Seafar area, comprise intricate courtyard-type arrangements of dwellings with split-level plans. For diversity, the areas were designed and built in relatively small numbers by different groups under Lyddon's overall aegis; each was designated by the name of the area (*not* 'neighbourhood' – Cumbernauld has none of those) followed by section number. The areas used standard types of terraced cottages, built throughout the town but scattered and individually laid out. One widely praised example was Seafar 2, built in 1961–3, comprising 147 dwellings in two-storey split-level terraced cottages.[25] Here, to exploit the dramatic hillside site, the blocks are irregularly staggered and set in very heavy landscaping, with boulders, cobbled slopes and pends inter-penetrating the rows.

There were only two exceptions or offshoots from this unified town plan –

25. This was a Saltire Society housing design winner in 1963. 'Pend' is a Scottish word for an archway spanning a (usually) pedestrian route.

both of them also treated in a highly nucleated manner. The first was the original Cumbernauld village, standing about a third of a mile to the north. This dense grouping of mainly nineteenth-century housing, arranged on the pattern of long, narrow 'burgage plot' patterns to north and south of a winding main street, was infilled around the edges with new development, providing an immediate, if loose, precedent for some of the new patterns of the town. The second stemmed from a 1965 decision to expand the town, while respecting the integrity of the original plan, with Abronhill, a miniature version of the main town, about a mile to the north-east, with its own microcosmic town centre abutted by low, dense housing clusters and ringed by woodland.

While the overall concept of the housing was that of the low-rise high density carpet – a very early example of a pattern which later became ubiquitous across Britain as an alternative to high-rise building – Cumbernauld also exhibited the older 1950s pattern termed mixed development, with various types and heights of blocks including tower blocks as a punctuation, seen most famously in the LCC's Roehampton complex. Wilson shared with his contemporaries a liking for varied visual effects, associated with the elastic word 'townscape' represented by the writings of Gordon Cullen, but which the most up-to-date Brutalists condemned as excessively pictorial and meretricious. Thus, the overall carpet of the housing areas was punctuated by larger accents.

These higher blocks of flats fell into two basic categories: high point blocks and medium- or low-rise walk-up flats. The point blocks provided the most prominent punctuation of the low housing, and adopted a more straightforward and even (by the early 1960s) old-fashioned modernism in their design. They were concentrated on the north-west side, dotted among the terraces in 1940s Swedish fashion as landmarks along the town's escarpment, to house middle-income 'executive' tenants and provide a skyline signature. Most were standard twelve-storey towers, with four flats on each floor, built from 1964, using the contractor-designed Bison prefabricated concrete panel system, manufactured in Falkirk at Concrete Ltd's works, and brought to Cumbernauld by road. Bison was liked among architects as a system amenable to site-specific design while maintaining a high standard of precision in detailing – the smooth grey-whiteness of the aggregate finish contrasted strikingly with the rougher finish of the low terraces. Examples include Seafar 3, a group of three towers of 1964–5 just next to Seafar 2. In 1967–8, a more highly individualised group was built at Kildrum 22, immediately overlooking the town's most important flyover expressway junction, the Muirhead-Braehead

Figure 12. Formal terraces of maisonettes in Abronhill facing a central promenade, 1966.

Figure 13. Patio housing, Kildrum.

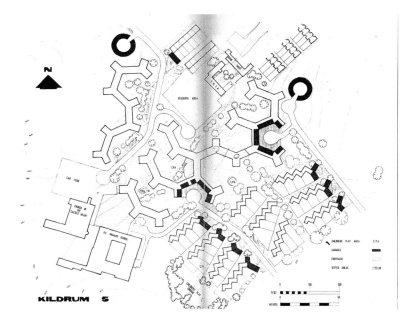

Figure 14. Kildrum 5, 1959–61, planned in polygonal interlocking groupings strikingly indebted to Backstrom and Reinius's Gröndal housing in Stockholm.

Interchange, at the north end of the summit of the ridge; it included two twelve-storey point blocks and one of twenty storeys, to give the town the crowning, San Gimignano-like visual punctuation that the crushing bulk of the town centre could not provide.[26]

Medium-rise flats were evenly interspersed throughout the entire housing belt. Some were arranged as isolated strips, others in denser squares, such as a 1961 development by Gillespie, Kidd and Coia adjacent to the Muirhead-Brae-head Interchange. Others took the form of medium-rise Bison slab blocks cutting across the low-rise fabric (all since demolished). One of the very earliest groups, Kildrum 5 (built in 1959–61), was planned in polygonal interlocking groupings strikingly indebted to the 1946 precedent of Backstrom and Reinius's influential Gröndal housing project in Stockholm. It contained 273 dwellings in terraced cottages and three-storey grouped 'Y' blocks designed by CDC project architect Ron Simpson, and grouped around open hexagonal courtyards, to create a sense of enclosure on a fairly sloping site. In contrast to Gröndal's 'rigid' hexagonal angles, Simpson designed Kildrum 5 using a 135 degree angle, which created more irregular groupings, creating a strong townscape heightened by carefully designed setts and other street details. Other punctuations to the low-rise housing fabric were provided by the relatively few local public buildings allowed under the centralised Cumbernauld formula – chiefly churches and schools. These were just about the only buildings in Cumbernauld not designed by the Development Corporation staff, and almost all went to private architects such as Gillespie, Kidd and Coia or Reiach and Hall.

DECAY AND DENIGRATION: CUMBERNAULD TODAY

Cumbernauld's planning concepts were diluted in subsequent British new towns, even as they spread more widely abroad – for example, to the hyper-density new towns programme of the Hong Kong Housing Authority from the 1970s to the 1990s, with mini-cities such as Sha Tin. More recently, Cumbernauld has fallen on hard times, with its international architectural reputation for the moment forgotten following successive phases of architectural polemic, and despite the 'revival' of the styles of modernism in a new 'iconic', capitalistic context. With the abolition of its Development Corporation in the mid–1990s the town was transferred to the unsympathetic control of the new unitary authority of North

26. Glendinning and Muthesius, *op.cit.*, pp.367, 380.

27. www.changeandcreation.org

Lanarkshire, dominated by traditional-style municipalities such as Motherwell and Coatbridge, and (seemingly) determined to cut the pampered new town down to size by allowing its meticulous landscaping and urban design to slide into decay. This trend was accentuated by its demographic shift towards an ageing population. More recently, a determined attempt has been made at surgery on the town centre, with all the terraced southern section of Phase 1 torn down, leaving the main portion, including the penthouse range, no longer used as housing, and hideously boxed-in with brown and beige sheeting. Predictably, Cumbernauld has become a target for game-show format architectural competitions such as *Demolition*, and has twice been nominated as 'the worst town in Scotland'. Its urbanist qualities have been publicly championed within Scotland only by DOCOMOMO, and have been flatly ignored by the Scottish heritage establishment. In an ironic sign of the political difficulties faced by the traditional conservation movement in accommodating the collective environments of the post–1945 era, the only buildings selected for listing by Historic Scotland in Cumbernauld have been churches and public buildings by private architects, good modern architecture but which could be found in any town. Here, as elsewhere, listing has failed to provide a means of conserving important pieces of town planning. New initiatives like English Heritage's Characterisation programme or its Change and Creation project recognise planning's importance, but even so, offer no programme of protection.[27]

BIBLIOGRAPHY

CUMBERNAULD NEW TOWN:
GENERAL (INCLUDING TOWN
CENTRE)

'Stockholm, Tapiola, Cumbernauld – from Three emerged One', *American Institute of Architects Journal*, **vol.**48, no.1, July 1967, pp.36–58. Report of the jury for the 1967 R.S. Reynolds Memorial Award for Community Architecture (meaning: design of towns), awarded to Cumbernauld. Jury members: Morris Ketchum, Jnr (Chairman), Archibald C. Rogers and John Fisher Smith.

Bruce Anderson, Michael Brammah, Karl Stevens, *Cumbernauld New Town Case Study*, Urban Design Program, Graduate School of Design, Harvard University, June 1966, unpub., copy held at RIBA.

'Cumbernauld New Town Centre', *Architects' Journal*, vol.136, no.23, 5 December 1962, pp.1279–88.

'RIBA: Wilson on Cumbernauld', *Architects' Journal*, vol.139, no.2, 8 January 1964, pp.65–6.

'Cumbernauld Centre' / 'New Town Central Area', *Architectural Design*, vol.33, no.5, May 1963, 209–25.

'Une importante experience anglaise: la nouvelle ville de Cumbernauld', *L'Architecture d'Aujourd'hui*, no.106, February-March 1963, pp.13–15.

L'Architecture d'Aujourd'hui, no.146, October-November 1969, pp.17–23.

'Cumbernauld: Neue Stadt mit neuer Konzeption', *Baumeister,* vol.62, no.10, October 1965, 1104–20.

'Britain's New Towns', *Barclays Bank Review*, vol.14, no.1, February 1970, pp.3–7.

L Buckthorpe and others, 'Cumbernauld New Town: some aspects of engineering development', *Institution of Municipal Engineers Journal*, vol.88, no.12, December 1961, pp.413–40.

Building Research Institute, 'New Towns: Frontiers or Failures?', *Building Research*, October-December 1969, pp.1–55, and January-March 1970, pp.55–126.

L Bullivant, 'Vom New Town Centre zum Betonfossil', in S Schneider and R Stegers, eds, *Glueck Stadt Raum in Europa 1945 bis 2000*, Basel, 2002, pp.46–9.

Christopher Carter, *Innovations in Planning Thought and Practice at Cumbernauld New Town, 1956-62*, Milton Keynes, Open University, 1983.

Christopher Carter and Michael Keating, 'Policymaking and the Scottish Office: the designation of Cumbernauld New Town', *Public Administration*, vol.65, 1987, pp.391–405.

Central Office of Information, *A Town for Tomorrow* (promotional film), 1967 (copy in Scottish Film Archives, Glasgow).

David Cowling, *An Essay for Today: the Scottish New Towns 1947–1997*, Edinburgh, Rutland Press, 1997, pp.48–70.

Cumbernauld New Town Development Corporation, *Preliminary Planning Proposals*, Cumbernauld, 1958.

Cumbernauld New Town Development Corporation, *Preliminary Planning Proposals, First Addendum*, Cumbernauld, 1959.

Cumbernauld New Town Development Corporation, *Report on the Central Area*, Cumbernauld, 1960.

Cumbernauld New Town Development Corporation, *Preliminary Planning Proposals, Second Addendum*, Cumbernauld, 1962.

Cumbernauld New Town Development Corporation, *Planning Proposals, Second Revision*, Cumbernauld, 1962.

Cumbernauld New Town Development Corporation, *Cumbernauld: Technical Brochure*, Cumbernauld, 1965.

Cumbernauld Development Corporation, *Investigating Cumbernauld New Town*, Cumbernauld 1967.

'Cumbernauld New Town', *Concrete Quarterly*, no.57, April-June 1963, pp.22-5.

Ivor Davies, 'Scottish New Towns', *Habitat* (Canada), vol.13, No.2, 1970, pp.10-16; and vol.13, no.3, 1970, pp.24-30.

Jack A. Denton, 'The Cost Planning of Cumbernauld New Town', *Chartered Surveyor*, vol.96, no.1, July 1963, pp.19-25.

John Donat, 'Cumbernauld', *Architectural Forum* (New York), vol.125, no.4, November 1966, pp.52-9.

Enterprise (Development Corporation newsletter), May 1966.

Lionel Esher, *A Broken Wave*, London, Allen Lane, 1981, pp.249-50.

Mary Gilliatt, 'Anatomy of a New Town', *Country Life*, vol.140, no.3631, 6 October 1966, pp.830-832.

Miles Glendinning, 'Megastructure and Genius Loci', in Docomomo-International, *Proceedings of the Fourth International Conference*, Bratislava, 1996.

Miles Glendinning, ed., *Rebuilding Scotland: the Postwar Vision, 1945-75*, East Linton, Tuckwell Press, 1997, pp.30-5, 85-92, 114-5, 170-2. Includes Geoffrey Copcutt, 'Cumbernauld New Town Centre in Retrospect' (1995, pp.89-92), and facsimile of *Architectural Design*, May 1963 (pp.87-8).

Jim and Krystyna Johnson, 'Buildings revisited: Cumbernauld New Town', *Architects' Journal*, vol.166, no.40, 5 October 1977, 637-649.

Michael Keating, *The Designation of Cumbernauld New Town*, Glasgow, 1986.

Ian Levitt, 'New Towns, New Scotland, New Ideology', *Scottish Historical Review*, vol.76 (2), no.202, October 1997, pp.222-238

Ian Levitt, 'The Scottish New Towns, a guide to records at the National Archives of Scotland', *Scottish Archives*, vol.5, 1999, pp.74-82.

Gordon Logie, Derek Lyddon and Roy Hunter, 'Cumbernauld New Town', *Architect and Building News*, vol.219, no.13, 29 March 1961, pp.407-26.

H. McCall, 'The Effects of some Recent Legislation in the Building of Scottish New Towns', *Institution of Municipal Engineers Journal*, vol.98, no.6, June 1971, pp.143-6.

H. B. Millar, *The History of Cumbernauld and Kilsyth from Earliest Times*, Cumbernauld Historical Society, 1980.

Ian Nairn, 'Britain's Changing Towns, Glasgow and Cumbernauld New Town' part 2, *Listener*, vol.64, no.1650, 10 November 1960, pp.830-2.

Patrick Nuttgens, 'Cumbernauld Town Centre', *Architectural Review*, vol.142, no.849, December 1967, pp.441-51.

Philip Opher and Clinton Bird, *British New Towns: Cumbernauld, Irvine and East Kilbride: an Illustrated Guide*, Oxford, Urban Design, 1980.

Frederic J. Osborn and Arnold Whittick, *New Towns: their Origins, Achievements and Progress*, London, Leonard Hill, 1963, 1969, 1977.

The Planning Exchange, *The New Towns Record*, Glasgow, 1997 (CD-ROM).

John Price, 'Cumbernauld: Whose Kind of Town?', *Surveyor*, vol.135, no.4053, 13 February 1970, pp.34-7.

Paul Ritter, 'Radburn Planning', *Architects' Journal*, vol.132, no.3421, 10 November 1960, pp.680-4 - vol.133, no.3434, 9 February 1961, pp.211-16 (series of eight articles).

Scottish Authorities Special Housing Group, *Newsletter 6, Cumbernauld, an A to Z*, Edinburgh, 1976.

Secretary of State for Scotland, *Draft New Town (Cumbernauld) Designation Order*, Edinburgh, 1955.

Roger Smith, 'The politics of an overspill policy', *Public Administration*, vol.55, Spring 1977, pp.79-94.

Roger Smith and Urlan Wannop, *Strategic Planning in Action, the Impact of the Clyde Valley Regional Plan 1946-1982*, Aldershot, Gower, 1985.

A J M Sykes/Strathclyde University, Occasional Paper 1, *Cumbernauld Housing Survey*, Glasgow, 1967.

Ray Thomas, *Aycliffe to Cumbernauld, a Study of Seven New Towns*, London, Political and Economic Planning Broadsheet 516, 1969.

Town Planning Institute, *Report of the Town and Country Planning Summer School*, University of St Andrews, 1960 (papers by L. H. Wilson, R. Grieve).

Town and Country Planning, vol.38, no.1, January 1970, pp.15-24; vol.39, no.1, January 1971, pp.8-12, 27-30, 35-53.

L. Hugh Wilson, 'Cumbernauld', *Prospect* (RIAS Journal), no.13, Spring 1959, pp.12-17.

L. Hugh Wilson, 'New Town Design - Cumbernauld and After', *RIBA Journal*, vol.71, no.5, May 1964, pp.191-206 (paper read 17 December 1963).

Michael Williams, *Contemporary Scotland: 2, New Towns*, Edinburgh, Heinemann, Third Edition 1981, pp.29-40.

Peter Youngman, 'Landscape Architecture at Cumbernauld New Town', *Journal of the Institute of Landscape Architects*, no.52, November 1960, pp.22-5.

F. Zweig, *The Cumbernauld Study*, London, Urban Research Bureau/ Wates Ltd), 1970.

HOUSING ZONE: GENERAL

Architect and Building News, vol.219, no.13, 29 March 1961, pp.407-26; vol.222, no.23, 5 December 1962, p.824.

Architects' Journal, vol.136, no.23, 5 December 1962, pp.1248, 1279-88; vol.139, no.2, 8 January 1964, pp.65-6; vol.147, no.5, 31 January 1968, pp.293-310.

Theo Crosby, 'Cumbernauld New Town', *Architects' Yearbook*, vol.10, 1962, pp.99-103; Geoffrey Copcutt, 'Planning and Designing the Central Areas of Cumbernauld New Town', L. J. Fricker, 'A Pedestrian's Experience of the Landscape of Cumbernauld', *Architects' Yearbook*, vol.11, 1965, pp.231-64.

Architectural Design, vol.30, no.9, September 1960, p.352; vol.32, no.1, January 1962, p.20.

Architectural Review, vol.135, no.803, January 1964, pp.14-15; no.804, February 1964, pp.93-9.

Cumbernauld New Town Development Corporation, *Housing Policy*, Cumbernauld, 1972.

Housing Review, vol.12, no.4, July/August 1963, pp.120-3.

Interbuild, vol.12, no.7, July 1965, pp.32-3.

Peter Wilmott, 'Housing in Cumbernauld', *Journal of the Royal Town Planning Institute*, vol.50, no.5, May 1964, pp.195-200.

Municipal Journal, no.3659, 5 April 1963, pp.982-4.

RIBA Journal, vol.71, no.5, May 1964, pp.191-206.

Surveyor, vol.118, no.3450, 7 June 1958, pp.577-8; vol.119, no.3561, 3 September 1960, pp.999-1001; vol.125, no.3813, 3 July 1965, pp.33-6

Town and Country Planning, vol.31, no.1, January 1963, pp.38-40.

INDIVIDUAL HOUSING AREAS
(ALL DESIGNED BY CDC ARCHITECTS UNLESS SPECIFIED)

Abronhill South: *Architectural Review*, vol.139, no.827, January 1966, p.48.

Abronhill: *Architects' Journal*, vol.144, no.1, 6 July 1966, p.16.

Carbrain 1, 2: *Architectural Review*, vol.129, no.767, January 1961, p.30.

Carbrain 13, 14: *Architectural Review*, vol.141, no.839, January 1967, p.29.

Muirhead 3: *Architectural Review*, vol.135, no.804, February 1964, 95-99.

Park 3 West: *Architectural Review*, vol.135, no.803, January 1964, p.15; *Interbuild*, vol.13, no.5, May 1966, pp.33-4 (this housing was by the Architecture Research Unit, Edinburgh University).

Park 4: *Architectural Review*, vol.137, no.815, January 1965, p.54.

Ravenswood 5: *Architectural Review*, vol.137, no.815, January 1965, p.54.

Seafar 2: *Architectural Review*, vol.129, no.767, January 1961, p.31; vol.135, no.804, February 1964, pp.93-9.

11 Byker: Surprising the Colleagues for 35 Years – A Social History of Ralph Erskine's Arkitektkontor AB in Newcastle

MICHAEL DRAGE

Byker: Surprising the Colleagues for 35 Years –A Social History of Ralph Erskine's Arkitektkontor AB in Newcastle

MICHAEL DRAGE

A PLACE TO COME HOME TO

Ralph Erskine would sometimes refer to architecture which would 'surprise the colleagues', as though that was never his intention. Ralph died in 2005 at the age of 91 and Byker in Newcastle upon Tyne, his best-known British scheme, has been surprising all and sundry since 1970.

Erskine's aim was never novelty for its own sake, but rather a fresh and inventive approach to social housing which treated the user as the most important client. This was done through a permanent on-site office with a dedicated team of staff pioneering community involvement in the redevelopment process. Also crucial to Byker's success was the establishment of excellent long-term working relations with the City Council officers responsible for Byker, notably the Planning, Housing and Engineer's departments. Unlike many such situations, the ethos was of client and consultants working towards a common goal, rather than forming opposing factions, the only exception to this harmony being from the local politicians and local press, of which more later.

A great deal has been written about Byker, but I hope to give more of an insider's view of the Erskine office and the way the project developed. Alison Ravetz in the *Architects' Journal* wrote that 'Erskine's architecture is in every sense humane: it creates a place to be homesick for, a place to come home to'.[1] For off-the-wall gonzo criticism Reyner Banham's piece cannot be bettered: 'a tidal wave of sheddery and pergolation' became an office catchphrase.[2] Andrew Saint's *New Statesman* article, 'the Byker Street Irregulars', is an excellent one-page summary of the redevelopment process and how the office saw its role in the community. 'Mention socialism and Erskine's lads will grow glassy-eyed and look the other way; but at Byker they have created the most practical socialism we have had in housing for many years.'[3]

My first visit to the Erskine office was as a Newcastle University architecture student in 1972. I was part of a group taking the old Byker Bathhouse as a fourth-year design project with Vernon Gracie, Erskine's Byker-based chief architect, acting as client. I worked for the office in the summer of 1972 and returned in late 1973. As one does with a first job, I intended to stay for around three years but in fact became fully absorbed into the Byker experience and remained until we closed the office in 1984. But first the back story.

ERSKINE APPOINTED, 1968–9

Ralph Erskine had won a competition for private housing in Killingworth, near Newcastle, and as a result his reputation and his consultation of the 'user client' became known in the North East. He was invited by the City Council to review plans for wholesale redevelopment of the run-down terraced housing area of Byker, where pressure from the residents to avoid the break-up of the community had been growing, articulated largely by an informal grouping of community-based professionals, social workers and clergy.

A three-month review by Erskine produced an initial strategy report that was accepted by the City Council in 1968. The aims were set out as working with, and for, the residents, maintaining the valued traditions and characteristics of

1. The best contemporary accounts are the *Architectural Review* articles (vol.156, no.934, December 1974, pp.346–54; vol.170, no.1018, December 1981, pp.334–43) and Alison Ravetz in the *Architects' Journal* (vol.163, no.15, 14 April 1976, pp.731–42), plus those footnoted below.

2. Reyner Banham, 'The Great Wall of Tyne', *New Society*, vol.31, no.644, 6 February 1975, pp.330–1.

3. Andrew Saint, 'The Byker Street Irregulars', *New Statesman*, vol.93, no.2409, 20 May 1977, p.687.

Figure 2. Old streets at the heart of Byker (Raby Street is still the central spine of the development).

Figure 3. Demolition reaches the architects' office, 1974 (author).

Byker, as well as family and neighbourly ties, whilst exploiting the physical opportunities of the south-west sloping site in a way which the existing terraces had failed to do.

The review also proposed that all residents who wished to remain should have that opportunity. 'Byker for the Byker people' had been a slogan in the campaign against the kind of wholesale clearance which had been seen in the west end of Newcastle.[4] This was to be achieved by reducing the size of the proposed clearance areas and establishing a rolling programme of new building handovers, by beginning on already vacant ground. This strategy was to be only partially successful, as delays caused by slow builders, strikes, materials shortages and funding approvals led to many residents accepting new houses outside Byker.

WORKING IN THE FUNERAL PARLOUR

In 1969, as soon as Erskine was appointed as architect and planning consultant to carry out a full reappraisal of the city's plans for the 200 acre (81 ha) site, an office was set up in a former funeral parlour in the middle of the Redevelopment Area. Vernon Gracie had worked for Erskine in Sweden and was invited to take charge, initially living in the flat above the corner shop and later becoming eligible for one of the new flats. He was soon joined by Dave Hill, a technician

4. Newcastle City Council, Proceedings, 3 July 1968.

who had worked for the contractor of the Killingworth scheme, and by Tony Smith, who had also worked in the Swedish office and then, by contrast, for James Stirling at Runcorn. Roger Tillotson and later Ken McKay arrived from Liverpool and that group formed the UK core of the office by 1973. Reinforcements from the Swedish office came for both short and longer-term visits, some such as Per Hederus and Arne Nilsson staying for eighteen months or more and in many cases living in Byker.

At a time when UK architects were not allowed to practice as a limited company, except as a branch of an overseas practice, the office was quite properly a branch of the Swedish company (Ralph Erskine's Arkitektkontor AB). So Byker was – and had to remain – its sole project, and we had neither time nor inclination to take on other projects in the North East. Even so, there was a certain amount of initial suspicion and hostility from the local architectural establishment, eventually eroded by support from such friends of Byker as Doug Cunningham (the City Housing Architect), Professor Douglass Wise, Peter Yates, Bill Ainsworth and the

Figure 4. A sketch of the proposed Byker, with a retained church, 1970, from Erskine's *Plan of Intent* (RE AB).

Figure 5. The Byker team in 1975. Ralph Erskine is in the centre, sitting left of the dog (RE AB).

Department of the Environment's regional office's professionals.

The practical aspects of the corner-shop office bear mention. Initially we were in just two rooms, one of which was in full view of the street and was open to any resident at any time. Later the flat upstairs was taken over, and a small extension built. Creature comforts were minimal and we shared the dust, noise and mud (and burglaries) of the demolition and redevelopment process with the residents. We operated with the technology of the time, so there were no computers, e-mails, faxes etc., which would now ease the logistics of such a large project being carried out between offices in two different countries. All drawings were done by hand, and often freehand, in pencil on home-made plywood drawing boards propped up on bricks. Copying technology was primitive, initially comprising a wet developer copier and a noxious dyeline machine. Communications with Sweden were by telephone or letter and bundles of drawings were mailed or couriered back and forth.

Initial design work was carried out by Ralph Erskine and key office members, mainly in Sweden, with regular visits from Vernon Gracie, Roger Tillotson and other members of the Byker team. Erskine paid visits to Byker regularly in the early years, their frequency diminishing as time went on. Apprehension accompanied these visits, the fascination of working with Ralph tempered by concern about what he might want to change and how that could affect the programme. Even work under construction was not immune to a better idea.

At its peak in the mid–1970s the Byker team was equal in size to Erskine's Swedish office, with around fifteen professional staff, plus four clerks of works. This number included the landscape team, who worked alongside the architects

Figure 6. Map of Byker, the final master plan as intended in 1980. Clydesdale, Harbottle and most of Janet Croft were not built (RE AB)

**Ralph Erskine
Final Masterplan
(as intended 1980)**

on all phases of the project. Arne Nilsson was the first landscaper, and after he returned to Sweden Par Gustaffson and Gerry Kemp were the principal landscape architects, assisted by horticulturalist Derek Smith and year-out landscape students.

The office operated as a flat pyramid, with Vernon Gracie and Roger Tillotson taking the lead design and management roles as well as acting as job architects for some phases. When a deadline was approaching on a particular phase all office members would assist, filling gaps as necessary, with nobody standing on ceremony. Byker had become not just a job but a way of life for all of us.

Particularly memorable were the sustained efforts to prepare presentation drawings for Housing and Planning Committees, where everyone joined in to produce large 1:200 scale hand-drawn and hand-coloured axonometric views of the schemes. These eventually were joined together into a vast, fragile drawing of the whole redevelopment which required several ladders and a large hall to display. These 3D drawings were used not just to impress the politicians but also as an invaluable tool in helping residents to understand the proposals, along with non-threatening models of a deliberately home-made, dolls-house character. Exhibitions, newsletters, information sheets and show flats furnished with an actual tenant's furniture (in exchange for a free new carpet) were other participation and information experiments. These communication methods were vitally important in the early stages of the scheme when demolition and building work were all around and it was hard to see what the finished product would be like.

The aim was always to demystify the process so that the residents not only understood what was happening but had more capacity to get involved. Countering rumour was another important feature, as in Byker rumours spread like wildfire. For example, one afternoon the *Evening Chronicle* billboards announced 'Local flats to be demolished', and the word spread around Byker in no time that the Wall had been built in the wrong place and would have to come down to make way for a motorway.[5] The flats in question were in fact in Gateshead, just to spoil a good rumour.

Caroline Gracie had come to Byker as a social scientist supervising a detached youth work project and stayed to work for the office on community participation and housing management initiatives. A code of practice for demolition was a successful initiative, intended to improve the lives of those living alongside the clearance areas. A key piece of Caroline's work was a paper on alternative forms of tenure and housing management, regrettably not adopted at the time, but now starting to be reflected in Labour's housing policies. We felt that if residents had been given more control of their own areas from the beginning many of the subsequent problems of maintenance and top-down housing management could have been reduced in impact.

Vernon Gracie has commented that the community involvement of the office relied on the enthusiasm and goodwill of the team, which could not be forced, and that these qualities were indicative of the scheme being generally well liked by the community. If the scheme had not been succeeding reasonably well our life in the corner shop could have become intolerable.[6] The ethos of the office could be characterised as teamwork in adversity. We were pressured by local politics, the housing cost yardstick and the building contractors, but determined to succeed, to continually innovate, to create individual identity areas within the overall scheme and to work with, and for, the Byker people. The city provided a small annual budget for 'participation' but the amount of time which went into the non-architectural work of the office far exceeded this. In effect the community participation work was subsidised from the architectural fees, helped by the low overheads of the on-site office. There was great enthusiasm in the office and a team spirit which led to all sorts of experiments and adventures. A prototype children's play area was built in the street outside the office by ourselves and residents in their spare time. It was mainly built from demolition timber and

5. The Byker Wall, up to eight-storeys high, is the dominating feature of Byker, intended to screen the low-rise housing from a motorway that was never realised, though a dual carriageway and metro were built.

6. Vernon J. Gracie: 'Pitfalls in Participation', C. Richard Hatch, ed., *The Scope of Social Architecture*, New York, Van Nostrand Reinhold, 1984, pp.186–201.

Figure 7. Courtyard Play equipment in Bolam area (Jeremy Preston).

Figure 8. Ralph Erskine's office in Byker, the trademark balloon mural painted on the side (Jeremy Preston).

included a sandbox convertible to a paddling pool, a tall climbing frame and little in the way of safety surfaces. Not an experiment to repeat in these more litigious times. A children's drawing club (half an hour at the end of the working day, twice a week) helped break down barriers and get parents talking to the architectural team, though nowadays in a less innocent age all kinds of formalities and checks would, no doubt, apply.

The Erskine team became known by the local planners for our interest in salvaging items for use in the scheme, and we were tipped off about opportunities to rescue sculptures from the Old Town Hall, the portico from Elswick Hall and sundry gates, railings and fireplaces, all of which, dubbed 'ruin-bits' by one of the Swedes, found their way into the development. When the terrace next to the office was demolished, leaving a raw gable end, we built a Byker-style lean-to office extension complete with corrugated metal roof and spent a couple of summer evenings painting a giant red white and blue hot-air balloon on to the rendered gable. To us it was just a bit of fun and a reinterpretation of Ralph Erskine's trademark balloon, so we were amused that Charles Jencks cited it as having deeper meaning in his *Post-modernism* book.[7]

We helped to organise the annual Byker Festival, running a massive treasure hunt side-show entitled the Byker Wall Game, again an opportunity to familiarise people with the architectural ideas and to make links with the residents. Other more formal contacts with the community included a monthly open meeting known as the Byker Forum, a Byker liaison committee, allocation meetings with groups of residents six months before their new houses were due for handover, meetings of residents' groups, a shopkeepers' group and even a competition to design a park. Annual office expeditions helped team building; whirlwind architectural tours of Denmark, Sweden, Paris, Amsterdam and Milton Keynes come to mind.

BUILDING BEGINS, 1970–3

A Pilot Scheme of 46 dwellings (Janet Square) was built in 1970, based on one-to-one detailed consultation with a group of pre-selected tenants who in effect acted as guinea-pigs for the 2500-dwelling social and architectural experiment which Byker was to become.

Also, by 1970 designs for the first phases of the sound-shielding perimeter block, immediately dubbed the Byker Wall, were being developed. In an attempt

7. Charles A. Jencks, *The Language of Post-Modern Architecture*, London, Academy Editions, 2nd Edition, 1978, p.104. The photograph and caption do not appear in the first edition.

154

Figure 9. Tenants' visit to the Pilot Scheme (Janet Square) construction site in 1970 (RE AB).

to keep the office small a contract requiring detailed design to be carried out by the contractor (the Swedish model) was adopted for the first phase. The contractor, Stanley Miller Ltd, employed Douglass Wise and Partners (DWP) to carry out the working drawings. This led to a good long-term relationship between DWP and the Byker team, with them carrying out a similar role as sub-contractors to

Figure 10. An axonometric of the Kendal Street area, with architects' office bottom centre. The type of drawing used to explain the scheme to residents and council committees (RE AB)

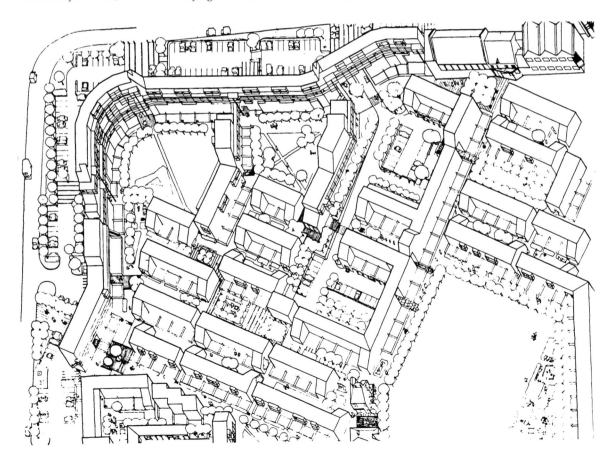

Figure 11. [opposite] Tom Collins House, old people's housing in Dunn Terrace phase, named after a particularly difficult Labour councillor (Jeremy Preston).

Figure 12. The architects' office in the midst of the redevelopment, 1976, with Erskine's characteristic balloon. From Erskine's Christmas card (RE AB).

the Erskine office for the later Dunn Terrace phase of the project.

The Wall, a cast in-situ concrete egg-crate structure with brickwork and Eternit cladding, began on site in 1971 with Roger Tillotson as job architect. It was immediately hit by delays caused by an overheated building industry, shortages of labour and materials and, if the contractors were to be believed, by the unusual design and the architects' unreasonably high standards!

The first full phase of timber-framed low-rise housing, Kendal Street, began on site in 1972 and overtook the Wall to give the first handovers just before Christmas of 1973, completing in 1975. Tony Smith ran this project and I assisted. I then went on to be job architect for the Chirton Street phase in 1976 (158 units) and the Clydesdale area, which was never built, but more of that later. Inside toilets and district heating were no doubt factors in the very high approval ratings from the early residents, but people had also warmed to the architecture and were keen to show visitors around their new houses and flats.

The spaces outside the houses were an important aspect of the design. Radburn-style vehicular separation allowed for a dense and village-like character, with a gradation outward from the houses to private gardens, via semi-private courtyards, to the public realm and, finally, to the largest open spaces. Key routes and landmark buildings such as churches, pubs and the bathhouse from old Byker were retained and the scheme was carefully stitched around these.

Vernon Gracie was anxious not to overwhelm the Pilot Scheme residents with architectural tourists so resisted all overtures from the professional press until 1974, when the first *Architectural Review* article was published. Thereafter, publications snowballed and consequently visitor numbers increased. Being in the middle of the redevelopment area visitors often called into our corner shop office unannounced, getting short shrift if we were particularly busy. However, we usually made time for those who made an appointment, and enjoyed discussions with all manner of visitors. Sir Hugh Casson featured Byker in his *Spirit of*

Figure 13. Wall exterior with private and access balconies, away from the motorway noise zone (Jeremy Preston).

Figure 14. Brickwork patterns on the north side of the Byker Wall (author).

the Age TV series and it made the front cover of the *Observer* magazine. Byker was officially opened by the Duke of Edinburgh in 1974, an opportunity the office took to extract funds from the Lord Mayor's contingency budget to enhance landscaping and build an access stair to the old Bathhouse for the reception. This effectively pump-primed the subsequent conversion of the Bathhouse to community use in 1976, the realisation of my 1972 student project but without the exterior supergraphics.

Subsequent phases then came thick and fast. Grace Street and Gordon Road (1974) could not attract tenderers as individual contracts, so were amalgamated into one contract of 239 dwellings. Shepherd Construction won this and Shepherd Design carried out a partial working drawings service. Ken McKay was job architect here and subsequently for Ayton Street (152 units plus the surgery and local centre, 1978). Shepherds also built Bolam Street (1976) with Nils Viking as job architect, and Raby Street (1978) under Trevor Harris.

BRIEF EXTENDED TO SOUTH BYKER

Erskine had initially been appointed to carry out just the northern half of the redevelopment, by a short-lived Conservative City Council led by Councillor Arthur Grey. The intention was to extend the appointment at a subsequent time. However, by 1974 a Labour leadership had returned to power, suspicious of Erskine's as a foreign private practice, and there was some doubt about the appointment for southern Byker being confirmed. Ironically Erskine, the Socialist architect championing community involvement was appointed by a Conservative council and nearly ousted by a Labour one. The brief was extended in 1974, but local political opposition to the Erskine office continued throughout the remainder of the development, manifesting itself in a variety of pressures and petty harassments, which mainly served to bond the Byker team, as adversity tends to. The root cause seemed to be that the politicians saw their role as representatives of the people being usurped by the direct contact between the residents and the architects. To complete the local picture, despite the almost unanimous approval of the national and professional press, the politicians ensured that the Newcastle newspapers were unremittingly hostile, and we eventually simply refused to speak to them.

At this stage a reappraisal of the master plan was made to try to counter the perceived undesirability of living in the southern area. Historically this was less favoured being at the foot of Byker Hill, with the smarter folk wanting to live at the top, nearer to larger shops and bus routes, and further from the, then, insalubrious Tyne. The Tyne was being cleaned up by this time, and the revised plans put a local centre, with shops, surgery, offices and workshop units, as well as a large open space, Ayton Park, into south Byker to try and redress its perceived disadvantages.

THE FINAL PHASES, 1975–83

Dunn Terrace, Bolam and Chirton phases (1975–8) and Carville and Ayton phases (1978–80) were built in a better contractual climate with fewer delays than previous areas. Janet Street started on site in 1978 but ended with a protracted and traumatic episode where the contractor pulled off the site and an arbitration ensued. Only 38 units were completed and the rest of the site was cleared. Avondale (1979–83) was the last phase built in northern Byker, with Tim Coulter as job architect, bringing the total number of new dwellings to 2010, of the 2400 originally envisaged.

By 1980 the final two proposed phases, Clydesdale and Harbottle, were designed, and in the case of Clydesdale fully detailed up, with an acceptable tender received. However, they fell foul of a change in Government policy which froze funds for almost all council housing. The sites were hived off to private developers who we were told were informally discouraged by the city from using Erskine as architect. Not surprisingly, the results were out of keeping with Byker, both visually and by interrupting important pedestrian circulation routes.

So it could be said that in the end the politicians prevailed and Byker ended with a whimper. The team gradually dispersed, spawning two new UK practices, the Vernon Gracie Partnership and The Byker Group. The corner-shop office closed in 1984 to become the area housing office, which it still is, though much altered and extended and with the loss of the famous balloon mural. Alison Ravetz commented that Byker had been a unique combination of political circumstances, a special architectural practice and a commitment which might never be repeated.[8] Vernon Gracie more cautiously suggested that we had made a modest advance in humanising the process of redevelopment, and that is perhaps a satisfactory epitaph.[9]

BEYOND 1984 TO LISTING

Byker attracted numerous awards, the Eternit Award, the Ambrose Congreve Award for Housing, the Veronica Rudge Green prize for Urban Design, a Civic Trust Award and two Britain in Bloom Awards. It was also cited as significant in Ralph Erskine's CBE, RIBA Gold Medal and Newcastle University Honorary Doctorate awards.

The influence of Byker perhaps continued through its diaspora, with office members moving on into practice and architectural education in the UK, Ireland, Sweden, Norway, Finland, Nigeria and Botswana. Vernon Gracie, Par Gustaffson and Trevor Harris became professors, while Tony McGuirk is head of design at BDP. Roger Tillotson went on to teach at Newcastle School of Architecture and was Chair of Newcastle Architecture Workshop, the pioneering environmental education and technical aid charity.

Byker was managed by the City Housing Department until 2004 when the new 'arms length' management organisation *Your Homes Newcastle* took over. During this time maintenance had been patchy and had often lacked understanding of the principles and nuances of the scheme. Proposals were even afoot to demolish a number of blocks, including Bolam Coyne, one of the 'Little Wall' landmark blocks in the low-rise housing. A determined campaign of opposition to this proposal, led by Professor Peter Fauset, who was at the time a Byker resident, led to the postponement of the proposed demolition and a renewed interest in Byker's qualities.

In 2000 Byker was put forward by English Heritage for Grade II* listing, finally realised in 2007 with little press comment. A Conservation Plan was prepared by the North East Civic Trust in 2002–3, funded by the City Council and English Heritage. From the original team Gerry Kemp and I contributed extensively to this work, which is now being used to guide maintenance and improvement programmes.

POSTSCRIPT

Key issues facing Byker now are the assimilation of new residents as the first occupants die out or move on, pressures from people wanting to park right next to their houses, the need for the restoration of hard and soft landscaping, a greater demand for privacy and a 'collective retreat' into the home, and a degree of private ownership via right-to-buy. The development and gentrification of Newcastle Quayside has already reached the Ouseburn valley area just west of Byker and is beginning to affect residents' perceptions of south Byker, hopefully for the better.

2005 saw the start of an estate-wide three-year upgrading programme to bring the housing up to the national Better Homes standard. At the same time a high-profile architect and developer competition was announced, to revitalise and infill the more run-down areas of south Byker, including Bolam Coyne and the vacant Janet Street site, as well as other areas outside the original development boundary.

8. Hatch, *op.cit.*, p.200.

9. Hatch, *op.cit.*, p.197.

In November 2005 many of the Byker team, from both Sweden and the UK, took part in a nostalgic reunion to unveil a commemorative plaque to Ralph Erskine at the old office and to attend the launch of the Conservation Plan publication.[10] Older and wiser, most agreed that Byker had been a massively educational and formative experience, as well as a difficult act to follow. We might not have embarked on it if we knew quite how challenging it was to turn out, but that on the whole we were very glad to have been part of it.

10. North of England Civic Trust, *A Byker Future*, Your Homes Newcastle, 2005.

12 Estate Regeneration in Practice: The Mozart Estate, Westminster, 1985–2004

JONAH LOWENFELD

Estate Regeneration in Practice: The Mozart Estate, Westminster, 1985–2004

JONAH LOWENFELD

The Mozart Estate, a massive, mixed-use development in the Queen's Park neighbourhood of Westminster, was designed between 1968 and 1969 by the city's Department of Architecture and Planning. The design was clearly influenced by another Westminster estate, Darbourne and Darke's critically-acclaimed Lillington Gardens.[1] Larger than the Lillington scheme, the Mozart Estate eventually housed 3,450 people in 870 houses and flats, and stretched for 24 acres from Kilburn Lane south towards Harrow Road. Lillington Gardens was a low-rise, high-density development, a marked departure from the 'high rises in green spaces' estates of the 1950s; the similar Mozart Estate was itself awarded a Department of the Environment Housing award in 1974 for its first phase.[2]

From a very early point in its life, however, the Mozart Estate encountered problems of damp, water damage, and insufficient heating, and began making local headlines only seven years after its completion.[3] Many estates built in Britain at this time encountered these problems. Even Lillington Gardens (now listed) was found wanting when in 1976 the *Architects' Journal* (*AJ*) commented on condensation problems in the flats, the limited growth of grass during the dry summer, the proximity of children's play areas to old people's flats, vandalism, and the absence of 'evident gossiping at front doors'.[4] If the building of Lillington Gardens was an attempt to incorporate the *aesthetic* and *economic* criticisms levelled against earlier housing estates while retaining a modern image and public status, the *AJ* article prefigured the powerful *social* critique of modern housing that was emerging in 1970s Britain. This erupted in a fierce debate over environmental determinism, or how the physical shape of modern public housing estates affected the daily lives of people living in and around them. It began in the pages of scholarly books and journals, but quickly led to a popular discussion about modern housing in Britain in newspapers and on television.

Out of that debate emerged a consensus about council housing, whose effects have been felt across Britain in the rehabilitation of existing housing, in the policies that shrank, divided, and privatised councils' housing stocks, and in the dramatic dynamiting of high-rise council flats. Both the debate and the consensus that followed have played themselves out on the Mozart Estate, which has been undergoing almost continuous building work for over a decade, with the first designs and proposals dating back nearly twenty years. Now that the last phase of this lengthy regeneration is complete, it is worth looking at the history of the estate and how this shaped its current form.

The social problems associated with post-war British housing dogged the Mozart Estate, almost from the moment of first occupancy. In 1973, there were complaints about 'vandals' and 'hooligans', and though some tenants tried to defeat the 'teenage wreckers', others simply sought to leave.[5] It quickly became a 'sink estate', a last option for those who could afford to live nowhere else. Stories in the local newspapers with bitterly ironic headlines reported residents wanting to move out of their homes on the 'prize estate'.[6] At its nadir, the Mozart Estate was for a time also known as 'Crack City', and in 1993 it 'had the greatest incidence of reported crime across all categories in Westminster'.[7] Issues of race and class

Figure 1. The Mozart Estate in the 1970s – this view up the Third Avenue side of the estate shows the access road for the garages on the ground floor and the sloping bank of grass that separates the estate from Third Avenue, which is nowhere to be seen. (From 'Building Dossier: Mozart Estate London,' *Building*, 26 April 1974.)

1. Darbourne and Darke won the Lillington Gardens competition in 1961, and construction on the first phase began in 1964. The influence of their estate on the Mozart design was recognised by the assessors of the 1974 DoE housing awards. 'Housing Study: Mozart Estate, Phase 1, W10,' *Architects' Journal*, vol.159, no.4, 23 January 1974, pp.169–173.

2. Anthony Williams and Burles, 'Building Dossier: Mozart Estate London,' *Building*, vol.226, no.6829, 26 April 1974, pp.78–87. The first phase was completed in 1972.

3. The flats were undergoing structural repair as early as 1978. 'Speed up Work on Damp Mozart Flats – Plea to Council,' *Marylebone Mercury*, no.7447, 3 August 1978, p.44; 'Speed up Mozart Repairs,' *Marylebone Mercury*, no.7431, 13 April 1979, p.5; ' "Waterlogged" flat tenant to sue council,' *Paddington Times*, no.3391, 24 August 1979, p.3. A plan for repairs had been agreed on in 1979: Chris Mihill, 'Show Flat highlights repairs,' *Paddington Times*, no.3395, 28 September 1979, p.3. Nonetheless, every clipped article from 1980 about the Mozart Estate in the City of Westminster Archives discussed its damp problems.

4. Peter Collymore, 'Building Revisited: Lillington Street, Pimlico,' *Architects' Journal*, vol.164, no.48, 1 December 1976, pp.1031–9.

Figure 2. A plan of the Mozart Estate's DoE award-winning first phase of construction. Note the space left open, and the relative closeness of the blocks to one another, characteristic of low-rise, high-density projects. (*Building* 1974)

Figure 3. A plan of the Mozart Estate from *Utopia on Trial*. The dark black marks the elevated walkways that traversed the estate before regeneration. The first phase of construction is at the bottom left (southwest) of this plan. Note that the surrounding streets do not penetrate into the interior of the estate at any point. (Alice Coleman, *Utopia on Trial*)

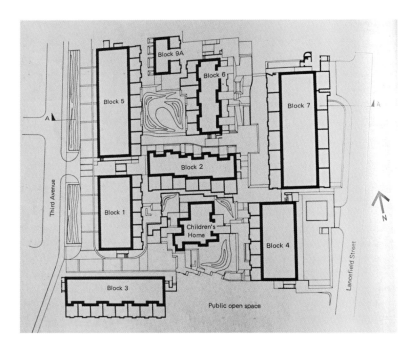

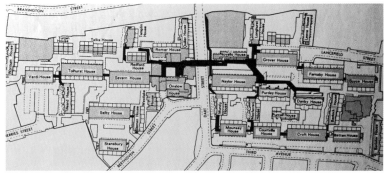

5. Mike Macnish, 'Families want to move out of new council homes', *Marylebone Mercury*, no.7150, 23 November 1973, p.60. The article reports the formation of a tenants' association to combat trouble-making youths, thought to be 15- and 16-year-olds who did not live on the estate. 'Battle against teenage wreckers', *Paddington Mercury*, no.7265, 6 February 1976, p.1; 'Tenants to Name Estate Wreckers', *Paddington Mercury*, no.7,268, 26 February 1976, p.1.

6. 'Tenants press to move from prize estate', *Paddington Times*, no.3257, 28 January 1977, p.1

7. Rachel Lohan, 'Tuning in to peoples needs at the Mozart', *Royal Institution of Chartered Surveyors Journal*, 11 October 2002.

8. 'Courthouse demo follows arrest of "Mozart Seven"', *Paddington Times*, no.3597, 12 August 1983, p.1.

9. David Bowler, interviewed by author, 1 September 2004, London.

10. Ferdi Dennis, 'Mozart's Paddington Symphony', *City Limits*, no.119, 13–19 January 1984, p.15; 'Anti-vandal phones for Council Estate', *Marylebone Mercury*, no.7386, 2 June 1978, p.5.

11. Alice Coleman, *Utopia on Trial: Vision and Reality in Planned Housing*, London, Hilary Shipman, 1985, p.1.

played a role in the estate's dire situation. Its demographic makeup seemed the result of an unofficial racist placement policy, and the population by the 1980s was largely African and Caribbean. Uneasy interactions between the estate's residents and the primarily white local police force were aggravated by accusations of 'swamping', a policing method that saturated the neighbourhood with officers.[8] Flawed tenant selection policies certainly contributed to this perfect storm: David Bowler, working on the estate at the time, commented that 'it had been housing the mad, bad and sad for the better part of a decade. Something about this social mix here wasn't quite right'.[9] Many problems on the estate did not stem from its design – 'If it was in Hampstead, it would be great', one tenant said, when asked about the design in 1984 – and yet, from the first installation of entryphones in 1978, the design of the Mozart Estate became a common feature of any discussion of its social problems.[10]

'What is wrong with modern housing estates?' With its opening sentence, Alice Coleman's 1985 book, *Utopia on Trial: Vision and Reality in Planned Housing*, set off an intense and sustained debate over environmental determinism in Britain.[11] Coleman, a professor of geography at King's College, London, presented the findings of a five-year study of 4,099 blocks of flats and 4,172 houses in the London Boroughs of Southwark and Tower Hamlets. Monitoring how fifteen 'design variables' of modern housing estates affected six measurable indicators of 'social malaise' present in these dwellings, Coleman concluded that more 'disadvantaging' design variables corresponded to higher levels of social malaise. Coleman's 'trial' put forward 'suspect' characteristics of estates like size, circulation and the types of entrances, and correlated them to the 'evidence', primarily 'material clues that could be objectively observed in each block of flats'. These were 'types of malaise that leave behind visible traces: litter, graffiti, vandal damage, and excrement'.[12] In (over)simplified terms, Coleman argued that design led to crime, and proposed corrective design measures as *the* solution – using the Mozart Estate, first as a theoretical example and later as a laboratory.

In February 1987, a group of scholars organised a conference in London entitled 'Rehumanizing Housing', whose papers were published the following year.[13] Though the organisers tried to downplay the significance of Coleman's book as an impetus for the event, nearly every essay addressed her work, and the event seems to have been designed as a venue for criticising her. Some did so on historical or theoretical grounds; others took Coleman to task for the structure of her study, and a few offered alternatives to physical alteration to improve life on housing estates – such as intensive management. Only one contributor addressed the two most important chapters of *Utopia on Trial*, where Coleman proposed Oscar Newman's decade-old model of 'defensible space' as a way of fixing the 'disadvantaging design' she saw in so many modern estates. In his paper 'Against Enclosure', Bill Hillier, a professor at the Bartlett School, put forward a model of physical alterations that could be made to housing estates based on a set of ideas collectively called space syntax.[14] When it was first published in 1973, Hillier had called Newman's *Defensible Space* 'a bad book about a very important subject', not because he disagreed with its basic premise – that the physical design of environments could foster antisocial and criminal activity – but because he worried that Newman's arguments would be 'accepted for the wrong reasons'.[15] In a 1986 review of *Utopia on Trial*, he had already critiqued Coleman's methodology, so in 'Against Enclosure', Hillier demonstrated space syntax analysis and presented the rules derived from it as positive alternatives to defensible space's guidelines.[16] He compared the Marquess Estate, built in the London borough of Islington in the 1970s, to Apt, a town in the south of France, showing that the former, a low-rise high-density housing estate, ended up a crime-ridden sink estate as a result of its spatial orientation, while the traditional town, the putative model for such estates, was actually based on different spatial principles, and worked well. Space syntax, Hillier wrote, was developed to fill 'a substantial gap in our knowledge of the social implications of strictly formal, hence, architectural, decisions'.[17]

At the end of his essay, Hillier, while emphasising the need for in-depth research to be done prior to any large-scale redesign project, set out a few 'rules of thumb' for those making architectural decisions. Areas being redesigned should have an 'integrating core', a significant destination at the centre of the area that could be approached without making too many changes in direction along the way. All spaces should have dwelling entrances opening directly on to them; these should also be directly visible and directly accessible from the area's major axial streets. Building facades should be designed and orientated to clarify the circulation routes, and to mark the spaces. Avoid too much enclosure, avoid too much repetition, and avoid creating a spatial hierarchy that would produce spaces that are empty most of the time.[18]

Hillier and Coleman proposed the same general means – architectural modification – to achieve the same general end – reducing social malaise and crime. The methodological and ideological differences between them – Hillier was an architectural scholar with a modern sensibility, Coleman was a social scientist with a radically conservative bent – are clear. More significant is their basic agreement on what needed to be done. Because neither questioned *whether* failing estates had to be physically modified, Hillier and Coleman could each address the logical follow-up question: *How?*

12. ibid., p.23.

13. Necdet Teymur, Thomas A. Markus, Tom Wooley, eds., *Rehumanizing Housing*, London, Butterworths, 1988.

14. Bill Hillier, 'Against Enclosure', in *Rehumanizing Housing*, ibid., pp.63–88.

15. Oscar Newman, *Defensible Space, People and Design in the Violent City*, London, Architectural Press, 1972. Bill Hillier, 'In Defence of Space', *RIBA Journal*, vol.80, no.11, November 1973, pp.539–44.

16. Bill Hillier, 'City of Alice's Dreams.' *Architects' Journal*, vol.186, no.28, 9 July 1986, pp.39–41.

17. Bill Hillier *et al.*, 'Space Syntax', *Architects' Journal*, vol.178, no.46, 30 November 1983, p.49.

18. Hillier, 'Against Enclosure', *op.cit.*, pp.86–7.

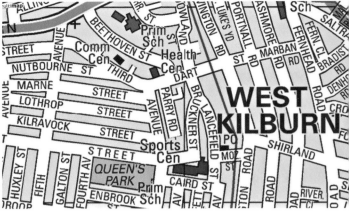

Figure 4. One of the controversial elevated walkways. (Courtesy HTA Architects)

Figure 5. A present-day streetmap of the area. Note the new streets: Lancefield Street, Bruckner Street, and Parry Road. Hillier would rightly note that there is a radical reduction of scale between the estate and the surrounding streets. (www. mulitmap.co.uk)

19. Williams, *op.cit.*, p.78.

20. Coleman, *op.cit.*, p.137.

21. Sue Balding, 'Tenants demand action as Attacks Mount', *Marylebone Mercury*, no.7546, 10 July 1981, p.25; Jim Howard, Crime Prevention Design Officer for City of Westminster, interviewed by author, London, 27 August 2004.

22. Coleman, *op.cit.* pp. 135–44. 'Walkways on Estate to be Axed', *Paddington Times*, no.3729, 21 February 1986, p.1.

23. 'Tenant Revolt over Coleman Master-plan', *Architects' Journal*, vol.184, no.46, 12 November 1986, p.34.

24. Bill Hillier and Alan Penn, quoted in 'Mozart Plan Out of Tune says Report', *Architects' Journal*, vol.184, no.49, 3 December 1986, p.18.

25. Coleman, 'Utopia Debate', *Architects' Journal*, vol.184, no.32, 6 August 1986, p.17. Hillier, 'City of Alice's Dreams', *op.cit.*, p.41.

Let us follow the Hillier-Coleman theoretical debate as it was played out in the Mozart Estate. It began in late 1986, and hinged on one design element: overhead walkways. Part of the Mozart's original planning brief, the walkways were intended to link:

> the new school and Queen's Park Underground station in the north with a linear park and proposed new district centre in the south. This route takes advantage of a gentle north-south fall in the land, by commencing at ground level and continues without gradient until it passes over Dart Street ... at which point it gently descends to ground level again at its southern end.[19]

In *Utopia on Trial*, Coleman identified elevated walkways as one of her design suspects, calling them 'the most vicious "open sesame" making a block vulnerable to outsiders'.[20] On the Mozart Estate, they connected most of the blocks to one another, and were concentrated just north of Dart Street where the shopping area and the Magic Flute pub were located. The need to remove the elevated walkways that hid parking garages and other spaces from view was one of Coleman's most distinctive claims; more ubiquitous in the United Kingdom than in the United States, walkways were not present in the housing examples that Oscar Newman had studied in the 1970s.

Coleman was not the first in the UK to call for the removal of elevated walkways. In 1981, the Chairman of the Tenants' Association of another estate in Westminster, Lisson Green, demanded that the long elevated walkways there be broken up. There was a drop in reported crime on the estate after demolition. Today, none of the elevated walkways are left on the Mozart Estate, but they have not been forgotten. Everyone mentions them, from those most involved in the regeneration effort, to the Jehovah's Witnesses knocking on doors of houses, to the young women working in The Learning Store on Mozart Street. The seams left in the brickwork from where the walkways once were are still visible.[21]

The Tenants' Association backed Coleman's demolition plan, and the first walkways were knocked down in 1986.[22] Soon afterwards, however, another group of tenants commissioned an alternative study from Hillier and Alan Penn, colleagues at the Bartlett Unit for Architectural Studies.[23] In their report, they accused Coleman of insufficient research:

> Had a study of the layout or pedestrian movement been carried out, it would have shown the importance of the upper level walkways for residents' movement patterns and cast serious doubts on the wisdom of removing them without the careful consideration of the effect on the tenants.[24]

Coleman claimed her strategies would create 'traditional streetscape' and Hillier said that they would not.[25] Although space syntax was gaining adherents in architectural circles, Hillier and the tenants he represented lost their battle.

After the successful application of her first principle of 'rehabilitation', with the demolition of four of the Mozart's elevated walkways, Coleman's influence on the physical modifications to the estate proceeded almost unchecked. Her ideas were very much in vogue, most notably with Prime Minister Margaret Thatcher. 'Thatcher . . . authorised a £50 million project to test out the Coleman thesis on seven selected estates in the north-west of England, the Midlands and in London.'[26] Although Mozart was not funded through the Thatcher-approved scheme, Coleman's influence with the Conservative-controlled Westminster City Council ensured that she could freely apply the defensible space-derived principles she had laid out in *Utopia on Trial*.

The architects of the first stage, which was limited to one-fifth of the estate, in the south-west quadrant, were Max Lock Easton Perlston & King (MEPK). They worked 'in conjunction' with Coleman, who was officially a consultant to the City of Westminster but whose significance went much further than the title suggests.[27] The four blocks facing Third Avenue were intensively refurbished to establish two street fronts. The blocks had been built at a distance from the street, separated from it by a bank of grass that sloped down toward an estate road providing access to the garages that occupied the blocks' ground floors. In the redesigning of the blocks, the elevated walkways that had connected them were eliminated and in their places, secure entrances shared by no more than six dwellings were built, turning what had been a permeable string of four blocks

26. Rachel Kelly, 'A way out of dead ends', *The Times*, no.64548, 22 January 1993, p.13; David Bowler, *op.cit.*

27. Mike Molloy of MEPK Architects, interviewed by author, London, 23 August 2004.

Figure 6. Mozart Estate – Regeneration Stage 1. Modifications done by MEPK Architects in conjunction with Alice Coleman. Note the prominently placed area map that reads 'Queens Park Area Map.' On the far right, you can see the access point for the flats on the upper stories. On the left is one of the 'bubbles' housing the living areas of the houses in the converted ground-floor garages, some of which still remain. (author)

Figure 7. View of one of the 'bubbles.' Note how close it is to the pavement and its glazed corners. (author)

Figure 8. Mozart Estate – Regeneration Stage 1. A view north onto Parry Road. On the left, the ground-floor entrances to the dwellings. Note the private gardens in accordance with defensible space guidelines. Also, although it is officially a two-way road, it is very narrow, lending credence to Bill Hillier's assertion that it would be 'villagey.' (author)

into an unbroken whole. Some of the ground-floor garages between the new entrances were converted into the bedrooms of eight new single-storey units, the living areas of which projected forward from the old blocks towards Third Avenue in four new semi-detached 'bubbles'. These structures eliminated the estate road (which had been called 'the racetrack' for the high speeds at which some cars navigated it), and the bank of grass, and attempted to reduce what Coleman termed 'facelessness' in favour of evoking a row of semi-detached houses.[28]

The other side of the blocks was converted into new houses, each with its own small, fenced-in front garden and fully glazed projecting entrance porch. They front on to Parry Road, a small new carriageway cut through the estate. Across the street are a number of refurbished flats and new houses occupying what had been open space. The architecture of the new dwellings follows a defensible-space strategy of design, to minimise shared space and maximise surveillance. Low fences proliferate. They demarcate where the public streets end and where the private gardens begin, while eyes inside the houses can still watch the street. Most of the houses also had glazed corners meant to act as the 1980s equivalent to the bay and bow windows of the inter-war, semi-detached and terraced houses Coleman had praised so highly in *Utopia on Trial*. Coleman sums up her opinion by quoting this perceptive epigram: 'Inter-war semis were cheap without being nasty, while post-war building may be nasty without being cheap.' 'In a modern servantless family, however, surveillance is much more important, and seems to be best satisfied by bay or bow windows that give a clear view up and down the street as well as across it.'[29]

These were only the most visible changes made in the first stage of the Mozart's regeneration. Less apparent was the complex reconfiguration of the infrastructure and circulation of the blocks' upper levels. Coleman demanded that blocks have only one exit. The legal requirement to provide an alternative means of escape in case of fire, however, demanded that there be two interconnecting exits. Eventually, Coleman and the architects had to compromise, and other means of escape were built securely, not allowing entry from the outside. This was not the only point of contention between Coleman and MEPK. Brian Foyle, principal architect of the project who had been designing housing with MEPK since the 1960s, confided that 'I'm not so sure about building on the open spaces. I think that small green spaces provide good relief on otherwise dense urban estates. I think I would have left them.'[30]

Coleman's biggest problem turned out to be much more basic: a cost-benefit analysis. In *Utopia on Trial*, she argued that design modification would produce long-term benefits to justify the initial cost of the work, including reduced management costs, reduced security costs, reduced stress on remaining housing staff and, most ambitiously, 'financial gains outside the housing budget':

> As children are reared in a more stable community, the scale of school vandalism should decline. The reduction in crime should permit police-force economies. Victims' calls upon the health service should lessen. The fire service would have fewer cases of arson to deal with. And so on.[31]

But in the early 1990s, the costs of physical modifications to the Mozart Estate became too high to justify. A second stage of work had begun, with Floyd Slaski Partnership as architects. David Bowler, who became the area's housing manager in May 1993, said that it was at this point that the willingness to implement Coleman's proposals began to falter. 'From 1993 to mid-'95, you got a developing sense that applying Coleman's principles in their undiluted entirety to the development of a living environment was unworkable.' 'Chunking up the building into units' to achieve 'the magic number' – the design disadvantagement thresholds – was very expensive: the second stage of refurbishment cost £54,000 per unit, a sum comparable to the cost of new-build. For a price that could have paid for new bathrooms and kitchens, residents of Mozart were getting exterior modifications as part of an 'incredibly complex reorientation' with the added headache of living

28. I owe these terms to Brian Foyle, the principal MEPK architect on the project. Brian Foyle, telephone interview, 31 August 2004.

29. Coleman, *Utopia on Trial*, *op.cit*., pp.107, 109.

30. Brian Foyle, interview, *op.cit.*

31. Coleman, *Utopia on Trial*, *op.cit*., pp.168–69.

Figure 9. Mozart Estate – Regeneration Stage 2, Floyd Slaski Partnership. A view down Bruckner Street. New houses on the left, with the 6-storey Farnaby House in the background. (author)

on a construction site for two years.

Coleman proposed a solution of a sort to the conflict between her design principles and fire codes in *Utopia on Trial*: she called for a 'fundamental re-thinking' of the issue. Her argument was that social breakdown resulting from design was causing social malaise, which was in turn increasing the incidence of arson. The very designs that the fire services demanded – extra walkways, stair-cases and exits – were, according to this line of thinking, causing more fires.[32] As the requirements for an alternative escape route in case of fire were not up for 'rethinking' or reconsideration, Coleman got creative. Consider the case of the six-storey Farnaby House, where she proposed both horizontal and vertical subdivision. The block would have private entrances to houses on the ground-floor and flats on new, shorter corridors above. Meeting Coleman's thresholds for dwellings per corridor/entrance, the architects again encountered problems with fire codes and escape routes. This time, the solution entailed providing smoke ventilators in the interior corridors, which meant running shafts through all six storeys of the occupied residences. 'At a certain point people just said, "No more"', Bowler recalled. The estate regeneration team ended their contact with Coleman in the mid–1990s. Her influence with the Westminster City Council waned after a change in leadership in the wake of the 'homes for votes' scandal revelation. According to Bowler, Coleman 'went from being the centre of the world to being an outside consultant'.[33]

Coleman's rise and fall was played out on a national level as well. In 1985, *Utopia on Trial* was a surprise bestseller, and she met Prince Charles and Mar-garet Thatcher, the most powerful critics of modern architecture and council housing at the time.[34] Thatcher helped launch the Design Improvement Con-trolled Experiment (DICE) in 1989, with £50 million of government funding that Coleman was to distribute to seven estates across the country. The first regen-erative work at the Mozart Estate was the first to be funded by Estate Action, a Department of the Environment initiative established in 1985 specifically to fund physical changes to problem estates. Estate Action prioritised '*capital invest-ment* (my italics) in physical improvements with social, economic and manage-ment measures designed to protect the capital investment in the long term, and improve living conditions on local authority estates in a more holistic way.'[35] It was also intended to fund social programmes, but in practice (especially on the Mozart Estate) primarily encouraged investment in bricks and mortar.[36] The Conservative Party had proposed in its 1980 Housing Act to move investment 'from bricks and mortar to people' by shifting housing subsidies to individuals

32. Coleman, ibid, pp.147–48.

33. Dame Shirley Porter, the Conservative leader of the Westminster City Council, transferred council houses from sitting council tenants to non-resident private owners in a process that was later declared illegal. She left the Council in 1993, and many other Conservative members – who were Coleman supporters – followed. Coleman lost much influence as a result. David Bowler, *op.cit*.

34. *Sunday Times*, no.8522, 6 October 1987, p.36.

35. Stephen Hill, 'Getting the Money for Refurbishment,' *Architects' Journal*, vol.197, no.6, 10 February 1993, p.34.

36. Paul Balchin and Maureen Rhoden, *Housing Policy*, London, Routledge, 2002, pp.330-1.

and away from local authorities. It was due to Coleman's influence in the Conservative Party that Estate Action focused on structural investment. However, the Department of the Environment was unenthusiastic about funding Coleman, since she held it responsible for the continuing failure of modern housing and called for its abolition: it acquiesced to the Party's programme, but contracted Price Waterhouse to evaluate DICE's accomplishments.[37] By the time *Utopia on Trial*'s second edition was published in 1990, the DICE project had been approved and funded. Coleman's vision for estate regeneration seemed to have prevailed, both over critics who had argued that any physical modifications were mere 'tinkering' and over Hillier and his colleagues who disagreed with the specific modifications she proposed.

But Coleman's and DICE's fortunes were about to be reversed. First, after Thatcher's ousting in 1990, Secretary of State for the Environment Michael Heseltine revoked those DICE funds not yet distributed.[38] There was also a shift in policy. The infrastructure improvement programmes for estates in the 1980s depended upon an influx of new, and in most cases private, sources of funding. But for estates like Mozart, privatisation initiatives like Right-to-Buy, Housing Action Trusts, and large-scale Voluntary Transfers were not viable sources of funds.

And yet, in the early 1990s, the Conservative Party was already shifting away from infrastructure, in large part because the expense seemed not to be paying off. The evaluation of Coleman's DICE programme ultimately supported this shift of spending priorities, concluding that the improvements did not pay for themselves as promised, and were not significantly more successful than the non-DICE Estate Action Schemes evaluated around the same time.[39] DICE – which spent between £13,200 and £41,500 per dwelling on the estates where Coleman's principles were implemented – was doomed, and Estate Action shifted its focus towards a more multi-faceted approach. David Bowler recalled that 'Estate Action went from being a cure-all panacea to being part of a more wide-ranging approach to solving management, social, and economic problems, as well as problems with crime'.[40] The Single Regeneration Budget (SRB), established in 1994 to 'facilitate a mix of economic, social and physical regeneration' changed the approach to public housing regeneration. It incorporated budgeted funds from many governmental offices – including the Departments of Environment, Trade and Industry, Employment and Education – so that social programming could be organised in conjunction with any physical modifications. Social problems were once again addressed with social solutions, and have continued to flourish in recent years. Recent developments in urban regeneration policy have furthered the effort to integrate physical improvement programmes with social investment. The New Deal for Communities, an experiment launched in 2000, attempts to integrate all community services under a single roof, including housing, policing, health care and education.[41]

I met Alice Coleman and Bill Hillier in 2004, and found that each regards the work at the Mozart Estate as a missed opportunity. Neither had visited the estate since the ending of their respective involvements with it.[42] But looking at recent estate regeneration projects around Britain, their two philosophies guide physical modifications, if not in the way either Hillier or Coleman would have hoped. Architects are not too concerned with any overarching philosophy of spatial analysis or physical modification. The either/or debate between space syntax and defensible space in the early days of estate regeneration has given way to a situation in which architects freely choose parts from both strategies.

David Levitt is one of the pioneers of estate regeneration, and co-founder of the firm Levitt Bernstein Associates, one of the most successful and prolific in the UK.[43] In a conversation in July 2004, Levitt did not mention either space syntax or defensible space. When I asked, he had not heard of space syntax – though his projects and our discussion showed he has put many of its concepts into action – while he regarded Alice Coleman as 'not very original.' He ignored Oscar New-

37. Coleman, *Utopia on Trial, op.cit.*, p.184. This criticism was contained in the book's closing paragraphs, which were significantly altered in the second edition. In the second edition's preface, Coleman called the DoE's funding DICE 'such a positive step forward'. Alice Coleman, *Utopia on Trial*, 2nd Edition, 1990, p.ix.

38. Alice Coleman, interviewed by author, London, 22 June 2004.

39. Price Waterhouse, *An Evaluation of Design Improvement Controlled Experiment (DICE) Schemes Regeneration Research Summary*, No.11, 1997. http://www.communities.gov.uk/index.asp?id=1128678

40. David Bowler, *op.cit.*

41. David Bowler, *op.cit.*

42. Alice Coleman, interview, *op.cit.*; Bill Hillier, interviewed by author, London, 24 June 2004.

man entirely, calling defensible space 'an idea that comes out of Jane Jacobs'.[44] Explaining his regeneration strategy, Levitt put it simply:

> *The layout of estates is fundamentally different to the layout of streets … The post-Corbusian notion of blocks freely located in spaces with lots of open green space around doesn't work for the client group we're dealing with because the space isn't defensible. We try to keep [existing] buildings where possible, and we introduce a permeable street-grid layout, to establish defensible space with overlooked streets and clear edges.*[45]

Levitt's ideas at once admit a degree of environmental determinism while being acutely aware of the socio-economic position of his estate's tenants and their needs. His claim to establish both permeability (Hillier's priority) and defensibility (Coleman's) is borne out in his master plan for regenerating Hackney's Holly Street Estate, which draws on concepts both from space syntax and defensible space. It also looks very much like a Jane Jacobs-inspired common-sense design, with streets taking paramount importance.

Rob Sprunt, another architect of regeneration projects, is very familiar with the different merits of the two design strategies, and explains the built legacy of the Hillier-Coleman debate much more explicitly. Sprunt has worked on the regeneration of ten estates in fifteen years, and before that studied with Bill Hillier. He dismisses the supposed opposition between space syntax and defensible space, saying that both strategies inform his work. 'Defensible space is not the whole answer' for Sprunt, and neither is space syntax. The regenerated King's Cross Estate, just south of Euston Road, for which Sprunt Ltd did the master planning (1995), takes cues from – and breaks rules of – both design philosophies. The guidelines of space syntax would have ruled out the addition of fences surrounding the blocks as reducing permeability, and Coleman would have insisted on establishing individual gardens and subdividing block entrances. Sprunt's goal, 'to take unusable space and out of it create clear uses and clear ownership, [bringing] clarity to the public realm', meant that at King's Cross, where the major problems were drugs and prostitution, fencing off individual blocks that had been 'in a sea of asphalt', building 'significant entrances' of which residents would be proud, and bringing the border between public and private back to the pavement, could best re-establish the street as the primary space of circulation and encounter. 'It's actually Jane Jacobs', Sprunt said when explaining his regeneration strategy. 'She said that those spaces that work are full and those spaces that don't are empty.' Again the emphasis is on occupied spaces and Jane Jacobs is the key influence. The successful spaces of her 'Great American Cities' were the busy streets, the very thing both Coleman and Hillier believed they were helping to make.[46]

The last stage of regeneration on the northern half of the Mozart Estate was another attempt to achieve Coleman and Hillier's stated aim – a more traditional system of streets – using strategies appropriated from the work of each while producing a result of which neither would completely approve. Planned and designed by HTA Architects, it was completed in late 2004. The taller blocks in the core of the estate were demolished and replaced with new two-storey houses. The medium-rise (three- and four-storey) blocks were converted by subdividing them horizontally into ground-floor accessed maisonettes and flats with access via secure new stair towers. The blocks of flats still look and act like blocks of flats – Coleman would have objected to their having interconnecting exits and exceeding the threshold of dwellings per entrance. David Mason of HTA architects suggested that there was an unofficial guideline for number of flats served by a single entrance of twelve, or double Coleman's threshold of six. There was also an understanding that the vertical subdivision of corridors wasn't viable because of fire regulations.[47] The layout of the new streets combines clear and circuitous elements, and has at least two culs-de-sac – Hillier would have labelled it 'villagey'.

43. In 1998, Prime Minister Tony Blair visited the Holly Street Estate in Hackney, then undergoing a LBA-masterplanned regeneration. 'This is the type of initiative we need to see replicated across the country', he said, while the regeneration – consisting of demolition, refurbishment, and some new construction – was underway. London Borough of Hackney, 'Prime Minister praises Holly Street as a "symbol" for the nation', [press release], 15 September 1998. Levitt Bernstein Architects have won many awards for estate regeneration.

44. Jane Jacobs, *The Death and Life of Great American Cities*, New York, Random House, 1961 (English edition London, Jonathan Cape, 1962).

45. David Levitt, interviewed by author, London, July 2004.

46. Rob Sprunt, interviewed by author, 20 August 2004, London.

47. David Mason, interviewed by author, London, 13 September 2004.

48. Oma Megbele of Haywards Property Services, interview by author, 3 August 2004, London. Alan Fernandes of Acton Housing Association, telephone interview by author, 22 July 2004, London.

49. Jim Howard, interviewed by author, 27 August 2004, London.

And the 'Rehumanizing Housing' crowd might have dismissed it all as tinkering, except that so much of the energy and money put into the Mozart Estate over the last ten years has gone into social programmes. Initiatives like Sure Start, which provides assistance with pre-school age children so their parents have time to find work or train for future employment, were funded under the SRB. The new Beethoven Centre, housed in the converted nineteenth-century 'play-shed' of a local school, is home to many projects, including the Queen's Park New Media Centre (in partnership with the Institute of Contemporary Art), which runs training courses for local residents. The yellow shirts of the City Guardians, young people who patrol the area in pairs, are always visible; and they are well-known in the community, ready to provide assistance, and reporting any problems so that appropriate action can be taken. Two advocacy groups – the general Queen's Park Neighbourhood Forum and the Queen's Park Estate Tenants' and Residents' Association, particular to residents and tenants of Westminster City Council-owned property – have offices at the Beethoven Centre. Other special interest groups – the Queen's Park Bangladeshi Association and the Somali Advisory Bureau, to name two – also have a presence there. In addition to all this, an outside company has been hired to provide regular maintenance. The process has also been highly collaborative, involving much resident consultation, and with the work on the estate divided among many organisations.[48]

Even the Metropolitan Police have had a hand in reshaping the Mozart Estate into what it is today. A Crime Prevention Design Officer (CPDO) advises the City's Planning Department on the security of any proposed construction or modification that requires permission. The focus of Jim Howard, the CPDO for the City of Westminster, ranges from the smallest details – the relative security of doors, the shape of drainspouts (to inhibit climbing), the presence of flat surfaces on building facades that could potentially be used as handholds to allow break-ins – to the broadest planning of space. He was familiar both with defensible space and with space syntax, and said many of the same things as did the architects, advocating a balance between enclosure and permeability: 'You don't want too many escape routes and you don't want to create the cul-de-sac effect.'[49] The informal combining of Coleman's and Hillier's principles, along with the division of responsibility on the estate, with many programmes being implemented simultaneously, has ensured that no single guiding design principle or social ideology takes the lead.

When Alice Coleman asked, 'What is wrong with modern housing estates?' the first instinct of the architectural community was to collectively respond, 'It's not our [buildings'] fault!' That argument reduced architecture to irrelevance. Today, with widespread estate regeneration, the next generation of architects is admitting that it was, in part, the fault of the buildings. In accepting responsibility for those failures, today's architects are also claiming to have power to rectify past mistakes and prevent future ones. Hillier and Coleman, who believed that physical modifications to modern housing estates would have significant socially beneficial effects, enabled architects to once again address the challenge of mass housing, confident that societies need them to help improve existing, and build new, housing. But now that they have been able to reassert a role for their profession in the provision of housing that is social, humane, and affordable, architects are careful (some might say cowardly) not to go too far. Architects involved in estate regeneration today are also making the point made by the other contributors to the 'Rehumanizing Housing' conference: it was not only architecture that caused the failure of modern housing, and any solution will necessarily be in part social. We are all environmental determinists now, just not exclusively so.

Select Housing Bibliography

MANUALS AND CONTEMPORARY
GOVERNMENT ACCOUNTS

A. W. Cleeve Barr, *Public Authority Housing*, London, Batsford, 1958

J. B. Cullingworth, *Housing and Local Government in England and Wales*, London, George Allen and Unwin, 1966

John P. Macey, and C. V. Baker, *Housing Management*, London, Estates Gazette, 1965

Ministry of Health, *rural workers' homes*, 1937

Ministry of Health, *Rural Housing Manual*, 1938

Ministry of Health/ Ministry of Works, *Housing Manual*, HMSO, 1944

Ministry of Health, *Housing Manual*, HMSO, 1949

Ministry of Housing and Local Government, *Design in Town and Village*, HMSO, 1953

Ministry of Housing and Local Government, *New Homes for Old, Improvements and Conversions*, HMSO, 1954

Ministry of Housing and Local Government, Circular No. 13/62, *Homes for Today and Tomorrow*, London, HMSO, 1962

Ministry of Housing and Local Government; *Space in the Home*, Design Bulletin No.6, HMSO, 1963

Ministry of Housing and Local Government (Cmnd.2837), *The Housing Programme 1965 to 1970*, HMSO, 1965

RIBA, *Cottage Designs awarded premiums in the Competitions conducted by the Royal Institute of British Architects with the concurrence of the Local Government Board*, London, RIBA, 1918

RIBA, *Rebuilding Britain*, London, Lund Humphries, 1943

Baroness Sharp, 'Housing in Britain, Successes, Failures and the Future', in Department of the Environment, *Housing, Building and Planning in the United Kingdom*, London, HMSO, 1971

HISTORIC STUDIES

Catherine Bauer, *Modern Housing*, London, George Allen and Unwin, 1935

John Burnett, *A Social History of Housing*, (3rd edition) London, Routledge, 1991

Nicholas Bullock, *Building the Post-War World*, London, Routledge, 2002

Donatella Calabi, ed. *Architettura Domestica in Gran Bretagna* 1890–1939, Milan, Electa, 1982

Mark Clapson, *Invincible Green Suburbs, Brave New Towns, Social Change and Urban Dispersal in Postwar England*, Manchester University Press, 1998

David Crawford, ed., *A Decade of British Housing, 1963–1973*, London, Architectural Press, 1975

John B. Cullingworth, *Housing and Local Government in England and Wales*, London, George Allen and Unwin, 1966

Elizabeth Darling, *Re-Forming Britain, Narratives of Modernity before Reconstruction*, London, Routledge, 2007

Elizabeth Denby, *Europe Rehoused*, London, George Allen and Unwin, 1938, 1944

Patrick Dunleavy, *The Politics of Mass Housing in Britain, 1945–1975*, Oxford, Clarendon Press, 1981

Arthur Edwards, *The Design of Suburbia*, London, Pembridge Press, 1981

J. S. Fuerst, *Public Housing in Europe and America*, London, Croom Helm, 1974

Miles Glendinning and Stephan Muthesius, *Tower Block, Modern Public Housing in England, Scotland, Wales and Northern Ireland*, London, Yale University Press, 1994

John R. Gold, *The Experience of Modernism, Modern Architects and the Future City, 1928–1953*, London, E & FN Spon, 1997

Greater London Council, *Home Sweet Home*, London, Academy Editions/ GLC, 1976

Peter Gresswell, *Houses in the Country*, London, Batsford, 1964

Dennis Hardy and Colin Ward, *Arcadia for All, the Legacy of a Makeshift Landscape*, London, Mansell, 1984

Jensen, Finn, *The English Semi-Detached House*, Ellington, Ovolo, 2007

David Jeremiah, *Architecture and Design for the Family in Britain, 1900–70*, Manchester University Press, 2000

Paul Mauger, *Buildings in the Country*, London, Batsford, 1959

Patrick Nuttgens, *The Home Front*, London, BBC, 1989

Laurence F. Orbach, *Homes for Heroes, a Study of the Evolution of British Public Housing, 1915–21*, London, Seeley, Service, 1977

Alison Ravetz (with Richard Turkington), *The Place of Home, English Domestic Environments 1914–2000*, London, E & FN Spon, 1995

Alison Ravetz, *Council Housing and Culture, the History of a Social Experiment*, London, Routledge, 2001

Peter G. Rowe, *Modernity and Housing*, Cambridge, MIT Press, 1993

Andrew Saint, ed., *London Suburbs*, London, Merrell Holberton, 1999

Anthony Sutcliffe, ed., *Multi-Storey Living, the British Working-Class Experience*, London, Croom Helm, 1974

Mark Swenarton, *Homes Fit for Heroes, the Politics and Architecture of Early State Housing in Britain*, London, Heinemann, 1981

Michael Young and Peter Willmott, *Family and Kinship in East London*, London, Routledge and Kegan Paul, 1957

SPECIFIC ARCHITECTS

Colin Amery and Lance Wright, *The Architecture of Darbourne and Darke*, London, RIBA, 1977

Mats Egelius, *Ralph Erskine, Architect*, Stockholm, 1990

Elain Harwood and Alan Powers, *Tayler and Green Architects 1938-1973, The Spirit of Place in Modern Housing*, London, Prince of Wales Institute of Architecture, 1998

Barbara Simms, ed., *Eric Lyons & Span*, London, RIBA, 2006

Robert Williams, *Herbert Collins, 1885-1975, architect and worker for peace*, Paul Cave with City of Southampton, 1985

SPECIFIC TOWNS, REGIONS AND SCHEMES

Tom Begg, *Fifty Special Years, A Study in Scottish Housing*, London, Henry Melland, 1989

Chamberlin, Powell and Bon, *Barbican Report 1959*, Barbican Committee, Corporation of London, April 1959

Carl Chinn, *Homes for People, 100 Years of Council Housing in Birmingham*, Birmingham Books, 1991

David H. Halley, *Scottish Special Housing Association, A Chronicle of Forty Years, 1937-1977*, Edinburgh, 1977

David Heathcote, *Barbican, Penthouse over the City*, Chichester, Wiley-Academy, 2004

Patrick Hodgkinson, 'Brunswick Centre, Bloomsbury: A Good Bit of City?' in *Twentieth Century Architecture*, no.6, *The Sixties*, 2002, pp.83-90

Sergei Kadleigh assisted by Patrick Horsbrugh, *High Paddington, A Town for 8000 People*, London, *Architect and Building News*/ Iliffe and Sons, 1952

Anrezej Olechnowicz, *Working-Class Housing in England Between the Wars, the Becontree Estate*, Oxford Historical Monographs, 1997

Simon Pepper, 'Housing at Roehampton', in Boris Ford, ed., *The Cambridge Guide to the Arts in Britain*, vol.9, *Since the Second World War*, Cambridge University Press, 1988

Alison Ravetz, *Model Estate, Planning Housing at Quarry Hill, Leeds*, London, Croom Helm, 1974

Andrew Saint, *Park Hill, What Next?* London, Architectural Association, 1996

Sheffield Corporation Housing Development Committee, *Ten Years of Housing in Sheffield, 1953-1963*, Corporation of Sheffield, 1962

POLEMICS

Lionel Brett, *The Things we see: Houses*, West Drayton, Penguin Books, 1947

Petra Griffiths, *Homes Fit for Heroes*, London, Shelter, 1975

Lynsey Hanley, *Estates, an Intimate History*, London, Granta, 2007

Chris Holmes, *A New Vision for Housing*, London, Routledge, 2006

Peter Hutchinson, *The Housing Battlefield*, London, Athena Press, 2003

Martin Pawley, *Architecture versus Housing*, London, Studio Vista, 1971

Nicholas Taylor, *The Village in the City*, London, Temple Smith, 1973

Colin Ward, *Housing: An Anarchist Approach*, Freedom Press, 1976

Colin Ward, *Talking Houses*, London, Freedom Press, 1990

Colin Ward, *New Town, Home Town, the Lessons of Experience*, London, Calouste Gulbenkian Foundation, 1993

PREFABRICATION

Hugh Anthony, *Houses, Permanence and Prefabrication*, London, Pleiades Books, 1945

Hugh Casson, *Homes by the Million*, Harmondsworth, Penguin, 1946

Colin Davies, *The Prefabricated Home*, London, Reaktion, 2005

Eric de Maré, ed., *New Ways of Building*, London, Architectural Press, 1951

Brian Finnimore, *Houses from the Factory, System Building and the Welfare State*, London, Rivers Oram, 1989

Richard Sheppard, *Prefabrication in Building*, London, Architectural Press, 1946

Greg Stevenson, *Palaces for the People, Prefabs in Post-War Britain*, London, Batsford, 2003

Brenda Vale, Prefabs, *A History of the UK Temporary Housing Programme*, London, E& FN Spon, 1995

R. B. White, *Prefabrication, a History of its Development in Great Britain*, London, HMSO, 1965

HOUSING ASSOCIATIONS

Johnston Birchall, *Building the Communities the Co-Operative Way*, London, Routledge and Kegan Paul, 1988

Ian Cole and Robert Furbey, *The Eclipse of Council Housing*, London, Routledge and Kegan Paul, 1994

David Page, *Building for Communities, a Study of New Housing Association Estates*, York, Joseph Rowntree Foundation, 1993

HOUSING REGENERATION

Department of the Environment, *Estate Action Handbook*, London, HMSO, 1992

John English, *The Future of Council Housing*, London, Croom Helm, 1982

Graham Towers, *Shelter is not Enough, Transforming multi-storey Housing*, Bristol, Policy Press, 2000

Colin Ward, *Tenants Take Over*, London, Architectural Press, 1974

Nick Wates, *The Battle for Tolmers Square*, London, Routledge, 1976,

JOURNAL ARTICLES

'Houses not Housing', *Architects' Journal*, vol.165, no.8, 23 February 1977, pp.702-3

'Tall Flats', *Architects' Journal*, vol.119, no.3176, 25 February 1954, pp.246-50

Thomas Adams, 'Some phases of England's Housing and Town Planning Problem', in *Landscape Architecture*, no.11, 1920-1, pp. 11-12

John Barr, 'Status Village', in *New Society*, no.370, 30 October 1969, pp.677-80 (New Ash Green)

Lionel Brett, 'Post-war Housing Estates', in *Architectural Review*, vol.110, no.655, July 1951, pp.17-26

Sherban Cantacuzino, 'Powell and Moya', in *Architecture and Building*, vol.31, no.7, July 1956, pp.250-3

R. A. H. Livett, 'Housing in an Industrial City', in *Architectural Association Journal*, vol.53, no.615, May 1938, pp.487-501 (Quarry Hill)

Eric Lyons, 'Back to Blackheath', in *The Architect*, vol.1, no.6, July 1971, pp.36-42

Evelyn Sharp, Frederick Gibberd, Margaret Willis *et al*, 'Symposium on High Flats', *RIBA Journal*, vol.62, no.5, March 1955, pp.195-214

Nicholas Taylor, 'the Failure of Housing', in *Architectural Review*, vol.142, no.849, November 1967, p.341

Lawrence Veiller, 'Building a Nation: Social Apects of England's Housing Program', *Architectural Record*, no.48, November 1920, pp.407-416